JOHN GAY
AND
THE SCRIBLERIANS

JOHN GAY
AND
THE SCRIBLERIANS

edited by
Peter Lewis and Nigel Wood

VISION PRESS · LONDON
ST. MARTIN'S PRESS · NEW YORK

Vision Press Ltd.
c/o Harper & Row Distributors Ltd.
Estover
Plymouth PL6 7PZ

and

St. Martin's Press, Inc.
175 Fifth Avenue
New York
N.Y. 10010

ISBN (UK) 0 85478 296 6
ISBN (US) 0 312 02422 3

Library of Congress Cataloging-in-Publication

John Gay and the Scriblerians edited by Peter Lewis
and Nigel Wood

   (Critical studies)
   1. Gay, John, 1685–1732—Criticism and interpretation.
2. Scriblerus Club.   3. English literature—18th century—History
and criticism.   4. Satire, English—History and criticism.
5. London (England)—Intellectual life—18th century.   I. Lewis,
Peter Elfed.   II. Wood, Nigel, 1953–   .   III. Series: Critical
Studies.
PR3474.J64   1989   821'.5—dc19   88-18198
ISBN 0-312-02422-3 (St Martin's): $35.00 (est.)   CIP

Printed and bound in Great Britain
at The University Printing House, Oxford.
Phototypeset by Galleon Photosetting,
Ipswich, Suffolk.
MCMLXXXVIII

Contents

Acknowledgements

Peter and I would both like to record thanks to the Finance Committee at Durham University for putting up the initial finance for the 1985 John Gay Tercentenary conference, Professor J. R. Watson for the necessary support when it was needed most, and all the delegates for their suggestions and formal contributions. I owe particular thanks to the University's Research Foundation for my Arts Fellowship, 1984–85, and the English Department's help and enthusiasm for the project during my stay there.

N.W.

Abbreviations

Editions:

DW   John Fuller (ed.), *John Gay: Dramatic Works*, 2 vols. (Oxford, 1983)

Letters   C. F. Burgess (ed.), *The Letters of John Gay* (Oxford, 1966)

PP   Vinton Dearing (ed.), with the assistance of Charles E. Beckwith, *John Gay: Poetry and Prose*, 2 vols. (Oxford, 1974)

Journals:

EC   *Essays in Criticism*
JEGP   *Journal of English and Germanic Philology*
MP   *Modern Philology*
PMLA   *Publications of the Modern Language Association of America*
PQ   *Philological Quarterly*
SP   *Studies in Philology*
TLS   *Times Literary Supplement*

Chronology of Gay's Main Works and Other Important Scriblerian Dates

(Except where otherwise noted, works cited are by Gay and dates are of first publication.)

1661 Robert Harley, first Earl of Oxford, born.
1667 John Arbuthnot and Jonathan Swift born.
1679 Thomas Parnell born.
1685 John Gay born.
1688 Alexander Pope born.
1704 Swift's *A Tale of a Tub*.
1708 *Wine*; Swift's *Argument against Abolishing Christianity*.
1709 Pope's *Pastorals*.
1711 *The Present State of Wit*; Pope's *An Essay on Criticism*; Swift's *The Conduct of the Allies*.
1712 *The Mohocks* (not performed); Arbuthnot's *The History of John Bull*; Pope's *The Rape of the Lock* (first version).
1713 *Rural Sports*; *The Wife of Bath* (produced at Drury Lane); *The Fan*; Pope's *Windsor-Forest*.
1714 Scriblerus Club formed; *The Shepherd's Week*; Pope's *The Rape of the Lock* (five-canto version).
1715 *The What D'Ye Call It* (produced at Drury Lane).
1716 *Trivia: or, The Art of Walking the Streets of London*.
1717 Gay, Pope and Arbuthnot's *Three Hours after Marriage* (produced at Drury Lane).
1718 Parnell died.
1719 *Acis and Galatea*, Handel's opera with a libretto by Gay, privately performed.
1720 *Poems on Several Occasions* (includes *Dione*).
1724 *The Captives* (produced at Drury Lane); Harley died.

1726   Swift's *Gulliver's Travels*.
1727   *Fables* (First Series); Pope-Swift *Miscellanies* (I–II).
1728   *The Beggar's Opera* (produced at Lincoln's Inn Fields); Pope's *The Dunciad* (first version); Pope-Swift *Miscellanies* (III).
1729   *Polly* (not performed); Swift's *A Modest Proposal*.
1730   *The Wife of Bath* (revised version, produced at Lincoln's Inn Fields).
1731   *Acis and Galatea* publicly performed at Lincoln's Inn Fields.
1732   *Acis and Galatea* published; Gay died; Pope-Swift *Miscellanies* (IV).
1733   *Achilles* (produced at Covent Garden); Pope's *An Essay on Man* (I–III).
1734   *The Distress'd Wife* (produced at Covent Garden but not published); Pope's *An Essay on Man* (IV).
1735   Pope's *Moral Essays* completed and *Epistle to Dr Arbuthnot*; Arbuthnot died.
1738   *Fables* (Second Series).
1741   *Memoirs of Martinus Scriblerus* (Scriblerus Club).
1743   *The Distress'd Wife* published; Pope's *The Dunciad* (four-book version).
1744   Pope died.
1745   Swift died.
1754   *The Rehearsal at Goatham* (not performed).
1777   *Polly* produced at the Theatre Royal in the Haymarket.

Introduction

by NIGEL WOOD

> His Body was brought by the Company of Upholders, from
> the Duke of *Queensberry*'s to *Exeter 'Change* in the *Strand*, and on
> the 23rd. of *Dec.* after lying in, very decent, State, was at Eight
> of the Clock in the Evening, drawn in a Herse, trimmed with
> Plumes of Black and White Feathers, attended with three
> mourning Coaches and six Horses to *Westminster-Abbey*.[1]

Nothing became Gay's life more than his leaving it. Arbuthnot
claimed that he had died 'as if he had been a peer of the
Realm'.[2] Pope was one of his pall-bearers, and, together with
Arbuthnot, wrote immediately to Swift with the sad tidings.
The letter lay unopened for five days. Swift guessed its contents.
The reply is stark and revealing: Swift acknowledges it and the
news of Gay,

> upon which event I shall say nothing. I am only concerned that
> long living hath not hardened me: . . . I know not any man who is
> in a greater likelyhood than my self, to die poor and friendless.[3]

Curll's *Life* of Gay (1733), quoted above, is really a paste-up of
hastily-assembled journalism plus a collage of quotation, and,
even if unauthorized, tallies with the testament of his closest
friends: 'His Personal Character was perfectly amicable; he was
one of the most natural, inoffensive and disinterested of Men. . . .'
This good-humoured independence Curll represented by selective passages from Gay's own 'Introduction' to the first series of
Fables, 'The *Shepherd* and the *Philosopher*'. Here, we learn that
'the little knowledge' he gained 'Was all from simple nature
drain'd' (33–4), and that he took his 'rule' from 'nature' and so
shunned 'contempt and ridicule' that he never shone 'with
important air' in social gatherings (51–4).[4]
 This is the same writer, however, whose *The Beggar's Opera*

11

was attacked by the King's Chaplain, Dr. Herring, because it provoked Newgate footpads to emulate Macheath,[5] whose *Polly* could not be performed until 1777 because of direct intervention by the Lord Chamberlain, whose dedication of *The Shepherd's Week* to Bolingbroke prevented any early favour from the Hanoverian court and whose refusal of the post of Gentleman-Usher to the Princess Louisa in 1727 earned him Pope's whole-hearted support: a garland of Liberty for his 'happy Dismission from all Court-Dependance'.[6] This dichotomy should not be particularly surprising. What on the face of it may be good-humoured and equable writing from all internal evidence may have a quite contrary effect, once we take account of external factors such as the calculated audience and its supposed standards of decorum. This is so much more the case if we bear in mind Marcus Walsh's distinction between an Ironist and a Satirist. The Democritean Ironist 'has a realist's sense of the universal fallibility of man, and rarely allows his reader the luxury of reposing upon an absolute value'.[7] Consistent commitment, the 'important air', of Pope's Horatian Heroism in his *Epilogue to the Satires* (1738) or of Swift's Drapier, is not Gay's until perhaps the *Fables*. The commitment is usually in the *act* and rarely in the *rhetoric*.

Gay's self-image is an unassuming one, and yet when summing up his life for Pope in the letter of October, 1727 he chose his 'Own Epitaph' from the *Poems on Several Occasions*: 'Life is a jest; and all things show it,/ I thought so once; but now I know it.'[8] This melancholic weariness still helps commemorate Gay on his monument, but it does not stand alone. Pope's compassionate epitaph follows and helps curb the bite of Gay's own lines:

> Of manners gentle, of affections mild;
> In wit, a man; simplicity, a child:
> With native humour temp'ring virtuous rage,
> Form'd to delight at once and lash the age: . . .
> . . . A safe companion, and an easy friend,
> Unblam'd through life, lamented in thy end.

This was not enough to prevent the epitaph incurring Johnson's displeasure. 'Pamphilus', in writing to the *Gentleman's Magazine*, (October 1738) wanted it erased. Gay had returned from the regions of death not much improved in his poetry, and very much corrupted in his morals; for he [had] come back with a lie in his mouth, *life is a jest*.[9]

This jesting from beyond the grave rankled, as such prescience was pert and against all Christian conviction. Gay could be inflammatory merely by misplaced good humour.

Gay's epitaph is apposite. If all human seriousness is at best wasted effort, at worst vapoury posturing, then moral distinctions disappear and the Great Man may as well be such. The difficulty lies in locating Gay; does he enjoy the holiday from high seriousness, or depict it sourly, forcing the reader to fill the ethical vacuum? Alternatively, do we need Gay the 'author' to ordain meaning at all? Certainly, Gay's confessions are not always to be trusted. In the 'Preface' to the 1729 printing of *Polly*, he is outrageously 'innocent' of the obvious politics of the piece:

> Since this prohibition I have been told that I am accused, in general terms, of having written many disaffected libels and seditious pamphlets. As it hath ever been my utmost ambition . . . to lead a quiet and inoffensive life, I thought my innocence in this particular would never have requir'd a justification . . . . this kind of writing is, what I have ever detested and never practic'd. . . .[10]

The combination of his fellow Scriblerians' verdicts and this kind of self-projection is, it would seem, testimony enough: Gay was an innocent abroad, and if the cunning world read more worldly wisdom into his work, then this was not calculated and got him into a surprising amount of trouble with potential patrons. The balance of probabilities is tilted towards a quite different conclusion: that Gay tried hard all his life to gain preferment, but that he found the going hard and much against the grain. Unlike Pope and Swift, he also gained a sufficient amount of encouragement early in his career to sustain the 'public' idiom of good-natured *bonhomie*. However covert, there is on the other hand a contrary impulse, one best shown perhaps in the opening passages of the 1713 *Rural Sports*:

> But I, who ne'er was bless'd from Fortune's hand,
> Nor brighten'd plough-shares in paternal land,
> Have long been in the noisie Town immur'd,
> Respir'd its smoak, and all its Toils endur'd,

Have courted Bus'ness with successless Pain,
And in Attendance wasted Years in vain;
Where news and politicks amuse mankind,
And schemes of state involve th' uneasie mind;
Faction embroils the world; and ev'ry tongue
Is fraught with Malice, and with scandal hung: ... (9–18)

This is the poem so often discussed only in terms of the manipulation of Virgil or of Gay's acute eye for detail.

From here it is only a short step to the bitter sweetness of *Trivia* or *The Beggar's Opera*, where the Walker and Beggar enjoy a sufficiently de-centred perspective to mock costume and pretence. 'Poverty' becomes the 'Title to Poetry' for the Beggar in his 'Introduction' and the Player agrees, for 'The Muses, contrary to all other Ladies, pay no Distinction to Dress, and never partially mistake the Pertness of Embroidery for Wit, nor the Modesty of Want for Dulness.' Frequently, however, such boldness of statement is reserved for the framing devices in his work; once he gets into his narrative stride Gay is no allegorist. He may distrust the fabric of a city's gracious living, but he can also delight in it. As Carolyn Williams notes in this volume (pp. 173–75), the disordering effects of fashionable life were often imaged as female cosmetic powers. It was no coincidence to Gay that the Muse was female. In Steele's *Poetical Miscellanies* (1714) Gay's contribution included two complementary images: the 'Town Eclogue', *Araminta*, and its elegiac rural counterpart, *Panthea*. The overall point to the poems apparently lies in their contrast, as the unequivocal pathetic fallacies of the latter are designed to show up the snares of urban opportunity in the other. Gay's mock-*aubade* in *Araminta* (1–6) is as careful to sketch in the speciousness of gracious living as in Pope's *Rape* (1712, 1714). Delia's wedding preparations partake of Belinda's toilet ritual and the sylphs that maintain it:

In haste she rose; unmindful of her Pray'rs,
Flew to the Glass, and practis'd o'er her Airs:
Her new-set Jewels round her Robe are plac'd,
Some in a Brilliant Buckle bind her Waist;
Some round her Neck a circling Light display,
Some in her Hair diffuse a trembling Ray;
The Silver Knot o'erlooks the *Mechlen* Lace,
And adds becoming Beauties to her Face:

14

Introduction

> Brocaded Flow'rs o'er the gay Mantoe shine,
> And the rich Stays her Taper Shape confine:
> Thus all her Dress exerts a graceful Pride,
> And sporting Loves surround th'expecting Bride, . . . (9–20)

Delia's beauty has captivated Daphnis at no little cost to Araminta, who wishes for 'some Retreat far from this hateful Town!' (86) and who now dismisses 'Vain Dress and glaring Equipage' as 'empty Shows' (87–8). For Araminta there is Right and assertion, but Delia inspires poetry. It would be inexact to claim that Gay is here being *contradictory*. Beauty and Show are here an indissoluble amalgam.

In their critique of *Trivia* in this volume (pp. 62–82) Stephen Copley and Ian Haywood demonstrate the lacunae in Gay's representations of luxury and its place in the social economy. Occasionally, Gay can be found to be aware of his productive 'predicament'. Glittering costume appears in *The Fan*, an early attempt at the mock-heroic. Lost in a panorama of the 'inconstant Equipage of female Dress' (I, 230) Gay muses (in every sense) at the 'Force of Thought' and expressive limitations of 'Numbers' when out to catch femininity on the wing. For Pope, in *The Rape* and *Epistle to a Lady* (1735), the evanescence of beauty is much more gender specific. Pope's poetic women inspire the male imagination and yet, given the 'praise and blame' structures inherited more or less directly from antiquity, there are yardsticks of praiseworthiness (Clarissa or Martha Blount) whom Pope offers as rocks against the waves.[11] Gay, perhaps, is less of an orthodox 'success' in this because his emphasis is very much more on Poetry than the traditions of Verse Satire or Women. 'How shall I soar,' he wonders, 'and on unweary Wing/ Trace varying Habits upward to their Spring!' (*The Fan*, I, 227–28), when he imagines himself addressed by the combination of female allure *and* supreme art met in the Fan. When Pope had counselled the tracing of Muses upwards to their source in *An Essay on Criticism* (1711) it led to Homer, Virgil, formed judgements and helpful maxims (126–27). For Gay it is debateable whether it leads anywhere:

> Should you the Wardrobe's Magazine rehearse,
> And glossy Manteaus rustle in thy Verse;
> Should you the rich Brocaded Suit unfold,

15

Where rising Flow'rs grow stiff with frosted Gold;
The dazled Muse would from her Subject stray,
And in a Maze of Fashions lose her Way.

(I, 239–44)

Ensnared by silken flowers, Gay feels inclined to fall on the grass of pastoral life. His art seems ensnared by the myriad of fashionable forms that urban prosperity can provide. Distinction and judgement are blurred; irony is the only appropriate mode that can both revel in its depiction and yet withhold full assent. Well may 'a just Distance be to Beauty paid' (I, 237).

The picture is clearer after reading Gay's *Guardian* 149 (1 September 1713), an apparently whimsical piece, proposing a sustained analogy between adorning the body and expressing sentiments suitably. Hidden in this is a satire on the cosmetics that gain preferment:

> Dress is grown of universal Use in the Conduct of Life. Civilities and Respect are only paid to Appearance. Tis a Varnish that gives a Lustre to every Action, a *Passe-par-tout* that introduces us into all polite Assemblies.[12]

This irony is placed in a context that deliberately mitigates its indignation. Initially, when concluding that the 'sciences of *Poetry* and *Dress*' are closely allied, it would seem that the trivia of the dressmaker's trade and genteel taste are undermined. This becomes less so as the paper develops. Indeed there is more than once an ambiguous allusion to the standard authority for decorum: Horace's *Ars Poetica*. The advice to the Pisones had included a serious parallel between the decorum of content and form in art, and the civilities of acceptable social behaviour, especially as concerns social duty.[13] Gay's version hovers very near to ridicule of this:

> As different Sorts of Poetry require a different Style; the *Elegy* tender and mournful; the *Ode* gay and sprightly; the *Epic* sublime, etc. So must the Widow confess her Brief in the Veil; the Bride frequently makes her Joy and Exultation conspicuous in the Silver Brocade; and the Plume and the scarlet Dye is requisite to give the Soldier a Martial Air. (II, 461)

The whole universe could be a suit of clothes. Gay here poses the possibility that clothes do indeed make all that is worthy of the fashionable Man:

16

Introduction

A Lady of Genius will give a genteel Air to her whole Dress by a
well fancied Suit of Knots, as a judicious Writer gives Spirit to a
whole Sentence by a single Expression. (II, 462)

Gentility is here reduced to singularity of dress, the ephemeral,
and, most damning of all, a failure to perceive the simple,
essential forms of life. For Swift in *The Tale of a Tub* (1704) the
written Will is sacerdotal, the Shoulder Knots unequivocal
excrescences.[14] For Pope in *An Essay on Criticism* expression's
dressing of thought leads the reader to conclude that decency
stemmed from suitability:

> A vile Conceit in pompous Words exprest,
> Is like a Clown in regal Purple drest;
> For diff'rent *Styles* with diff'rent *Subjects* sort,
> As several Garbs with Country, Town and Court.
>
> (320–23)[15]

The contrast between such urban manners and 'the awkward
Appearance of her Rural humble Servant' in *The Fan* is very
much to the disadvantage of the former (II, 462). Whether it is
to the advantage of the latter is a moot point. As with many of
Gay's rural details, its significance is heuristic, a means by
which the frailties of Modern life may be writ large without a
firm commitment to an alternative.

This elusiveness can be both fascinating and maddening.
William Empson's *Some Versions of Pastoral* (1935) went some
way towards discovering the radical Gay, where the 'main thing
[about *The Beggar's Opera*] is the political attack and the principles
behind it'.[16] More recent criticism has almost converted Gay
into a proto-aesthete. Even if Gay as the good-humoured japester
can no longer be entirely credible, another image has risen to
take its place which is derived from it. Martin Battestin's position
is clear: 'For Gay, no less than Pater, art was necessary because
life was deficient in form.' Gay's subversion of inherited tropes
formed part of a search for transcendent ideals as 'The ideal in
Gay's poetry is found rather in that curious discrepancy between
his subject matter, which can be gross and sordid enough, and
his elegant, witty manner'.[17] In *Trivia* this means Doll's macabre
death (II, 381–98) transformed to a moment of artistry, and in
Rural Sports the Angler an analogue for the skilful Artist. More
recently, Gay has resembled a post-Modern in his pervasive

17

slipperiness. Anne McWhir's provocative reading of *The Shepherd's Week* and *Trivia* notes the uneasy mix of both sophistication and simplicity and the polite and vulgar, and yet finds the impulse one of defence, the creation of 'plots that trick us in order to amuse or instruct us—benevolent webs of words to take the place of the "Wiles and subtil Arts" of genuine predators'.[18] The same might be said of the winning melodies in *The Beggar's Opera*. As Margaret Anne Doody describes it, we cannot shove them away because we congratulate ourselves on our moral bearings: 'The melody touches us before we can stop it.'[19] This insidious artifice plays with received notions of Art and Nature and reminds the reader that both are generic and frequently unable to help us assess their validity in an advanced modern economy. Gay's answer is to enable us to step outside such paradigms and travel with his Walker down city streets that are neither wholly contemporary nor wholly mythical and observe Newgate in song. The intention may have been satiric, but recently all we are likely to see is playfulness.

1985 saw the tercentenary of Gay's birth, and a conference held at Collingwood College in the University of Durham, England. Most of these essays started life there either as formal papers delivered then or themes that arose from the ensuing discussions and that were written up later. The enthusiasm evinced by the participants and delegates to revalue Gay's achievement has not resulted in a uniform New Direction for Gay studies but rather revisions of staunchly-held beliefs once considered irrefutable. Brean Hammond and Alan Downie, for example, both look afresh at the political and cultural contexts for Gay's writing career. For Hammond, Gay is caught up in a rapidly changing system of patronage, which fostered for him two Scriblerian rôles: that of 'neglected poet', proof that 'existing forms of patronage are tainted', or 'the independent writer, poor but virtuous, who was born to blush unseen'. Downie analyses this independence in terms of recent research on the political ideologies in Gay's time. No longer can he be dubbed 'Tory' without further detail or without a glance at 'Old Whig' thinking. This is bound to affect the interpretation of individual works. In the essays by Copley/Haywood and Tom Woodman, and also in mine, the ideological colouring given to the City and Country is evinced with special reference to *Trivia* and *The*

Shepherd's Week. Copley and Haywood depict the unease Gay felt at urban prosperity and his own position in its midst, especially as regards Mandeville's cynical realism about luxury and all its apparent works. Woodman notes Gay's mock-georgic indecorum and its fleeting identifications of nature with modern manners. I try to equate pastoral theories of Simplicity with the political animus of Gay's *The Shepherd's Week*. One casualty of these studies is Gay's 'realism', as these texts emerge as containing carefully contrived perspectives and idioms.

The Beggar's Opera has long been considered Gay's masterpiece. Its originality as the first ballad opera (or at least the first popular one) still leaves us ambivalent about Gay's own reading and interest in 'straight' opera. Was he antagonistic, or paying amused homage to its novelty and high-flown *bravura*? Or did he attempt both? For Pat Rogers, the World of Opera held definite attractions for Gay, even if he felt the need for recantation in his own version, feeding 'upon lost loyalties and forsaken allegiances'. In the contribution by Peter Lewis there is evidence of Gay's own independent way with allusion. In *The Beggar's Rags* . . . there is a study of the dramatic metamorphoses Gay visits on much of his source-material throughout his dramatic career. This fascination at theatrical effect is admirably mapped by both Yvonne Noble and Carolyn Williams in their essays on the later drama and Gay's depiction of women. For Noble the condition of dependency, peculiarly that of women, structures Gay's *Achilles* deeply. His 'characteristic duality' in symbol and genre allows him a bifocal line of vision. He is enabled to speak and yet 'withholds what he would say' about gender rôles *and* his own predicament. For Williams Gay's very flexible Muses were the tutelary spirits of a disinterested aestheticism, where there was no objection to 'morality, so long as it was compatible with good drama'. The surprise and humour of the resulting work resides in this capacity to keep the ethical motivation of the work hidden most but not all of the time.

Gay will doubtless still be canonical for his humour, but this re-assessment of the whole range of his writing deepens its hue profoundly. Perhaps Swift and Pope discovered Gay's more steadfast qualities belatedly. Most certainly there is still much to be done on the *Fables*, where the fun is mordant and at its thinnest. Swift found Gay a contender for his 'own hum'rous biting Way' (54) in *Verses on the Death of Dr. Swift* (1731)[20] and, just as for Pope, Gay came to epitomize a courageous rage for liberty, for Swift he came to suggest in *Tim and the Fables* (1728) and *To Mr. Gay on his being Steward to the Duke of Queensberry* (1735) much for which he himself would like to be known: the sardonic realist isolating the Yahoo beneath the skin. The Painter 'who pleased No body and Every body' from *Fable XVIII* in the first series learns to deal in flattery not truth: 'Truth should not always be reveal'd' (24) because you lose friends and custom. In *Fable XLIII*, 'The Council of *Horses*', the 'colt, whose eye-balls flam'd with ire' (7) spreads dissension through his herd by objecting to Man's exploitation. He is answered by a steed 'With age and long experience wise' (39) who points to the rewards quiescence brings and who counsels him, 'Appease your discontented mind/ And act the part by Heav'n assign'd' (61–2). Gay's closing couplet shows he can hardly have shared the steed's equanimity: 'The tumult ceas'd. The colt submitted,/ And, like his ancestors, was bitted' (63–4). Gay understood both the tumult and the submission.

NOTES

1. Edmund Curll, *The Life of John Gay* (London, 1733), p. 72.
2. Harold Williams (ed.), *The Correspondence of Jonathan Swift*, 5 vols. (Oxford, 1965), IV, 101 (13 January 1732–33).
3. *Correspondence*, IV, 103–4 (January, 1732–33).
4. The text of all references to Gay's poetry is that found in *PP*.
5. See Gay's letter to Swift (16 May 1728): 'I suppose you must have heard that I have had the honour to have had a Sermon preach'd against my works by a Court Chaplain . . .' (*Letters*, p. 75). For the immediate context, see William Henry Irving, *John Gay: Favorite of the Wits* (Durham, N.C., 1940), p. 252.
6. George Sherburn (ed.), *The Correspondence of Alexander Pope*, 5 vols. (Oxford, 1956), II, 453 (16 October 1727).
7. Marcus Walsh (ed.), *John Gay: Selected Poems* (Manchester, 1979), p. 7.
8. *Letters*, pp. 65–7. See also the annotation by Norman Ault and John Butt in *Minor Poems* (London and New Haven, 1954), pp. 349–52, Vol. VI of the Twickenham Pope.
9. Donald Greene (ed.), *Samuel Johnson* (*The Oxford Authors*, Oxford, 1984), p. 52.

10. *DW*, II, 70. Subsequent references to Gay's drama are to the text in *DW*.
11. For Pope's 'Imaginative' women, see the recent work by David Fairer, *Pope's Imagination* (Manchester, 1984), pp. 82–112, Brean Hammond, *Pope* (Brighton, 1986), pp. 150–94, and Rebecca Ferguson, *The Unbalanced Mind: Pope and the Rule of Passion* (Brighton, 1986), *passim*.
12. *PP*, II, 459. Subsequent references are cited in the text.
13. See especially the passage on the *Socraticae chartae* (308–19).
14. See Herbert Davis (ed.), *The Prose Writings of Jonathan Swift*, 16 vols. (Oxford, 1939–75), I, 49–51.
15. E. Audra and Aubrey Williams, *Pastoral Poetry and An Essay on Criticism* (London and New Haven, 1961), p. 275. Vol. I of the Twickenham Pope.
16. *Some Versions of Pastoral* (London, 1935), p. 195.
17. 'Menalcas' Song: The Meaning of Art and Artifice in Gay's Poetry', *JEGP*, 65 (1966), 662, 665. Possibly the first commentator to notice this was Hazlitt in his *The Round Table* essay 'On *The Beggar's Opera*' (1817): 'He chose a very unpromising ground to work upon, and he has prided himself in adorning it with all the graces, the precision and brilliancy of style . . . The elegance of the composition is in exact proportion to the coarseness of the materials' (P. P. Howe (ed.), *The Complete Works of William Hazlitt*, 21 vols. [London, 1930–34], IV, 65).
18. 'The Wolf in the Fold: John Gay in *The Shepherd's Week* and *Trivia*', *Studies in English Literature*, 23 (1983), 423.
19. *The Daring Muse: Augustan Poetry Reconsidered* (Cambridge, 1985), p. 213.
20. Herbert Davis (ed.), *Swift: Poetical Works* (Oxford, 1967), p. 498.

1

'A Poet, and a Patron, and Ten Pound': John Gay and Patronage

by BREAN S. HAMMOND

Those who have occasion to consult the new *Oxford Companion to English Literature* may be surprised to notice the large amount of space, in the relatively short entry, that is absorbed by information about Gay's finances. We do not have absolutely precise information about his earnings, but some figures are recorded in Lintot's memorandum book and printed by Nichols in the *Literary Anecdotes*.[1] Since no such memorandum book exists for Tonson, and printers' ledgers are not to hand to record such information as the size of edition-runs, the precise terms of copyright agreements are unavailable. The figures, therefore, will remain soft, but some sense of magnitude can be obtained. The subscription edition of *Trivia*, for instance, made enough, as Arbuthnot joked (February 1715–16), to keep Gay off the streets: 'Gay has gott so much money by his art of walking the streets, that he is ready to sett up with equipage.'[2] Even more successful in cash terms was the Lintot and Tonson volume of Gay's *Poems on Several Occasions* (1720), another subscription venture. It is quite true that Gay invested the profits in the ill-fated South Sea Company, but the speculation was probably not, as the *Oxford Companion* calls it, 'disastrous'.[3] Vinton Dearing thinks that Gay probably lost most of what he made

23

out of the *Poems*, but 'it is not necessary to infer that he was even temporarily destitute.'⁴ At any rate, he picked up the pieces rapidly, and even works like his play *The Captives*, not an outstanding success artistically, earned him in excess of £1,000. We all know that *The Beggar's Opera* made 'Gay rich and Rich gay'; while *Polly* was a *succès de scandale* to the tune of some £1,200. By April 1731, he was able to write to Swift as an independent man of substance, possessed of a fortune amounting to 'above three thousand, four hundred pounds'; and his estate was worth more than £6,000 when he died.⁵

Assuredly, then, Gay was no stereotype of the neglected poet, starving to death in a garret, his genius all unrecognized. For the record, he died in the Duke of Queensberry's fine Palladian town-house, designed by Leoni and situated in the splendid new development of Burlington Gardens. Nevertheless, it has to be said that the lines Pope devoted to Gay in the *Epistle to Dr. Arbuthnot* (1735) do create the stereotyped impression:

> Blest be the *Great*! for those they take away,
> And those they left me—For they left me GAY,
> Left me to see neglected Genius bloom,
> Neglected die! and tell it on his Tomb;
> Of all thy blameless Life the sole Return
> My Verse, and QUEENSB'RY weeping o'er thy Urn! (255–60)⁶

Mary Barber, poetess and friend of Swift, had a more palpable sense of what that neglect amounted to. Her poem 'A True Tale', published in her 1734 *Poems on Several Occasions* (to which Pope subscribed), recounts the story of a mother who takes care to select appropriate reading for her son. She gives him Gay's *Fables* and the boy is shocked by the autobiographical fable that chronicles Gay's neglect, 'The Hare with many Friends'. His mother, 'RESOLV'D to lull his Woes to rest', comforts him:

> This has been yet GAY'S Case, I own,
> But now his Merit's amply known:
> Content that tender Heart of thine,
> He'll be the Care of CAROLINE.
> Who thus instructs the Royal Race,
> Must have a Pension, or a Place.
> —MAMMA, if you were Queen, says he,
> And such a Book were wrote for me,
> I find, 'tis so much to your Taste,

> That GAY would keep his Coach at least.
> . . . WHAT I'd bestow, says she, my Dear?
> At least, *a thousand Pounds a Year*.[7]

Gay's merit is no longer so 'amply known', and many readers will encounter him for the first time in Pope's lines quoted above. The terms 'neglected' and 'the sole Return', the use of the metaphor of 'blooming'—these do create an impression of the great man perishing in Mozartian poverty. This impression is partly reinforced by a reading of Gay's correspondence. His letters are a litany of complaint about his failure to gain suitable employment at Court, with expressions of financial insecurity intercalated, so that the two factors appear to be connected. In the early letters, he records, on 30 December 1714, that Rowe has become Clerk of the Council to the Prince and, on 29 January 1714–15, Philips a Lottery Paymaster, while he is passed over. His epistolary trajectory takes in the financial returns on *The What D'Ye Call It* and *Trivia* and becomes gradually disenchanted with place-hunting in the 1720s, until he can comment on all those great men who have conferred upon him 'many Civilitys . . . but very few real Benefits' (22 December 1722). He is cynical enough, by August 1723, to offer Mrs. Howard, of all people, a 'Court Creed', which gives lessons in insincerity, and by October 1727 the climax occurs when he abandons all his hopes of preferment:

> O that I had never known what a Court was! Dear *Pope*, what a barren Soil (to me so) have I been striving to produce something out of! Why did I not take your Advice before my writing Fables for the Duke, not to write them? Or rather, to write them for some young Nobleman? It is my very hard Fate, I must get nothing, write for them or against them. I find myself in such a strange Confusion and Depression of Spirits, that I have not Strength even to make my Will; though I perceive by many Warnings, I have no continuing City here. I begin to look upon myself as one already dead.[8]

What is the justification for the sense that Gay clearly possessed of being neglected? The question is a difficult one to pose, because, as Pope said in the *Epistle to Dr. Arbuthnot*, 'A man's true merit 'tis not hard to find,/ But each man's secret standard in his mind' (175–76) is another matter![9] The *Dictionary of National*

Biography entry on Gay sounds a note of stern, not to say finger-wagging, caution on this point, and is worth citing:

> The lamentations of Gay's associates over his 'unpensioned' condition . . . require to be taken by the modern reader with a grain of salt. Gay had never rendered any services to entitle him to those court favours which he wasted his life in expecting, and on more than one occasion must have made himself a *persona ingrata* to those in power. Beginning as a mere mercer's apprentice, from such slender poetical credentials as 'Wine' and 'Rural Sports', he became the friend of all the best-known writers of his age, from Bolingbroke to Broome, and the companion of dukes and earls. Between their real and their fictitious value, his works succeeded on the whole remarkably well. . . . If he was unrewarded by an ungrateful court . . . it must be remembered that for the most part he lived in clover in great houses, and that he left at his death a very fair fortune acquired by his pen. . . .[10]

We might not like the tone of this very much, but it is instructive. When Gay commenced his writing career in or around 1708, literary patronage had diversified into an unprecedented multiplicity of forms—and Gay benefited from virtually all of them.[11] We might look at private patronage—the support of learning and the arts by the wealthy and the titled. There is surely very little to sustain any accusation of neglect here. Visible encouragement of the arts was dominated, in the early eighteenth-century, by a handful of high-profile patrons, and one of them, the Earl of Burlington, took Gay under his wide umbrella. In July 1715, we hear of Gay and the lawyer Fortescue taking a trip to Devon at Burlington's expense. Gay was resident at Burlington House during the period when the Earl was also extending protection to Handel and making major alterations to the architecture and landscape of Chiswick House, with Pope's energetic collaboration.[12] The opening of Gay's *Epistle to Burlington* celebrates the grandeur of Burlington's Palladian aspirations, yet the tone, with its joke at the expense of Pope's diminutive size, is intimate and domestic:

> While you, my lord, bid stately Piles ascend,
> Or in your *Chiswick* Bow'rs enjoy your Friend;
> Where *Pope* unloads the Bough within his reach,
> Of purple Grape, blue Plumb, or blushing Peach;
> I journey far.—You knew fat Bards might tire,
> And, mounted, sent me forth your trusty Squire. (1–6)[13]

Subsequently, Gay lived a rootless, wandering life, often depending on the bounty of the various aristocratic and wealthy hosts who provided for him. Thus, he was travelling on the Continent in 1717 and 1719—his biographer, W. H. Irving, does not know who paid the bills[14]; most of 1721 and 1722 was spent at Burlington House, while in 1723 he is to be found in Tunbridge Wells with the Burlingtons, again staying at Chiswick in 1724; 1728 is a typical year, with Gay residing at Cashiobury (Pulteney's house) in March, and visiting Bath with the Duchess of Marlborough and Congreve in May. Mrs. Howard had the pleasure of paying Gay's bills at Marble Hill on various occasions, and from 1729 onwards Gay became permanently established in the Queensberry household, dividing his time between their London town-house and the estate in Amesbury, Wiltshire. An impressionistic reading of Gay's biography suggests that he never had a home of his own at all, but in fact, he did: the Earl of Lincoln obtained lodgings for him at Whitehall. If we compare his life to Pope's, we find that although Pope's habit, post-1733, was also to spend his summers visiting friends, Twickenham remains a still-point in this turning world. By contrast, Gay is not associated with any house or garden through which he may have expressed his personality. This contributes to the somewhat desultory feeling that attaches to Gay's later life.

Private patronage extended beyond the bounds of hospitality and presumably of payment for dedications. Sometime near the end of 1722, the position of Commissioner for State Lotteries was secured for Gay, commanding a yearly salary of £150. This was no inconsiderable sum—the best paid Government sinecure raised £400 annually—and John Chamberlayne's *Magnae Britanniae Notitia* (26th. edn. of *Angliae Notitia*, 1723) lists Mrs. Howard's pension as Lady of the Queen's Bedchamber at only £300.[15] Gay's post does not seem to have involved burdensome duties. Information about the State Lottery is surprisingly difficult to come by, but it seems to have been a carry-over from the various fund-raising lotteries promoted to fight the War of the Spanish Succession.[16] The public were invited to buy tickets at a certain unit cost, which earned interest and participated in an annual draw for a cash prize of some £10,000. Unlike the notorious Harburgh Lottery of 1723, which was a fiddle, this

State Lottery was respectable and was drawn annually in September. Gay writes to Swift on 16 September 1726 that 'the Lottery begins to be drawn on Monday next, but my week of attendance will be the first in October.'[17] Other than supervision of the draw, Gay's only duty seemed to be to go to the Exchequer to collect his salary.[18] Who procured this post for him remains unknown, but it was probably a patron who was on friendly terms with Treasury or Exchequer officialdom—James Stanhope, William Aislabie, James Craggs or Walpole himself. The Earl of Burlington out of Craggs seems to me the likeliest stable. Earlier in his career, Gay had been employed as secretary to the Duchess of Monmouth, and thereafter in Government service as secretary to Lord Clarendon on his mission to the Elector of Hanover. He had experience, therefore, both of sinecures and of genuine political appointments. Despite Pope's remark in *The Dunciad* (1728) that 'Gay dies un-pension'd, with a hundred Friends' (III, 326),[19] he *was* offered a stipend from the Civil List of £150 p.a.—the same amount that conferred independence on Samuel Johnson—for the post of Gentleman Usher to the Princess Louisa. It is difficult to say why Gay thought this so derisory—his only comment was that he was too old for the job—but perhaps he felt entitled to a post in the Lord Chamberlain's office more suited to a literary man.

Private patrons were willing to go to very considerable lengths for Gay. The story of the Queensberrys' brazen show of support for *Polly*, touting it around Court and soliciting subscriptions, is well known. Admittedly, Charles Douglas seemed to be looking for an excuse to break with George II's Court and jettison his Privy Counsellorship, and the couple enjoyed delicious notoriety as a result; but the incident called forth a splendid expression of *hauteur* from the Duchess:

> . . . the Dutchess of Queensberry is suprized, and well pleased, that the King has given her so agreeable a Command as to stay from Court, where she never came for Diversion, but to bestow a great Civility upon the King and Queen. She hopes by such an unprecedented Order as this, the King will see as few as he wishes at his Court, particularly such as dare think or speak Truth; I dare not do otherwise, & ought not, nor could have imagined, that it would not have been the very highest

Compliment I could possibly pay the King, to endeavour to
support Truth and Innocence in his House.

Particularly when the King & Queen both told me, that they had
not read Mr. Gay's play. . . .[20]

It is difficult to establish what, exactly, were the grounds on
which the Queensberrys patronized Gay. He was certainly
entrusted with the Duke's business affairs, but was quick to
repudiate the title 'Manager' in a letter to Swift (18 July 1731),
claiming that he was merely acting as a stand-in for 'an unjust
Steward' who was sacked.[21] The Queensberrys were early
Patrons of the Royal Society of Music and, as such, would have
had a clear interest in Gay's operatic experiments.[22] How widely
they patronized the other arts—whether, for example, they were
notable collectors—is not an easy question to answer. Wyatt
Papworth's drawings of the principal apartments at Amesbury
are not labelled and it is impossible to decide the use to which the
rooms were put. However, the section drawing does depict a
picturesque landscape and a more classical one prominently
displayed, suggesting some interest in the visual arts.[23] Possibly
their main incentive for extending hospitality to Gay was purely
personal—the undoubted pleasure of his company.

Other forms of patronage are also relevant to the question of
how much benefit Gay derived from the multiplex eighteenth-
century system. Subscription publishing is now generally
recognized to be a form of patronage: a hybrid form that called
for co-operation between private patrons, who lobbied friends
to subsidize the author prior to publication, and booksellers,
who agreed to bear printing costs on this basis.[24] Capitalizing
on the outstanding success of Pope's Homer—'(thanks to
Homer) since I live and thrive', as Pope later put it in one of the
Imitations of Horace (II, ii, 68)[25]—Trivia and Poems on Several
Occasions were both subscription editions. If we compare the
subscription list for the latter with that for Pope's Iliad translation (1715–20), the massive overlap suggests that Gay used
Pope's list as the basis for his own recruiting drive. Finally,
accepting the broad definition of the term 'patronage' which
would extend it to include the reading public and the theatre
audience, we have already said that Gay was successful in the
market-place.

Insofar as we can speak of objectivity in this matter, it seems that there are no objective grounds for the sense of injury or neglect that Gay felt, which leaves us with something of a conundrum. Why did he feel it? This is, I have come to think, a sub-question of a wider issue in Gay biography. The general assumption made about his personality is summed up in James Sutherland's phrase for Gay—'a sort of Augustan Peter Pan'. Sutherland's John Gay would indeed be more at home in Disneyland than walking the streets of eighteenth-century London:

> It must be added that Gay's own friends rarely asserted his claims as a poet. They thought of him, and when he was dead they remembered him, as a man—gentle, good-natured, indolent, lovable in the extreme, shiftless, impracticable, innocent, volatile, a sort of Augustan Peter Pan riding in the coaches of his noble friends, dining at their tables, shooting their pheasants, but quite incapable of attending to his worldly affairs. They all loved him, and they all looked after him; he was a sort of joint responsibility, and he repaid them by his wit and geniality and by his unselfish interest in their own concerns.[26]

For a Peter Pan, his letters are remarkably crammed with grown-up anxieties. It sometimes seems as if Gay is a kind of Jonsonian character, compelled to live up to a surname that is prescriptive over his behaviour, nor would I agree that his disappointment was altogether the result of starry-eyed naïveté. On the contrary, it may have been the result of over-ambitiousness.

Matthew Prior was an example of a slightly older contemporary who could show Gay what sort of career was compatible with being a celebrated poet. Like Gay, Prior was of humble origins but, through the intervention of the notable patron the Earl of Dorset, gained an education and a secretaryship with King William's ambassador to Holland, a post that initiated a sparkling career for him as a diplomat. A remarkable succession of secretarial posts and commissionerships culminated in his being a principal negotiator of the Treaty of Utrecht. Even after his impeachment and imprisonment, Prior benefitted from Lord Harley's patronage both in cash terms and in putting together the subscription list for his *Poems* (1718); and he finished life as a gentleman-gardener on his estate at Down

30

Hall. There are enough incipient similarities between Gay's career and Prior's to suggest the latter as a rôle-model, though of course Gay did not achieve as high a quality of patronage. Gay's poetry is influenced by Prior's tales, and in the delightful *On a Miscellany of Poems* he paid tribute to Prior's unique blend of the robust and the mellifluous, a marriage of Chaucer and Spenser:

> Let *Prior*'s Muse with soft'ning Accents move,
> Soft as the Strains of constant *Emma*'s Love:
> Or let his Fancy chuse some jovial Theme,
> As when he told *Hans Carvel*'s jealous Dream;
> *Prior* th'admiring Reader entertains,
> With *Chaucer*'s Humour, and with *Spencer*'s Strains.
>
> (60–5)

But perhaps the answer lies not so much in the kind of *expectations* Gay entertained, as in the changing nature of the patronage system itself and the difficulties literary men felt in adjusting to it. No definitive account of the history of literary patronage from, say, the Stuart era to the Hanoverian era has yet been written and I certainly do not presume to know the *truth* about the way the system developed.[27] I do have some suggestions to make, however, about that development as determined by the Pope circle's view of it. To them, there was a relatively uncomplicated relationship between the vigour of the Court, especially of the King, and the health of the nation's intellectual life. Despite the great differences that existed between the moral tone of James I's Court and that of Charles I, the literary and performance arts received a good deal of direct encouragement from the Crown and from Courtier-patrons. Ben Jonson is an example of the kind of literary figure that the Pope circle would have envied and now considered to be extinct: regular annual employment on Court masques brought Jonson into contact with all the major literary patrons of the day, allowing him to develop relationships with the Herbert and Sidney families and with a remarkable collection of great literary ladies—Lucy, Countess of Bedford, most prominent amongst them. Yet none of this seemed to compromise Jonson's independence in making a fairly impressive bid to become the English Horace.[28]

31

Swift's admiration for the Caroline Court's patronage of learning comes out in his *Proposal for Correcting the English Tongue* (1712), wherein Charles I's Court is compared favourably to the 'very ill Taste both of Style and Wit, which prevailed under King *James* the First'.[29] An unqualified Golden Age view of the Stuart era is recorded in the only unambiguous celebration of patronage to be found in Gay's poetry, in *Trivia*:

> Come, F[ortescue], sincere, experienc'd Friend,
> Thy Briefs, thy Deeds, and ev'n thy Fees suspend;
> Come, let us leave the *Temple*'s silent Walls,
> Me Bus'ness to my distant Lodging calls:
> Through the long *Strand* together let us stray,
> With thee conversing, I forgot the Way.
> Behold that narrow Street, which steep descends,
> Whose Building to the slimy Shore extends;
> Here *Arundell*'s fam'd Structure rear'd its Frame,
> The Street alone retains an empty Name:
> Where *Titian*'s glowing Paint the Canvas warm'd,
> And *Raphael*'s fair Design, with Judgment charm'd,
> Now hangs the Bell-man's Song, and pasted here,
> The colour'd Prints of *Overton* appear.
> Where Statues Breath'd, the Work of *Phidias* Hands,
> A wooden Pump, or lonely Watch-house stands.
> There *Essex*' stately Pile adorn'd the Shore,
> There *Cecil*'s, *Bedford*'s, *Villers*', now no more.
> Yet *Burlington*'s fair Palace still remains;
> Beauty within, without Proportion reigns.
> Beneath his Eye declining Art revives,
> The Wall with animated Picture lives;
> There *Hendel* strikes the Strings, the melting Strain
> Transports the Soul, and thrills through ev'ry Vein;
> There oft' I enter (but with cleaner shoes)
> For *Burlington*'s belov'd by ev'ry Muse. (I, 475–500)

Mention of the Earl of Arundel here is especially significant. Arundel was perhaps the greatest of all Stuart collector-patrons, whose house (Arundel House) situated between the river and the Strand, incorporated a two-storeyed long gallery designed by Inigo Jones. This building housed the Earl's unrivalled collection of paintings and statuary, both in architectural style and in function the result of the Arundels' earlier tour to Italy in the company of Inigo Jones.[30] Celebrating

'Arundell's fam'd Structure', and lamenting its supercession by 'a wooden Pump, or lonely Watch-house', Gay is addressing himself to a particularly important instance of the *sic transit gloria mundi* theme. Since Arundel was the original patron of Palladianism, there is a natural transition to Burlington, who can be usefully exploited both as the last of a noble line—'Yet *Burlington's* fair Palace still remains'—and as the phoenix from whose ashes the new era of patronage will emerge: 'Beneath his Eye declining Art revives.' It is a remarkably flexible and economical passage, instinct with the poet's own personality—'ev'n thy Fees suspend' and '(but with cleaner Shoes)'—but widening out to embrace the themes of architectural decline and artistic *risorgimento*.

The history of patronage after the Civil War has a post-lapsarian complexity about it. Charles II's reign proved very difficult to assess in terms of the effects of his personality on the arts. Pope opts, in the *Epistle to Augustus* (1737), for emasculation, but not without observing that 'Love and Sport' produces its own ravishingly sensuous art forms:

> The Soldier breath'd the Gallantries of France,
> And ev'ry flow'ry Courtier writ Romance.
> Then Marble soften'd into life grew warm,
> And yielding Metal flow'd to human form:
> Lely on animated Canvas Stole
> The sleepy Eye, that spoke the melting soul.
> No wonder then, when all was Love and Sport,
> The willing Muses were debauch'd at Court;
> On each enervate string they taught the Note
> To pant, or tremble thro' an Eunuch's throat. (145–54)[31]

There was little doubt that the contributions made by later monarchs were negative; and in any event, since England was engulfed in a prolonged period of war, the impoverishment of the Crown entailed that those arts in the Royal service were not liable to flourish. Coeval with the development of constitutional monarchy and the two-party system was an unprecedented politicization of the arts, but naturally, in proportion to its semantic content, literature was particularly affected, so that as Royal patronage was declining and writers had to look increasingly towards powerful noblemen like Dorset, Halifax, Chandos, Burlington or the Harleys, private patronage was becoming politically conditional.

33

The decline of absolutism was, doubtless, a factor in the gradual change from art commissioned to art marketed that accelerated in the century following the Restoration, but, as Bertrand Goldgar has argued, the Pope circle saw the politicization of patronage as the besetting evil of the Walpole era.[32] They believed that Walpole had systematized this tendency by putting patronage in ministerial hands and harnessing authors to the treadmill of the Government press. In the 1730s, Opposition writers regarded Walpole as having broken faith with an earlier tradition of patronage under which writers were not forced to trade off free speech against square meals. He was regularly accused of encouraging inferior writers whose pens could be bought, and neglecting men of independent genius. Pope's letter to Gay of 23 October 1730 puts the point with panache:

> There may indeed be a Wooden image or two of Poetry set up, to preserve the memory there once were bards in Britain; and (like the *Giants* at *Guildhall*) show the bulk and bad taste for our ancestors: At present the poet Laureat and Stephen Duck serve for this purpose; a drunken sot of a *Parson* holds forth the emblem of *inspiration*, and an honest industrious *Thresher* not unaptly represented *Pains* and *Labour*. I hope this Phaenomenon of Wiltshire has appear'd at Amesbury, or the Duchess will be thought insensible to all bright qualities and exalted genius's, in Court and country alike.[33]

It is sometimes overlooked that Gay was himself very early into print with this view. His *Epistle to . . . Paul Methuen* urges precisely this case:

> Why flourish'd verse in great *Augustus*' reign?
> He and *Mecaenas* lov'd the Muse's strain.
> But now that wight in poverty must mourn
> Who was (O cruel stars!) a Poet born.
> Yet there are ways for authors to be great;
> Write ranc'rous libels to reform the State:
> Or if you chuse more sure and ready ways,
> Spatter a Minister with fulsome praise;
> Launch out with freedom, flatter him enough;
> Fear not, all men are dedication-proof.
> Be bolder yet, you must go farther still,
> Dip deep in gall thy mercenary quill.

> He, who his pen in party quarrels draws,
> Lists an hir'd bravo to support the cause;
> He must indulge his Patron's hate and spleen,
> And stab the fame of those he ne'er has seen.
> Why then should authors mourn their desp'rate case?
> Be brave, do this, and then demand a place.
> Why art thou poor? exert the gifts to rise,
> And banish tim'rous vertue from thy eyes. (15–34)

Gay's main complaint is that Britain is not a soil in which genius can flourish, and the interest of the argument is that it is primarily *ideological*. It might be thought that particular arts are the natural accomplishments of particular nations, but Gay advises Methuen that the economic conditions of production are far more significant:

> Why must we climb the *Alpine* mountains sides
> To find the seat where Harmony resides?
> Why touch we not so soft the silver lute,
> The cheerful haut-boy, and the mellow flute?
> 'Tis not th'*Italian* clime improves the sound,
> But there the Patrons of her sons are found. (9–14)

William Kent, for instance, whom the poem improbably compares to Raphael, has to go to Italy to find work as a history painter; and even if Burlington does recall him to play a part in the Palladian revival, the general level of taste is so low that artists of genius suffer detraction rather than encouragement. Here is the poem's second ideological contribution, one which is later to bulk so large in Opposition writing, that we can now distinguish 'sublime' art from 'nonsense'. These are Gay's prophetic lines (prophetic, certainly with respect to Chandos's future fate):

> While *Burlington*'s proportion'd columns rise,
> Does not he stand the gaze of envious eyes?
> Doors, windows are condemn'd by passing fools,
> Who know not that they damn *Palladio*'s rules.
> If *Chandois* with a lib'ral hand bestow,
> Censure imputes it all to pomp and show;
> When, if the motive right were understood,
> His daily pleasure is in doing good.
>   Had *Pope* with groveling numbers fill'd his page,
> *Dennis* had never kindled into rage.

35

> 'Tis the sublime that hurts the Critic's ease;
> Write nonsense and he reads and sleeps in peace:
> Were *Prior*, *Congreve*, *Swift* and *Pope* unknown,
> Poor slander-selling *Curll* would be undone.
> He who would free from malice pass his days,
> Must live obscure, and never merit praise. (67–82)

This distinction, later evolving in Pope's *Dunciad* into that between the hireling scribbler and the independent writer of genius, is doubtless not new—Jonson had a strong sense of it—but a new 'moment' is conferred upon it by significant changes in the basis of literary production. By the end of the seventeenth century, the size of the London reading public had greatly increased and a considerable market for writing had developed. But this was not a circumstance that the Scriblerians regarded as happy. They feared a situation where talented writers would be increasingly driven towards reliance on bookseller-publishers as brokers for public patronage. Vinton Dearing's introduction to his edition of the *Poetry and Prose* contains an important paragraph on the prominence of money in Gay's life. He puts the point in sociological terms:

> It may be asked why Gay's finances should play so large a part in so brief a biography. In the first place, he made constant reference to them in his poetry. In the second place, his life was one long suspense for himself and his friends. Merely to have wealthy and generous patrons was not enough; he had to be able to enter into their pleasures in some respects as an equal—if necessary, even to lose money at gaming. A gentleman might look down on many, but he pretended to look up to none. . . . In addition, it is fair to say, Gay's affectionate nature would have been stifled by absolute indigence. We cannot imagine him sharing as he did in the life of the Queensberrys had he been on the level of a poor relation.[34]

Dearing is employing his powers of empathetic understanding to reconstruct the situation as it may have appeared to Gay, but the issue is more properly an *ideological* one.

I use the term 'ideology' here in the sense employed by the French critic Pierre Macherey.[35] According to Macherey, ideology is present in literary works not only in so far as it is shaped by an author's consciously held beliefs, but also on an inexplicit and unconscious level. A writer's expression is partly shaped by the juncture at which he enters history, and for John Gay, I contend, the changing conditions of literary patronage were an important determinant of his expression—both of what he was able to express and of what he could only express unsatisfactorily through contradiction. One parameter of what Gay was able to say on this subject was created by the way in which Pope and Swift managed his image. To his Scriblerian associates, Gay was an important test case for their view of the changing economics of authorship; and the conundrum that this essay addresses, that of the 'neglected' Gay, is partly produced by their exploitation of his predicament. The best place to observe this exploitation—admittedly posthumous—is in Pope's *Epistle to Dr. Arbuthnot*, where a key distinction is made between *dependence* and *independence*. Pope's poem is dominated by three satiric portraits which are thematically connected in that they are all models of perverse dependence—in domestic friendship, in literature and in politics. Defined against these is the poet himself, who is seen to be *independent*. Unlike the professional 'hacks'—that is, writers whose skills and opinions are entirely specified by their employers—Pope represents himself as a man of genius who is not subject to the market forces that bring lesser writings into existence. The *Epistle*'s ideology of independence can be crudely paraphrased thus: 'There exists a tribe of professional writers who make a living by the pen. They need to write to pay the rent. Regrettably, their endeavours are encouraged by some of their social superiors who ought to know better—Atticus, who befriends men of inferior talent; Bufo, who finances them—even if according to a law of diminishing returns; and Sporus, another model of perverse dependence whose dealings with The Prompter and The Queen poison the world of letters at source. Alexander Pope, the model of virtuous independence, alone resists the attempts to drag him into the nexus of mercenarism.'

Within this ideology, Gay functions exactly as does Dryden, as an example of genius less robust than Pope's own, whose talents are not nourished as they should be by the soil of patronage—'the region where genius meets power', in Irvin Ehrenpreis's suggestive phrase.[36] The lines on Gay are an attempt to appropriate his image for Pope's own independence mythology, as we can see if we attend to the tombstone reference—'Neglected die, and tell it on his Tomb'. This is presumably to Gay's own mordant epitaph—'Life is a Jest, and all Things show it;/ I thought so once, but now I know it'—but of course it also summons up the inscription placed by the Queensberrys:

> Here lie the ashes of Mr. JOHN GAY,
> The warmest friend,/ The most benevolent man;
> Who maintained/ independency/ In low circumstances of
>   fortune;
> Integrity/ In the midst of a corrupt age;

and so forth. After Gay had refused the Gentleman Usher post, Pope's letter of condolence (16 October 1727) energetically recruited him for the independence pose—and quite successfully, given that Gay also took it up in his later correspondence:

> I have many years ago magnify'd in my own mind, and repeated to you, a ninth Beatitude, added to the eight in the Scripture; *Blessed is he who expects nothing, for he shall never be disappointed.* I could find in my heart to congratulate you on this happy Dismission from all Court-Dependance; I dare say I shall find you the Better and the Honester Man for it, many years hence; very probably the healthfuller, and the chearfuller into the bargain. You are happily rid of many cursed ceremonies, as well as of many ill, and vicious habits, of which few or no men escape the Infection, who are hackney'd and trammelled in the ways of a Court. Princes indeed, and Peers (the Lackies of Princes) and Ladies (the Fools of Peers) will smile on you the less; but men of Worth, and real Friends, will look on you the better. There is a thing, the only thing which Kings and Queens cannot give you (for they have it not to give) *Liberty*, which is worth all they have; and which, as yet, I hope *Englishmen* need not ask from their hands. You will enjoy That, and your own Integrity, and the satisfactory Consciousness of having *not* merited such Graces from them, as they bestow only on the mean, servile, flattering, interested, and undeserving.[37]

Swift also tried to manage Gay's image, though in a somewhat different direction. Swift's experience of patronage, at any rate after he left Temple's protection, was of repeated disappointment. When he might have seen his career progress as spectacularly as John Robinson's, who became Bishop of London and Lord Privy Seal, he was disappointed by the Earl of Berkeley. Later, he was always eager to have his embittered view of patronage confirmed, as it was by Mrs. Howard.[38] Swift's correspondence repeatedly blames Mrs. Howard for Gay's eventual disappointment at Court, and in *A Libel on Dr. Delany* (1730) he projects these sentiments into a Solomon Grundy-ish view of Gay's career:

> Thus *Gay*, the *Hare* with many Friends,
> Twice sev'n long Years the *Court* attends,
> Who, under Tales conveying Truth,
> To Virtue form'd a *Princely* Youth,
> Who pay'd his Courtship with the Croud,
> As far as *Modest Pride* allow'd,
> Rejects a servile *Usher*'s Place,
> And leaves *St. James*'s in Disgrace. (53–60)[39]

For Swift, genius *never really could* meet power, because, as *A Libel* argues, political figures only ever entertain wits as an escape from business—and a poet asking a politician for a place *is* business. In the poem Swift wrote *To Mr. Gay* in 1731, celebrating his supposed employment as Steward to the Duke of Queensberry, he suggests that stewardship to a benevolent private individual is an ideal post for a poet, because poets feel about money as eunuchs do about concubines—it does not excite them.[40]

Thus, Gay's Scriblerian partners created for him a choice of rôles—the neglected poet who is the living proof that existing forms of patronage are tainted, or the independent writer, poor but virtuous, who was born to blush unseen. It is an ambivalence that his friends *articulated* rather than invented, because it threads through the entirety of his poetic career. As Patricia Meyer Spacks observed twenty years ago, Gay 'typically wrote directly about his own literary problems'.[41]

For many years, Gay wrestled in his life and in his verse with the Scylla and Charybdis of being a hack, on the one hand, and a client, on the other. A lucrative and guaranteed position would have delivered him from financial insecurity and kept him above the market place—the literary prostitution that Pope's *Dunciad* encouraged him to despise. Several self-reflexive later works, notably *Fable* L (1727)—'The Hare and many *Friends*'—and *Fables* VII and X (1738)—'The *Countrymen* and

John Gay and the Scriblerians

Jupiter' and 'The *Degenerate Bees*'—find the poet trying to exorcise the earlier experience of disappointment and neglect, dispersing his life's experience in interesting ways. The posthumously performed play *The Distress'd Wife* is the clearest example.[42] Sir Thomas Willit is a country landowner who has found his attendance at Court, in the hope of securing a position through Lord Courtlove's patronage, financially ruinous. The play's action dramatizes Willit's decision to withdraw from the Court and the resultant difficulties he has in prising his wife's tenacious hold away from the fashionable world. Relationships are dominated by the attempts of various characters to *buy* others: and the normative characters are those, like Willit's merchant-uncle Barter, and the heiress Miss Sprightly, who act independently and refuse to be bought. Barter's defence of commerce, translated into a theory of literary production, points towards acceptance of the new market-economy, in which independent writers would exchange their skills for payment:

> *Barter.* Luxury, Necessity, and Dependance, are Advantages inconsistent with our Way of Life.—Industry and Commerce (however unfashionable) oblige us to OEconomy and Justice; and (notwithstanding the politer Examples of the *World*) our Credit does *still*, in a great measure, depend upon our moral Character. (IV, xvi, 12–17)[43]

Friendless is the Willits' indigent and dependent niece, and there is a harrowing scene when she is made to turn out the contents of her pockets by the odious Lady Willit, to be made the object of ridicule. The name, Friendless, is reminiscent of Gay's autobiographical *Fable*, 'The Hare and many Friends', where the friends are to be spoken of in inverted commas. I would suggest that in the Willit/Lady Willit polarity, Gay projects the clash between his rational desire for independence and retreat and his emotional desire for Court patronage and the *beau monde*. He is sexist enough to associate these desires with, respectively, the male and female genders:

> *Sir Thomas.* I have quitted all my Pretensions to an Employment; and did your Lordship weigh the Affair rightly, you would give up yours to a Wife.—An Employment frequently runs you into every fashionable Extravagance, Luxury and Debt: Does not a Wife do the same?—An Employment influences your Words

and Actions, even against Reason and common Sense: A Wife hath done, and can do the same. (I, iv, 71–8)

Here, Sir Thomas establishes an homology between a Government place and a wife, which perhaps suggests why this megrimm'd Peter Pan never found his Wendy.

NOTES

1. John Nichols, *Literary Anecdotes of the Eighteenth Century; comprising biographical memoirs of W. Bowyer, and many of his learned friends* . . ., 9 vols. (London, 1812–15), VIII, 296. The most valuable single item is his revival of *The Wife of Bath*: £75–0–0 (compared to its first production: £25–0–0). *Trivia* brought in £43–0–0, *Three Hours After Marriage*, £43–2–6, and *The What D'Ye Call It*, £16–2–6. The total came to £234–10–0.
2. *Letters*, p. 27.
3. Margaret Drabble (ed.), *The Oxford Companion to English Literature*, 5th edn. (Oxford, 1985), p. 384.
4. *PP*, II, 609.
5. *Letters*, p. 105.
6. John Butt (ed.), *Imitations of Horace* (London and New Haven, 1961), p. 114, Vol. IV of the Twickenham Pope.
7. *Poems on Several Occasions* (London, 1734), pp. 11–12.
8. *Letters*, pp. 16, 18, 41, 46, 66.
9. Butt, p. 109.
10. *Dictionary of National Biography*, compact edn., 2 vols. (Oxford, 1975), I, 762.
11. An important article that codifies some forms of eighteenth-century patronage is Paul J. Korshin, 'Types of Eighteenth-Century Literary Patronage', *Eighteenth-Century Studies*, 7 (1974), 453–73.
12. Jacques Carré makes clear how important a form of patronage was the extending of hospitality under the conditions offered by the Palladian villa in 'Burlington's Literary Patronage', *British Journal for Eighteenth-Century Studies*, 5 (1982), 21–33.
13. Line references are to the texts of Gay's poems in *PP* from which all quotations are taken.
14. W. H. Irving, *John Gay: Favorite of the Wits* (Durham, N.C., 1940), p. 174.
15. *Magnae Britanniae Notitia: Or, The Present State of Great Britain* . . . (London, 1723), Part II, Book III, No. XXVIII, p. 567. Mrs. Howard is one of six 'Bed-Chamber Women' to the Princess of Wales.
16. See P. G. M. Dickson, *The Financial Revolution in England* (London, 1967), p. 54n., and C. L. Ewen, *Lotteries and Sweepstakes in the British Isles* (London, 1932), *passim*.
17. *Letters*, p. 55.

18. See *Letters*, p. 50.
19. James Sutherland (ed.), *The Dunciad*, 3rd edn. (London and New Haven, 1963), p. 189 (1729 Variorum), Vol. V of the Twickenham Pope.
20. Wiltshire Record Office, Salisbury Museum Collection, 164/13/5. Quoted by kind permission of the Archivist.
21. *Letters*, p. 12.
22. Although the Queensberrys are not listed among the original list of subscribers to the Royal Academy of Music (P.R.O. LC 7/3, fols. 52–3), the Duke was among the Governors and Directors for the 1720–21 season, and was defeated in an election for Deputy Governor in 1724/25. See O. E. Deutsch, *Handel: A Documentary Biography* (London, 1955), pp. 123, 175.
23. These drawings are to be found in the British Library's Department of Prints and Drawings. More information on the Queensberrys' life on their country estate is provided in John Chandler and P. S. Goodhugh, *Amesbury: History and Description of a South Wiltshire Town* (Amesbury, 1979), pp. 22–3, 26–7.
24. See Pat Rogers, 'Pope and his Subscribers', *Publishing History*, 3 (1978), 7–36. This is the view taken by Korshin and Carré above and is endorsed by David Foxon in his unpublished 'Pope and the Eighteenth Century Book Trade'.
25. Butt, p. 169.
26. Sutherland, 'John Gay', in James L. Clifford (ed.), *Eighteenth-Century English Literature: Modern Essays in Criticism* (Oxford, 1959; rep. 1971), p. 131. It must be admitted that some evidence for this derives from contemporary or near-contemporary accounts. An early biographer, William Coxe, comments that 'the temper and manners of Gay were exactly the temper and manners of a child, as he retained in advanced age all the feelings and sentiments peculiar to that early period' (*The Life of John Gay*, 2nd edn., (Salisbury, 1797), p. 56). More recent biographical sketches of Gay transmit a similar picture of boyish irresponsibility. C. F. Burgess, in his introduction to the *Letters*, speaks of his love of life, and his inability to accept that the world was not 'a place where dreams are realized and promises are kept' (p. xvii). Maynard Mack declares that 'Gay resembles Pope in wit and vivacity, and in a boy's zest for puns, spoofs, jokes, double entendres, and highjinks generally . . . happy-go-lucky, infinitely good-natured, distinctly a bon vivant . . . improvident . . . and during much of his life the means to his support . . . were the anxious concern and some-times the free gift . . . of his more provident friends' (*Alexander Pope: A Life* (New Haven and London, 1985), p. 187). This is not, I think, the whole truth about Gay.
27. The only full-length study of patronage in the period known to me is Michael Foss, *The Age of Patronage; The Arts in Society 1660–1750* (London, 1971). The shortcomings of his narrative social history are made clear in Paul Korshin's review, *Eighteenth-Century Studies*, 7 (1973–74), 101–5. James Sutherland's essay, 'The Impact of Charles II on Restoration Literature', in Carrol Camden (ed.), *Restoration and Eighteenth-Century Literature* (Chicago and London, 1963), pp. 251–63, suggests some of the

difficulties involved in trying to extrapolate from Charles's general *appreciation* of the arts a view of how far they benefited from his *patronage*.

28. Jonson's importance in structuring the phenomenon of English Augustanism is ably demonstrated by Howard Erskine-Hill, *The Augustan Idea in English Literature* (London, 1983), pp. 108–33.

29. Herbert Davis (ed.), *The Prose Writings of Jonathan Swift*, 16 vols. (Oxford, 1939–75), IV, 9.

30. See Graham Parry, *The Golden Age Restor'd: The Culture of the Stuart Court, 1603–42* (Manchester, 1981), pp. 114, 126–27.

31. Butt, pp. 207–9. There is perhaps an allusion here, in the image of marble softening into life, to Caesar's lines on 'Sweet *poesies*' (V.i.17) in *Poetaster* (1601):

> Shee can so mould *Rome*, and her monuments,
> Within the liquid marble of her lines
> That they shall stand fresh, and miraculous,
> Even when they mix with innovating dust;
>> (V, i, 21–4, *Ben Jonson*, ed. C. H. Herford,
>> Percy and Evelyn Simpson, 11 vols.
>> (Oxford, 1925–52), IV, 290)

32. Goldgar, *Walpole and the Wits: the Relation of Politics to Literature, 1722–42* (Lincoln, Neb., 1976), *passim*.

33. George Sherburn (ed.), *The Correspondence of Alexander Pope*, 5 vols. (Oxford, 1956), III, 143.

34. *PP*, I, 11.

35. *A Theory of Literary Production*, trans. Geoffrey Wall (London, 1978, rep. 1980). *Pour une théorie de la production litteraire* was first published in 1966.

36. Ehrenpreis, *Swift: The Man, his Works and the Age*, 3 vols. (London, 1962–83), III, 648. He discusses Mrs. Howard's failure to achieve suitable patronage for Gay at III, 696–99.

37. *Correspondence*, II, 453.

38. Ehrenpreis, III, 646–65.

39. Herbert Davis (ed.), *Swift: Poetical Works* (Oxford, 1967), p. 418.

40. See *Poetical Works*, pp. 480–85.

> Not Love of Beauty less the Heart inflames
> Of Guardian Eunuchs to the *Sultan*-Dames,
> Their Passions not more impotent and cold,
> Than those of Poets to the *Lust* of Gold. (19–22)

41. Spacks, 'John Gay: a Satirist's Progress', *EC*, 14 (1964), 162.

42. John Fuller comments that this play 'seems at once personal and national', *DW*, I, 64.

43. Act, scene and line references of *The Distress'd Wife* are to the text in *DW*.

2

Gay's Politics

by J. A. DOWNIE

When, in the summer of 1714, Gay accompanied the Earl of
Clarendon to Hanover as his secretary, a rumour went round
the Hanoverian court that he was to stay on after Clarendon
returned to England. 'I have received many Compliments upon
that occasion', Gay wrote to Charles Ford, 'my Denial of it they
look upon as a Sketch of my Politicks'.[1]

To judge by what has subsequently been written about Gay's
politics, this allegedly disingenuous denial might indeed be
taken as the extent of his political interests and understanding.
William Henry Irving notes that

> he always made friends irrespective of party and displayed so
> much casual agility in the difficult art of sitting on fences
> comfortably that some of his modern biographers have wondered
> what his opinions were on politics, or even whether he had any[2]

and over a quarter of a century later, C. F. Burgess, in his
edition of Gay's *Letters*, showed how far awareness of these
matters had developed. 'Gay's political naïveté was almost
total', he explained.

> In an age of strong party allegiances he professed not to care
> 'one Farthing' for a man's politics; and in an era in which an
> interest in politics was often a ruling passion his apathy toward
> political matters is remarkable.[3]

Three centuries after Gay's death, we seem to be no further
advanced than this when it comes to our perception of his politics.

It might be objected, then, that an attempt to offer a more

detailed account of his politics is unnecessary, if not irrelevant. If Gay was not sufficiently interested in politics to record his opinions openly, why should we bother to try to reconstruct them? And even if it should be granted that a knowledge of Gay's politics might be desirable, how is this to be acquired? The first point to make quite clear is that I do not merely intend to repeat the amused King of Brobdingnag's question to Gulliver; I am not primarily interested in establishing whether Gay was a Whig or a Tory. Historical scholarship in the past twenty years or so has moved well beyond any simple model of post-Revolution politics which represents them as a choice between two parties. Alternatively, we should try to discern Gay's views on political issues because of the insight they would give us into the nature of his writings. In short, the establishment of Gay's world view serves a critical, as much as a biographical purpose, because of its application in the interpretation of his works, for, of course, the two are closely linked.

There are numerous examples of this. Let me illustrate two or three. Take what we accept to be Gay's first published piece, *Wine*, which contains a toast to a number of prominent men in 1708:

> The Hero *MALBRO* next, whose vast Exploits
> Fames Clarion sounds, fresh Laurels, Triumphs new
> We wish, like those *HE* won at *Hockstets* Field.
>
> Next *DEVONSHIRE* Illustrious, who from Race
> Of Noblest Patriots sprung, whose Soul's Endow'd,
> And is with ev'ry Vertuous gift Adorn'd
> That shon in His most worthy Ancestors,
> For then distinct in sep'rate Breasts were seen
> Virtues distinct, but all in *HIM* Unite.
>
> Prudent *GODOLPHIN*, of the Nations weal
> Frugal, but free and gen'rous of his own
> Next Crowns the Bowl, with Faithful *SUNDERLAND*,
> And *HALIFAX*, the Muses darling Son,
> In whom *Conspicuous*, with full Lustre shine
> The *surest* Judgment, and the *brightest* Wit,
> Himself *Mecaenus* and a *Flaccus* too,
> And all the Worthies of the *British* Realm
> In order rang'd succeeded, *Healths* that ting'd
> The *Dulcet* Wine with a more charming Gust. (232–50)[4]

With good reason, the editors of the standard edition of Gay's *Poetry and Prose* note that the 'politics behind these five toasts is curious and confused'. They are forced back on the old assumption that, in this poem at least, 'Gay's sympathies are Whig', and they try to explain away interpretative difficulties by suggesting that 'either he is less a supporter of or hopes less for patronage from those in the ministry than those out of it'.[5] This scarcely serves to clarify the meaning of the text, and a number of assumptions are made about Gay's intentions here, as well as about his political allegiances in 1708.

Wine is a burlesque of the style of *Paradise Lost*. Why, then, should it be automatically assumed that the toasts at the end of the poem are to be read unambiguously? Irving pictures Gay taking the opportunity 'to pay prettily turned compliments to Marlborough, Devonshire, Godolphin, Sunderland, and Halifax' (p. 32). In terms of the burlesque, however, it is far from clear whether this is a list of faithful or fallen angels. The lines referring to Marlborough are straightforward enough, although the war was by no means as popular in 1708 as it had been immediately after Blenheim ('*Hockstets* Field'). Then Gay, strangely enough, turns his attention to the largely anonymous Lord Steward, Devonshire. Why he (of all people) should be thought to be 'with ev'ry Vertuous Gift Adorn'd' is a question. This may be 'the hyperbole normal in this kind of flattery of nobility at the time' (as Dearing has it) (II, 483), but what is the purpose? When we proceed to Gay's next 'prettily turned compliments', further problems arise. It is distinctly unusual, in the literature of the period, to find Lord Treasurer Godolphin described as 'free and gen'rous of his own' resources; he was not a notably altruistic man. Worse, to call Sunderland 'Faithful' borders on the perverse, as he was notoriously irreligious! I do not think the editors of Gay's *Poetry and Prose* have done enough in pointing out that Sunderland was more faithful to his violent whiggish principles than obedient to the wishes of Marlborough or Godolphin.[6] Given that *Wine* is a burlesque poem, is it stretching the point to suspect that irony is at work here?

Another type of 'panegyric' was popular in the early eighteenth-century. Swift outlined the idea in his *Directions for a Birth-Day Song* (written 1729; published 1765):

Thus your Encomiums, to be strong,
Must be apply'd directly wrong:
A Tyrant for his Mercy praise,
And crown a Royal Dunce with Bays:
A squinting Monkey load with charms;
And paint a Coward fierce in arms.
Is he to Avarice inclin'd?
Extol him for his generous mind:
And when we starve for want of Corn,
Come out with Amalthea's Horn.
For Princes love you should descant
On Virtues which they know they want. (117–28)[7]

Is it possible that Gay, in *Wine*, is applying *his* encomiums 'directly wrong'?

Is he to Avarice inclin'd?
Extol him for his generous mind.

Prudent *GODOLPHIN*, of the Nations weal
Frugal, but free and gen'rous of his own.

Gay would not have had to wait until Swift mockingly explained how to write panegyric. Two years prior to the publication of *Wine*, Dr. Joseph Browne had been pilloried for his involvement in the publication of *The Country Parson's Honest Advice to that Judicious Lawyer, and Worthy Minister of State, My Lord Keeper*. These verses consisted entirely of the names of contemporary Whig politicians associated with qualities they conspicuously lacked:

Be Wise as *Somerset*, as *Somers* Brave,
As *Pembroke* Airy, and as *Richmond* Grave;
Humble as *Orford* be; and *Wharton's* Zeal
For Church and Loyalty wou'd fit thee well

There seems little distance between this ironic praise of Wharton's religious zeal, and Gay's extolling of 'Faithful *SUNDERLAND*'. Curiously enough, *The Country Parson's Honest Advice* concludes thus:

To sum up all; *Devonshire's* Chastity,
Bolton's Merit, *Godolphin's* Probity,
Halifax his Modesty, *Essex's* sense,
Montague's Management, and *Culpepper's* Pence,

47

Tenison's Learning, and *Southampton*'s Wit,
Will make thee for an able States-man fit.[8]

What price Devonshire's 'Virtues' or Godolphin's frugality
now? Perhaps even Gay's apparent flattery of 'modest' Halifax
is double-edged, pointed up (as Swift often does) by the
judicious use of italics:

> In whom *Conspicuous*, with full Lustre shine
> The *surest* Judgment, and the *brightest* Wit
> Himself a *Mecaenas* and a *Flaccus* too.

Halifax certainly had pretensions as a 'Patron of the *Muses*', 'a
great ENCOURAGER OF LEARNING and learned men', as
Macky put it, but remember also Swift's remarks on this
description: 'His encouragements were onely good words and
dinners—I never heard him say one good thing or seem to tast
what was said by another' (Marginal note to John Macky's
Characters of the Court of Britain . . . (1733)).[9]

Could it be that Gay, far from being the political naif or inept
flatterer, was fully aware of what he was doing in 1708, just as
he was in the posthumously published *Fables* of 1738? I wonder
if his description of Prince George, Queen Anne's consort, is not
meant as a clue. True, it accords with what we know to have
been the taste in complimentary verses, but it also reeks of
encomiums being applied 'directly wrong': 'For by *HIS* Prudent
Care, united shores/ Were sav'd from Hostile Fleets Invasion
dire' (230–31). The '*ROYAL DANE*' (223) was indeed Lord
High Admiral, but the post was almost entirely nominal, and
widely known as such. 'For Princes love you should descant/
On Virtues which they know they want.' Swift's *Directions* seem
to have been anticipated by Gay.

How can we be sure? I am afraid we cannot, because it is not
known what his politics were in 1708. It is customary to portray
him as a Whig who, by 1714, had been 'drawn . . . into the Tory
camp'.[10] I have looked in vain for evidence to support such a
view. Indeed, I rather suspect this alleged Whiggery is founded
largely on the evidence of the toasts I have considered at some
length. Unfortunately, like Irving's account of his early years, a
large part of Gay's biography is made up of the 'must-have'
variety. 'He must have been continually conscious . . . of the
bitterness of religious division' (p. 20). Why? He 'must have been

at least vaguely aware that the time had come to choose
between Cato's little senate at Button's, and the group of
writers playing for Tory smiles around Swift's powerful figure'
(p. 91). Perhaps. Who can say? And so the idea originated
that he was at first a Whig until he fell under the influence of
Swift.

The Present State of Wit is accepted as Gay's work. Published in
May 1711, it was (as far as we know) the second of his pieces to
be printed. In the second paragraph, 'J.G.' asserts

> that as you know I never cared 'one Farthing' either for *Whig* or
> *Tory*. So I shall consider our Writers purely as they are such,
> without any respect to which Party they may belong.[11]

Note that, *pace* Burgess, 'J.G.' does not claim not to 'care "one
Farthing" for a man's politics'; instead he claims that he does
not and never has cared for either the Whig or the Tory parties.
It does not mean that 'J.G.' has no politics, only that he is not a
party-man, and does not wish to be considered as one. Swift, in
the *Journal to Stella* (1710–13), remarked that the 'author seems
to be a Whig', presumably because 'J.G.' praised the *Tatler* and
the *Spectator* 'above all things'—even the *Examiner*! Swift
suspected that 'Steele and Addison were privy to the printing of
it'.[12] As far as I can gather, this is the reason for Irving's
suggestion that: 'Perhaps at this time Gay felt himself slipping
away from his old party allegiances', so that 'his description of
himself [in *The Present State of Wit*] as a man of no party may be
true' (p. 59).

What 'old party allegiances'? It appears that Gay has been
labelled a Whig on account of the toasts in *Wine*, and Swift's
comment that the author of the *Present State* 'seems to be a
Whig'. From this tenuous evidence, the 'must-have' theory of
biography has offered a narrative of Gay's conversion from
Whig to Tory which is not borne out at all by one of his next
publications, *On a Miscellany of Poems. To Bernard Lintott*. Also the
work of 1711, these verses list the Whigs Congreve, Addison
and Garth, to be sure, but Pope, Prior, Granville and Buckingham as well. Gay's references span the political spectrum, from
a supporter of the Junto Whigs (Addison) through a Harleyite
(Prior) to men later to reveal Jacobite sympathies (Granville
and Buckingham). What conclusions can possibly be drawn

from such inconclusive evidence? That Gay was a Whig? Or a Tory? Or that he was a man who 'never cared "one Farthing" either for *Whig* or *Tory*'?

Other examples of confusion stemming from ignorance of Gay's politics are to be found in considerations of the political significance of plays such as *The Captives* and *The Beggar's Opera*. Leaving his best-known work to last, let us turn our attention to *The Captives* for a moment. In his edition of Gay's *Dramatic Works*, John Fuller notes that 'contemporary newspapers provide clear evidence that the setting was topical', as 'the Turks were again in Persia' in January 1724. He seems disappointed therefore that

> no one who saw the play was to reflect (as they were all too likely to do four years later at *The Beggar's Opera*) upon a possible political significance of *The Captives*.

This does not stop Fuller pointing out that the

> false accusation of Sophernes as being implicated in the conspiracy upon the King's life bears some resemblance to the arrest of Atterbury on the charge of treasonable correspondence with the Pretender.[13]

Indeed, when Orbasius remarks that

> Our Priests are train'd up spies by education,
> They pry into the secrets of the state,
> And then by way of prophecy reveal them;
> 'Tis by such artifice they govern Kings. . . . (I, v, 8–11)[14]

it is more than likely that comparisons between Median priests and English ministers of state are being suggested. In *Gulliver's Travels*, Swift, too, was to draw attention to 'the Kingdom of *Tribnia*, by the Natives called *Langden*', where

> the Bulk of the People consisted wholly of Discoverers, Witnesses, Informers, Accusers, Prosecutors, Evidences, Swearers; together with their several subservient and subaltern Instruments; all under the Colours, the Conduct, and pay of Ministers and their Deputies.[15]

Such apparently opaque comments were really more or less transparent references to the Atterbury affair, and Gay could well be implying that, despite Atterbury's undeniable involvement with Jacobitism, the trumped-up evidence used against him was based on nothing more than mere 'prophecy'.

However, when Fuller tries to elaborate on these things to outline a sustained political allegory in *The Captives*, he is on ground which is decidedly shaky. Why should there be 'something metaphorically apt in representing the Tories in opposition as captive Persians'? 'Atterbury's wife had recently died', Fuller notes unhelpfully, and 'the particular opposition of the odious Araxes may represent the single-minded prosecution of the energetic Walpole, "Author of all I suffer", according to Atterbury'.[16] Sophernes, then, according to this ingenious reading, must somehow be the antitype of Atterbury, with Araxes as Walpole. But, in *The Captives*, Sophernes's wife is not dead, and there seems to be little reason for calling Araxes 'odious'. This is a clear misrepresentation of Gay's dramatic intentions. Araxes is an upright, honest soldier who knows his duty, and who tries to do it. True, he originally suspects Sophernes—for political reasons that are undoubtedly sound—but he is subsequently prepared to revise his opinion when it is shown to be wrong. 'Come forth, unhappy Prince, excuse my words', he says, ''Tis with reluctance that I bring the message./ Your death's at hand' (IV, v, 1–3). Impressed by Sophernes's stoicism, Araxes, far from being the single-minded prosecutor, observes that

> Such unconcern,
> Such steady fortitude amidst afflictions
> Was never seen till now. (IV, v, 10–12)

If anything, Araxes is the moral centre of Media. He maintains the old values while all around him falter.

No wonder, then, that 'the pro-government *Pasquin* found no hint of such political nuances in *The Captives* and indeed went out of its way to praise it'.[17] John Fuller's hints of a political allegory are strained, and imitate the allegorical interpretations of *Gulliver's Travels* that have recently been discredited. Yet, like Swift's satire, *The Captives has* political significance and it is not surprising that a Whig journal like *Pasquin* sought to praise it. The keynote of *The Captives* is the concept of liberty, and that had considerable contemporary importance. It is Araxes, once again, who explains why he expects the Persians to rebel:

Captivity's a yoke that galls the shoulders
Of new-made slaves, and makes them bold and resty.
He that is born in chains may tamely bear them;
But he that once has breath'd the air of freedom,
Knows life is nothing when deprived of that.
Our lord the King has made a people slaves,
And ev'ry slave is virtuously rebellious. (I, iii, 13–19)

This is a ringing phrase, shot through with potential political significance: 'ev'ry slave is *virtuously* rebellious'. When Araxes goes on to say that he 'fear[s] the *Persian* Prince', Orbasius assures him that Sophernes is virtuous: 'Who suspects his virtue?'. Araxes rejoins, ''Tis not dishonest to demand our right;/ And freedom is the property of man' (I, iii, 20, 26–8).

The watchwords of Liberty and Property had been bruited many times in Gay's lifetime. It is well known that in *Cato* (1713) the lines on liberty (III, v, 72–81)[18] were praised by the Whigs and echoed by the Tories to show that the satire was unfelt. *The Captives* uncomfortably turned the tables on the Whig regime of the 1720s. The political meaning of the play, I suggest, is at once a challenge to the Hanoverians and a warning. The Revolution had raised questions of how far the obedience of the subject could be taken for granted, and resistance to a tyrannical monarch had been justified by Parliament. When Araxes draws attention to the boldness of 'new-made slaves', Gay seems to be joining in the growing chorus of voices raised against what was seen as the rising tide of absolutism under the Hanoverians.[19] The Opposition made great efforts to try to portray the regime as an incipient tyranny. Swift feared that he 'might outlive liberty in England', but was comforted 'to see how corruption and ill conduct are instrumental in uniting Virtuous Persons and lovers of their country of all denominations'. This sounds remarkably like the virtuous rebellion outlined by Araxes. 'If this be disaffection', Swift wrote, 'pray God Send me allways among the disaffected'.[20] ''Tis not dishonest to demand our right', Araxes points out in terms which strongly echo both the Revolution Principle and Locke's *Two Treatises of Civil Government* (1690), 'And freedom is the property of man' (I, iii, 27–8).

Pasquin, the government journal, applauded *The Captives*, I suspect, to show that the comment upon contemporary politics

was unfelt. It was a formula that would become a
in the years to come. The Opposition write
governmental tyranny in a variety of guis
ministerial apologists denied that any threat t
conceivably exist under the most enlightened c
political significance of works like *The Captives* and *The Beggar's
Opera* was common knowledge, and yet, because criticism of the
ministry was not openly voiced, it could, for most of the time, be
simply ignored by those in authority. Recently, in the *Times
Literary Supplement*, Sir David Hunt asked where allusions to
contemporary politics were to be found in *The Beggar's Opera*.[21]
This is the same sort of question which leads F. P. Lock
virtually to discount topical political significance in *Gulliver's
Travels*, despite Swift's own fears that his satire could be accused
of 'particular reflections'.[22] Gay himself denied that either *The
Beggar's Opera* or *Polly* could be construed as politically subversive or libellous. 'I am sure I have written nothing that can
be legally supprest', he claimed in a letter (2 December 1728),
'unless the setting vices in general in an odious light, and
virtues in an amiable one may give offence'[23]—yet *Polly* was
suppressed. Why? Was it because, as Hervey put it, Walpole
was not prepared to 'suffer himself to be produced for thirty
nights together upon the stage in the person of a highwayman'?[24]
John Fuller rightly remarks that '*Polly*, as it was eventually
published, appears to be no more, indeed perhaps rather less,
slanted against Walpole than its predecessor'.[25]

Polly makes its point largely in two ways, and in this it follows
the lead of both *The Captives* and *The Beggar's Opera*, not to
mention the *Fables* (especially the 1738 *Fables*). Firstly, under the
guise of general satire, it condemns the manners of contemporary
society, and implicitly blames those in power for the corruption
of the people. Secondly, it makes 'particular reflections', attack-
ing Walpole and his colleagues, not by name, but through
allusion—precisely the sort of allusion that Sir David Hunt
thought was absent from *The Beggar's Opera*. But, to a contemporary audience, such innuendo was unmistakable (my italics):

> ... my Papa kept company with gentlemen, and ambition is
> catching. He was in too much haste to be rich. I wish *all great men*
> would take warning. 'Tis now seven months since my Papa was
> hang'd. (I, v, 37–40)

Whatever *other great men* do, I love to encourage merit. (II, v, 42–3)

You may talk of honour, as *other great men* do: But when interest comes in your way, you should do as *other great men* do. (II, ix, 50–2)

Your *great men* will never own their debts, that's certain. (III, xi, 10)

Gay, then, was equivocating when, in his preface, he denied that *Polly* was 'fill'd with slander and calumny against particular great persons'.[26] References to 'great men' were accepted as allusions to Walpole. True, *Polly*, as it was printed, is not *filled* with these catchphrases, but they are scattered throughout the play.

Similarly, when Gay denies that 'Majesty it-self is endeavour'd to be brought into ridicule and contempt,'[27] he is not being quite honest. The Scriblerians often forced implicit comparisons between rulers of the past, or fictional rulers, and the current King of England (whether George I or George II). When, in conclusion, Pohetohee observes that ''Tis my duty as a king to cherish and protect virtue' (III, xv, 11–12), Gay is insinuating that this is not always the case as far as George II is concerned, in the same way that Swift, in *Gulliver's Travels*, implicitly compares George I with first the Lilliputian Emperor, and then with the model King of Brobdingnag, who is

> posssessed of every Quality which procures Veneration, Love and Esteem; of strong Parts, great Wisdom and profound Learning; endued with admirable Talents for Government, and almost adored by his Subjects.[28]

The rhetorical strategy is the same in both cases: contemporary Englishmen are being invited to compare the real-life King of England with his fictional counterparts, and too often he is found wanting. That is how, in *Polly*, 'Majesty it-self is endeavour'd to be brought into ridicule and contempt', and Gay's preface is itself part of the strategy. Far from refuting such accusations, it encourages its readers both to look for and to find examples in the text, for, of course, prefaces are meant to be read first.

The Beggar's Opera and *Polly* are primarily satires of the manners of the Britain of 1728. As such they are political plays, and provide important clues to Gay's political ideas. The *Fables* serve a similar purpose. Like many of his contemporaries, Gay had an ideal view of the way society should be structured and how it should operate, and he believed that the old ways were under threat from *parvenus* who were prepared to sacrifice their integrity in the pursuit of their own advantage. As W. A. Speck succinctly puts it, the 'natural aristocracy' who had hitherto 'governed in the national interest', had been 'usurped by upstart monied men who, led by Walpole himself, had ousted the traditional rulers and governed entirely for their own self-interest'.[29] Gay's plays document this development. In *The Beggar's Opera*, Lockit warns his daughter against doing anything 'but upon the Foot of Interest' (III, i, 41). Peachum finally decides to 'peach Macheath, and justifies his action because 'we must comply with the Customs of the World, and make Gratitude give way to Interest' (I, xi, 12–13). In *Polly*, Ducat advises Polly to 'consult your own interest, as every body now-a-days does' (I, xi, 2–3). The connection with the behaviour of the prime minister, Walpole, is clinched, when Jenny Diver admonishes Vanderbluff: 'You may talk of honour, as other great men do: But when interest comes in your way, you should do as other great men do' (II, ix, 50–2).

Thus Gay outlines two conflicting modes of social behaviour, one based on self-interest, the other on benevolent paternalism. Usually his method is to force the reader to acknowledge the discrepancy between the real and the ideal, but occasionally, like Pope, he offers a positive picture of social harmony, as in his *Epistle to Pulteney*:

> Happy, thrice happy shall the monarch reign,
> Where guardian laws despotic power restrain!
> There shall the plough-share break the stubborn land,
> And bending harvests tire the peasant's hand;
> There liberty her settled mansion boasts,
> There commerce plenty brings from foreign coasts.
> O *Britain*, guard thy laws, thy rights defend,
> So shall these blessings to thy sons descend! (247–54)

Gay's ideal is couched in terms every bit as idyllic as those employed by Pope in the concluding lines of the *Epistle to*

Burlington (1731) and for once it might be said that Pope is the poetic debtor. Note the insistence on the protection of the laws, for they are the bulwark of liberty. On this point, the Scriblerians are as one.

Dull as it is, *The Captives* best illustrates Gay's concern for liberty. He may not have boasted with Swift that 'Fair LIBERTY was all his Cry'[30], but Gay, too, comments on the importance of liberty throughout his writings. 'Let *Paris* be the Theme of *Gallia*'s Muse,/ Where Slav'ry treads the Street in wooden Shoes' (I, 85–6), he writes in *Trivia*, for 'Here *Tyranny* ne'er lifts her purple Hand,/ But Liberty and Justice guard the Land' (III, 149–50). Gay expresses his own fears for the continuation of liberty in England in terms less vibrant than Swift, perhaps, but nonetheless vital to his thought for being uttered *sotto voce*. Dione has no desire to be 'a nuptial slave' (*Dione*, V, i, 62). The Mohocks, in Gay's portrayal, scoff at law and order:

> Then a *Mohock*, a *Mohock* I'll be,
>   No Laws shall restrain
>   Our Libertine Reign,
> We'll riot, drink on, and be free. (*The Mohocks*, i, 75–8)

Confusing liberty with licence, the Mohocks are a threat to society, much as a standing army would be. Gay, perhaps surprisingly, even has words for that perennial fear of the country gentleman:

> Why need we armys when the land's in peace?
> Soldiers are perfect devils in their way,
> When once they're rais'd, they're cursed hard to lay. (*To my ingenious and worthy friend, W[illiam] L[owndes]* 55–8)

Gay's writings reflect a political ideology which, like that of his fellow Scriblerians, is remarkably consistent when analysed in detail. Louis I. Bredvold referred to them as 'Tory satirists',[31] but this can be misleading. Despite their close links with the Oxford ministry, and their continuing association with Bolingbroke, Swift and Pope persisted in describing themselves as Whigs. The reasons they gave for this are of particular interest when it comes to describing Gay's politics. Swift wrote that,

> having been long conversant with the Greek and Roman authors, and therefore a lover of liberty, I found myself much inclined to be what they called a Whig in politics; and that, besides, I

thought it impossible, upon any other principle, to defend or submit to the Revolution (*Memoirs Relating to That Change Which happened in the Queen's Ministry* (1714)).[32]

Shades, surely, of Araxes's explanation of Persian unrest in *The Captives*. A free people could not be expected to submit to slavery without resisting, as had been the case in 1688 in England. In *The Drapier's Letters* (1724–25), Swift observed that '*Freedom consists in a People being governed by Laws made with their own Consent; and Slavery in the Contrary*'.[33] This, in essence, he accepted as Whiggery. It was based on the love of liberty. Pope seems to have concurred. 'If you are a *Whig*', he wrote to Gay in September 1714,

> as I rather hope, and as I think your Principles and mine (as Brother Poets) had ever a Byas to the Side of Liberty, I know you will be an honest man, and an inoffensive one.[34]

Once again, a Scriblerian apparently equates liberty with the principles of the Whigs. Pope hopes that Gay is a Whig, despite his connection with Oxford's ministry.

True, Pope's words have a curious ring. It appears that even after the death of Queen Anne, he was uncertain of Gay's politics. 'Upon the whole', he continues, 'I know you are incapable of being so much of either Party as to be good for nothing'.[35] We are back with the uncommitted poet who professes not to care ' "one Farthing" for *Whig* or *Tory*'. Irving could 'scarcely imagine' that Gay 'would be stupid enough to confuse party with principle any more than Swift did' (p. 20). But this smacks more of twentieth-century cynicism than Augustan idealism. Swift *did* equate party with principle, and was disillusioned with contemporary Whigs when he recognized that they did not pay as much attention to principle as he would have wished. He stood out against 'Standing armies in time of peace; projects of excise, and bribing elections', 'not forgetting septennial Parliaments, directly against the old Whig principles, which always have been mine' (23 March 1733/34).[36] He stood out against them because they all posed threats to the *sine qua non* of liberty. Yet the threat was being posed, not by Tories, but by Whigs under Walpole. He could not stand idle when 'all things' were 'tending towards absolute Power' (12 May 1735).[37]

It is really only in the last twenty years that historians have turned their attention to political ideology in the early eighteenth-century in England, and have recognized that the simple dichotomy between Whig and Tory, which largely dominated politics during the reign of Queen Anne, was not necessarily the norm either before 1700 or after 1715. Whig ideology originally incorporated older attitudes towards authority and the social order. Suspicion of the Court goes back to Pym and beyond. J. G. A. Pocock, Isaac Kramnick, H. T. Dickinson and others have investigated political ideas in terms other than those simply of Whig and Tory.[38] Very recently, Colin Brooks has added a further refinement to studies of 'Country' political attitudes.[39] Borrowing the terminology of American political historians, he refers to the Country 'persuasion', rather than suggesting that there was anything so solid or organized as a 'Country' party. His analysis is fruitful whether applied to the fluctuating politics of the 1690s or the years of opposition to Walpole.

Gay's politics appear to conform to his pattern. From the evidence of the range of his writings, from *The Present State of Wit*, if not from *Wine*, onwards to *The Beggar's Opera* and *The Fables*, we can discern his adherence to the set of attitudes and assumptions about politics, religion and morality that characterize the 'Country persuasion' described by Brooks. Despite Carole Fabricant's recent reminder that it is fallacious to try 'to define a single, monolithic "Augustan outlook" presumably shared by all the major writers of the period',[40] it is curious that the Scriblerians, at least, seem to have shared certain ideological traits. Gay was at one with Pope and Swift in his nostalgic advocacy of a hierarchical, paternalistic society based on the doctrines of Christianity. *The Beggar's Opera* satirizes the movement in British society away from the assumptions which made up what Brooks calls the 'Country persuasion', but, strangely enough, the clearest exposition of all is to be found in Gay's posthumous play, *The Distress'd Wife*, when Barter upbraids Lord Courtlove (note the significance of the name) for his espousal of modern manners:

> *Barter.* This whole Proceeding, in the Eye of the World, appears
> so very mercenary, so very corrupt, that your Honour suffers.—
> Pardon my Freedom, my Lord.

Courtlove. As to notional Honour, you are undoubtedly in the
right of it; but what is that to the Practice of Mankind?—

Barter's response is telling in its explicit condemnation of
manners under the Robinocracy:

'Tis you, my Lord, and such as you, that influence the Manners
of Mankind.—Common Charity obliges those of your Rank to
show clear and conspicuous Proofs of Honour and Disinterested-
ness; for whenever you are mean and mercenary, the Vulgar are
hang'd for following your Example. (IV, xvi, 62–73)

The parallel with the moral of *The Beggar's Opera* is com-
pelling: ''Twould have shown that the lower Sort of People
have their Vices in a degree as well as the Rich: And that they
are punish'd for them.' (III, xvi, 24–6). Statesmen like Walpole
get away with crimes for which their meaner counterparts are
hanged. That is why Macheath (alias Walpole) should have
been executed. But Gay argues that the root cause of the
corrupted manners to be observed throughout the play is really
the failure of men in positions of authority to fulfil their proper
function of setting an example to their dependents. The
paternalistic ideal of the 'Country persuasion' is being super-
seded by a materialistic system which recognizes no social
responsibilities with respect to the lower orders. In Gay's eyes,
the very fabric of society is in jeopardy because, as Algernon
Sidney put it in his posthumously published *Discourses Concerning Government* (1698), 'Liberty cannot be preserv'd, if the
manners of the People are corrupted.'[41] Seen in this light, Gay's
supposed political naïveté can be seen as an expression of a
coherent *political* view of the way in which society should
function. He may have 'never cared "one Farthing" either for
Whig or *Tory*', but his works reflect the extent of his political
commitment. Far from containing genuinely subversive elements,
as some critics have argued, *The Beggar's Opera* is at one with
Gay's other writings in bemoaning the deviation from an ideal
paternalistic system in which 'Self-love and social' are the same.

NOTES

1. *Letters*, p. 12.
2. Irving, *John Gay: Favorite of the Wits* (Durham, N.C., 1940), p. 20. Subsequent references are recorded in the text.
3. *Letters*, p. xvi.
4. Line references are to the texts of Gay's poems in *PP* from which all quotations are taken.
5. *PP*, II, 483. Subsequent references are recorded in the text.
6. See *PP*, II, 483–84.
7. Herbert Davis (ed.), *Swift: Poetical Works* (Oxford, 1967), p. 405.
8. Frank H. Ellis (ed.), *Poems on Affairs of State: Augustan Satirical Verse, 1660–1714*, VII (1704–14) (New Haven and London, 1975), pp. 156–59.
9. Herbert Davis (ed.), *The Prose Writings of Jonathan Swift*, 16 vols. (Oxford, 1939–75), V, 258. Subsequently referred to as *PW*.
10. *PP*, I, 6.
11. *PP*, II, 449.
12. *PW*, XV, 269.
13. *DW*, I, 38–9, 40.
14. Act, scene and line references are to the texts of Gay's plays in *DW*, from which all quotations are taken.
15. *PW*, XI, 175.
16. *DW*, I, 41.
17. *DW*, I, 41.
18. A. C. Guthkelch (ed.), *The Miscellaneous Works of Joseph Addison*, 2 vols. (London, 1914), I, 397.
19. See J. A. Downie, ' "Walpole", the Poets' Foe', in Jeremy Black (ed.), *Britain in the Age of Walpole* (London, 1984), pp. 171–88.
20. Harold Williams (ed.), *The Correspondence of Jonathan Swift*, 5 vols. (Oxford, 1963, 1965, repr. corr. 1965, 1972), IV, 336; III, 506.
21. 21 October 1983, p. 1161: cf. *TLS*, 11 November 1983, p. 1247.
22. *The Politics of 'Gulliver's Travels'* (Oxford, 1980), p. 3, cf. *The Correspondence of Jonathan Swift*, III, 189.
23. *Letters*, p. 78.
24. Hervey, John, Lord, *Some Materials Towards Memoirs of the Reign of George II*, ed. Romney Sedgwick, 3 vols. (London, 1931), I, 98.
25. *DW*, I, 53.
26. *DW*, II, 70.
27. *DW*, II, 70.
28. *PW*, XI, 119.
29. *Stability and Strife: England 1714–1760* (London, 1977), p. 225.
30. *Verses on the Death of Dr. Swift*, 351, in *Poetical Works*, p. 507.
31. 'The Gloom of the Tory Satirists', in J. L. Clifford and Louis A. Landa (eds.), *Pope and his Contemporaries: Essays Presented to George Sherburn* (Oxford, 1949), pp. 1–19.
32. *PW*, VIII, 120.
33. *PW*, X, 87.

34. George Sherburn (ed.), *The Correspondence of Alexander Pope*, 5 vols. (Oxford, 1956), I, 254.
35. *Correspondence* (Pope), I, 254.
36. *Correspondence* (Swift), IV, 230.
37. *Correspondence* (Swift), IV, 333–34.
38. Pocock, 'Machiavelli, Harrington, and English Political Ideology in the Eighteenth Century', *William and Mary Quarterly*, 22 (1965), 549–83; Pocock, *The Machiavellian Moment* (Princeton. N.J., 1975); Kramnick, *Bolingbroke and his Circle: The Politics of Nostalgia in the Age of Walpole* (Cambridge, Mass. and Oxford, 1968); Dickinson, *Liberty and Property: Political Ideology in Eighteenth-Century Britain* (London, 1977).
39. 'The Country Persuasion and Political Responsibility in England in the 1690s', *Parliaments, Estates and Representations*, 4 (1984), 135–46.
40. *Swift's Landscape* (Baltimore, Mld. and London, 1983), p. 3.
41. *Discourses Concerning Government*, 2nd. edn. ('carefully corrected'), (London, 1704), II, xxv, p. 180.

3

Luxury, Refuse and Poetry: John Gay's *Trivia*

by STEPHEN COPLEY and IAN HAYWOOD

Readers of *Trivia* can scarcely fail to notice that they cannot proceed for more than a few lines at a stretch in the poem without coming across some reference to the human and commercial waste products of the urban society Gay is describing in London. In the course of his peregrinations the poet, in the figure of the Walker, is assailed by this waste in all its forms, and he spends a good deal of the poem offering advice on the best ways to escape being contaminated by it: advice which adds up to a large part of 'THE *ART* of *WALKING* the STREETS of LONDON'. As he picks his way through the 'Mire' of the streets, the Walker's clean clothes are continually under threat from the staining wastes of the various dirty tradesmen who brush against him in the 'mingling Press' (II, 27) and he has to warn us to avoid the piles of 'heapy Rubbish' (III, 336) that are deposited all around him.[1] At the same time he repeatedly draws our attention to the state of the 'kennels', telling tales of people falling into them and warning of their general unpleasantness and danger. Typically, in Book I, he informs us that, after rain,

> you'll hear the Sounds
> Of whistling Winds, e'er Kennels break their Bounds;
> Ungrateful Odours common Sewers diffuse,
> And dropping Vaults distil unwholesom Dews. (I, 169–72)

62

In addition, the poem contains several passages concerning Fleet Ditch,

> the black Canal of Mud,
> Where common Sewers a lulling Murmur keep,
> Whose Torrents rush from *Holborn*'s fatal Steep. (II, 172–74)

The most elaborate of these passages is the long 'mythological' episode in Book II (99–216), depicting Cloacina—the goddess of the sewers—and her illegitimate son: the bootblack boy. In this essay we want to inquire into the status of these cloacal references in Gay's verse and through that, to broach various questions about the nature of the poem as a whole. One immediate possibility is to say that *Trivia* simply lives up to its reputation for 'realism', and is empirically accurate in its representation of the London scene. After all, as numerous historians have pointed out, early eighteenth-century London was a filthy place. The history of Fleet Ditch itself has been admirably charted by T. F. Reddaway and summarized by Pat Rogers.[2] As they explain, the Ditch was originally a navigable river joining the Thames at Holborn, but was progressively choked with refuse, until, in the seventeenth century, the authorities intervened, cleared it, canalized it and built landing wharves and warehouses on its banks. By the early eighteenth century, however, the new structures had fallen into disrepair, and the polluting powers of the market stalls and densely packed population around it had transformed it into an open sewer, described by Defoe in 1722 as a 'nauseous and abominable sink of public nastiness'.[3] The most obvious feature of a modern sewer—its being rooted underground, out of sight and ultimately out of consciousness—was only achieved with Fleet Ditch in part in 1737, and fully in 1766.

The Ditch was only the most spectacular example of the general squalor of the London environment, the result of unprecedented rates of urban expansion and ramshackle and inadequate arrangements for waste disposal and sanitation—matters which were only gradually and selectively improved in the course of the eighteenth century. In 1721, five years after the publication of *Trivia*, the Grand Jury of the City of London gave orders to the constables and watchmen to arrest those throwing 'soil' into the street during the night. Nevertheless legislation took a long time to bite. As Pat Rogers has noted (pp. 144–46), the right of traders to empty their garbage into the street was jealously guarded. In 1722 Defoe addressed a plea to the Grand Jury, urging it to take a tougher line to 'put the laws in execution for paving and cleaning the streets, that no noisome, offensive stench may rise from the dirtiness and heaps that are usually found there'.[4] In 1741, however, Lord Tyrconnel, speaking in the House of Commons, could still find good reason to berate the

> neglect of cleanliness, of which, perhaps, no part of the world affords more proofs, than the streets of the British capital; a city famous for wealth, commerce, and plenty, and for every other kind of civility and politeness, but which abounds with such heaps of filth, as a savage would look on with amazement.[5]

Despite reported reactions such as this all through the first half of the century, the situation in London was not tackled significantly in legislative terms until the 1760s. Until 1762, when the Westminster Paving Act was passed, responsibility for paving remained with individual house owners, who were expected to cover the patch in the immediate vicinity of their property—an arrangement guaranteed to be unsuccessful. Only after that date was a series of Parliamentary Acts enforced to ensure that drains were deepened, sewers constructed, eaves fitted with spouts, and private 'scavenging' for refuse was organized into a more regular system of waste disposal. In *Grub Street* Pat Rogers has argued forcefully for the importance of deploying this kind of empirical historical knowledge in the reading of eighteenth-century literature. However he has also warned of the inherent danger that this approach will lead to purely referential or unduly literal-minded readings of the literary texts involved. This is a particular danger in the case of *Trivia*. As Rogers remarks

> both the tone and content [of the poem] have misled readers into imagining that its leading strategies are journalistic. Yet, as perceptive critics have recently drawn to our attention, it is a complex feat of rhetorical engineering. (p. 162)

As with all Augustan verse, the poem cannot be seen simply as a piece of 'realistic' loco-descriptive poetry—there is no available poetic mode in which such a possibility is conceivable.

Instead, it demands to be read primarily as a literary construction, in the light of the poetic models and forms that it adopts, imitates or parodies. Max Byrd makes this point emphatically when he writes that Gay's London is, to a far greater extent even than Pope's or Swift's, 'a purely literary artifact', and claims that 'our experience of it is filtered almost entirely through allusions, recollections, imitations—of Virgil, Juvenal, Dryden.'[6] Confirming this, the poem continually refers us to its literary origins in Georgic, mock-Georgic, satire, mock-heroic and burlesque. Its deployment of these forms— and in particular its choice of the *Georgics* and of Juvenal's *Third Satire* as the models for its imitation—leads us to expect that the city landscape it describes will be inscribed with emblematic values, or with satiric anti-values. However its juxtaposition of different models and modes prevents us all along from assuming that we can interpret it securely in relation to any one of them. Rogers recognizes this when he continues his commentary on the poem by describing its rhetorical complexity. He writes:

> *Trivia* is no more a straightforward mock-heroic than it is straight reportage. As with Pope, Gay takes the actual and topical as a limiting case: the poetry employs social observation to make permanent moral comment; it employs moral emblems, such as the Fleet, to state a sociological truth. (p. 162)

The rhetorical effects described here are noticed by various other critics of the poem, who often dwell on them in the course of attempting to define the tone of Gay's verse, and in particular in the course of trying to decide whether it is satirical or celebratory in its depiction of society. In discussing this, several draw attention to the striking changes in tone that can be observed if the poem is compared with the model of Juvenalian satire, while others compare the cloacal passages in it with on the one hand Swift's *Description of a City Shower* (1710) and on the other, the Fleet Ditch diving competition in Book II of *The Dunciad* (1728–43).[7] Both these examples provide instances of the emblematic use of cloacal imagery for satirical ends. In the first, as Roger Savage has shown,[8] the bland proposition in Swift's title—that the poem will simply be a passage of empirically descriptive verse—prepares us for a characteristically pointed and allusive exercise in the violation of literary

65

decorum, which rises to a head of impropriety and satirical disgust in the final lines cataloguing the contents of Fleet Ditch. In the second, the Ditch is established overwhelmingly as an emblem of cultural, moral and social corruption, and its contents are deployed as symbolic tokens in a vocabulary of satiric defilement. Comparisons with either of these passages serve only to heighten the peculiarly innocuous decorativeness of the similar passages in *Trivia*, and to reinforce an impression of them such as that noted by Rogers. Writing about the Cloacina episode, he argues that in it Gay's verse cannot be made to fit neatly with its expected models of scatological satirical or burlesque writing, but that it

> articulates a strand of thought otherwise present in the poem only inchoately . . . [suggesting] that there is something energetic and life-giving in the currents of filth that course beneath the streets of London (or beside them). Gay makes something almost pretty out of the showers of mud that bespatter citizens. (p. 164)

We will pick up this suggestion of the effect of Gay's verse later when we compare it with some non-literary writings about London. Initially, it is worthwhile returning to the general terms in which the poem has been read by critics. If we do so, we find that many recognize that a major difficulty we have with it lies in our inability to know what to make of its organizing persona— the Walker/Poet. Martin C. Battestin reads the whole poem allegorically, regarding it as 'a parable of the relation between actuality and art' which continually draws attention to the Walker's own artistry, and treating his travels round London as a journey through the city of life. In this reading, London is seen as being 'the very type and habitation of moral disorder, depravity, and disease'. Others read Gay's verse less heavy-handedly. Sven Armens writes that its tone is 'playful rather than vehemently satiric' and calls it 'basically a pleasant poem of observation'. Alvin B. Kernan agrees, but suggests that the poem makes sense if we see that what satire there is in it is directed at the Walker himself. John Chalker strikes a balance, acknowledging that 'Gay knows what is bad in London life. There is dirt everywhere, crime and immorality are prevalent and ill-health is common', but claiming that this should not blind us to 'the essentially celebratory character of the poem'. He also writes suggestively about the ironies that inform but do not dominate the presentation of the Walker throughout.[9]

We would suggest that the poem is a good deal more contradictory than any of these critics acknowledges, particularly in its representation of aspects of the social economy, in which it seems to occupy a variety of different and at times mutually exclusive positions simultaneously. In relation to this, the main difficulty we have to take account of in reading it is its pointed inconsequentiality. This does not come about because it consists of a series of scenes of documentary reportage, as Rogers makes clear. Rather it is because, in its combination of available poetic modes it continually raises our expectation that its accumulation of local detail will be open to large scale satiric or emblematic readings, but then does not allow us to sustain any such readings for any length of time. In this context the figure of the Walker certainly does not provide us with a coherent point of interpretation or a coherently ironic perspective on the miscellaneous matters dealt with in each book. Instead, the constantly shifting ironies that surround that figure serve only to accommodate the contradictions that run through the whole poem, while deflecting our attempts to establish coherent and consequential connections within it, and eluding the judgemental expectations that it seems to encourage.

This pattern of contradictions and ironic deferments can be read as evidence of the poem's ideological confusion over the problems of representing and, at least in part, celebrating the values of a commercial society. The ironies that inform the verse are most apparent—and most evasive—precisely when it touches on economic matters in the course of its description of the London scene. In particular, these ironies are pervasive in their representation of the place of luxury, labour and waste in society; and as an offshoot of that, in its treatment of the position of art and the artist within the economy. The problems and contradictions that we find when these subjects are raised directly or indirectly in the poem can be highlighted by looking briefly at a couple of other eighteenth-century descriptions of the appearance of London, in both of which similar matters are treated explicitly in the course of discussions of the city's economic life. The remarks of Lord Tyrconnel, quoted above, provide a good starting-point for looking at these passages. He is as interesting for what he does not say as for what he does. He sees contradictions between the 'wealth' and 'commerce', the 'politeness' and the 'filth' of London. However, for him, all three of those categories remain discrete; he does not consider that there might be some positive connection between them. For that connection to be made we have to look at a text that suggests that within the domain of economic discourse the three might be complementary phenomena. We can find something of this suggestion posed provocatively in Mandeville's *Fable of the Bees* (1714).

In the Preface to the first edition of the *Fable*, published two years before *Trivia*, Mandeville considers the necessity for a flourishing production of waste in a commercial society. His remarks are fashioned from the point of view of a pedestrian offended by the level of filth in the streets of London, and incorporate a number of details which parallel the leading motifs in Gay's poem. He writes:

> There are, I believe, few People in *London*, of those that are at any time forc'd to go a-foot, but what could wish the Streets of it much cleaner than generally they are; while they regard nothing but their own Clothes and private Conveniency: but when once they come to consider, that what offends them is the result of the Plenty, great Traffick and Opulency of that mighty City, if they have any Concern in its Welfare, they will hardly ever wish to see the Streets of it less dirty. For if we mind the Materials of all Sorts that must supply such an infinite number of Trades and Handicrafts, as are always going forward; the vast quantity of Victuals, Drink and Fewel that are daily consum'd in it, the Waste and Superfluities that must be produced from them; the multitudes of Horses and other Cattle that are always dawbing the Streets, the Carts, Coaches and more heavy Carriages that are perpetually wearing and breaking the Pavement of them, and above all the numberless swarms of People that are continually harassing and trampling through every part of them: If, I say, we mind all these, we shall find that every Moment must produce new Filth; and considering how far distant the great Streets are from the River side, what Cost and Care soever be bestow'd to remove the Nastiness almost as fast as 'tis made, it is impossible *London* should be more cleanly before it is less flourishing. Now would I ask if a good Citizen, in consideration of what has been said, might not assert, that dirty Streets are a necessary Evil inseparable from the

Felicity of *London*, without being the least hindrance to the cleaning of Shoes, or sweeping of Streets, and consequently without any Prejudice either to the *Blackguard* or the *Scavingers*.

But if, without any regard to the Interest or Happiness of the City, the Question was put, What Place I thought most pleasant to walk in? No body can doubt but, before the stinking Streets of *London*, I would esteem a fragrant Garden, or a shady Grove in the Country. In the same manner, if laying aside all worldly Greatness and Vain-Glory, I should be ask'd where I thought it was most probable that Men might enjoy true Happiness, I would prefer a small peaceable Society, in which Men, neither envy'd nor esteem'd by Neighbours, should be contented to live upon the Natural Product of the Spot they inhabit, to a vast Multitude abounding in Wealth and Power, that should always be conquering others by their Arms Abroad, and debauching themselves by Foreign Luxury at Home.[10]

The passage is a striking extension of the *Fable*'s central project—the establishment of luxury as the source of all the advantages of life in commercial society. It emerges as a sardonic commentary on the traditional emblematic opposition of ideally innocent country and corrupt and luxurious city. These are represented here on the one hand by the 'Garden' and 'shady Grove', and on the other by the 'stinking Streets of *London*'. Nevertheless, the explanation that Mandeville provides for the state of the streets renders the expected emblematic opposition irrelevant; he naturalizes the scene he describes as the site of beneficial economic activity, on which 'the Felicity of *London*' depends, and marginalizes any desire for an ideal alternative to it. He describes a society of consumers, in which the greater the quantity of goods consumed, the more waste must be produced. This leads him to a characteristically paradoxical formulation of the relation between waste and prosperity, and between private interest and public spirit in commercial society. In his argument, it is only the self-interested myopia of individuals which will lead them to 'regard nothing but their own Clothes and private Conveniency' and cause them to regret the state of the streets. Those with a more extensive perception, who are prepared to acknowledge the economic connection between the filth that they see and the prosperity of society, admit that 'what offends them is the Result of the Plenty, great Traffick and

Opulency of that mighty City', and understand that 'if they have any Concern in its Welfare, they will hardly ever wish to see the Streets of it less dirty.' Filth is a corollary and, indirectly, an emblem of prosperity and of the 'Felicity' to which it gives rise.

That 'Felicity' takes different forms at different levels of society. For some it consists of a continuing provision of luxury commodities: for others, the opportunity to work in order to supply them. The demand for luxury guarantees the continuing need for such work, and even the waste that goes with its production provides an opportunity for further labour—here graphically illustrated in the figures of the *'Blackguard'* and the *'Scavingers'*, who literally depend for a livelihood on the continuing production of filth that they cannot finally dispose of. Even while extolling the advantages of this economy, Mandeville insists that we recognize that the 'Happiness of the City' can only be purchased at the price of the 'true Happiness' of its inhabitants, which would be far better served by life in a subsistence economy.

A rather later description of London, in Johnson's *Adventurer* 67 (26 June 1753), extends some of the points that we see here, and forms a focus for a number of problems characteristic of polite writing about the economy in the period, which can be fed back into a reading of *Trivia*.[11] The essay starts with an account of the overwhelming impression made on a newcomer to London by the variety of trades and occupations apparent all round him. This leads Johnson into a reflection on the nature of the 'secret concatenation of society' (p. 386) which binds them all together. In the course of this he considers the mysterious economic balances that keep trade moving and the rôle that luxury plays in supporting the whole edifice. Two aspects of his account are particularly interesting. First, he shows signs of considerable uneasiness in his treatment of luxury in general, of the labour that supports it, and of his own position as an observer of that labour. Second, and as an offshoot of this, he develops the idea of a link between luxury and waste in an intriguing way—albeit in a less provocative tone than we find in Mandeville.

With regard to the first point, there is a conflict all through the essay between Johnson's general moral endorsement of

70

labour and his consciousness of the triviality of the ends to which it is applied in an economy stimulated by luxury consumption. He marvels that

> many of the arts by which families are supported, and wealth is heaped together, are of that minute and superfluous kind, which nothing but experience could evince possible to be prosecuted with advantage, and which, as the world might easily want, it could scarcely be expected to encourage.

However, he accepts that 'so it is, that custom, curiosity, or wantonness, supplies every art with patrons, and finds purchasers for every manufacture', giving as an extreme example the strange demand for tobacco and snuff. This leads him to insist that 'the world is so adjusted, that . . . he that is resolutely busy, can scarcely be in want' (p. 385), and to enlarge on the material and moral benefits of 'industry'. However, his observations are hedged around with comments which reveal the contradictions in his own position as a privileged commentator on society who is ironically aware of his own unproductive status in the economy, where he acts merely as an observer of the labour of others. He begins one paragraph by stating 'When I look round upon those who are thus variously exerting their qualifications, I cannot but admire the secret concatenation of society.' Two paragraphs later, however, he appears to undercut the basis of this earlier commentary, as he writes:

> In the midst of this universal hurry, no man ought to be so little influenced by example, or so void of honest emulation, as to stand a lazy spectator of incessant labour; or please himself with the mean happiness of a drone, while the active swarms are buzzing about him. (p. 386)

This position of the commentator, with its combined sense of privileged exclusion from the demands of the economy and ironically conceded unimportance in it is a posture that we will find in a lot of polite writing in the period: it is clear in the very titles of Johnson's own *Idler* (1758) or of the *Spectator* (1711–12), for example, and we will find a version of it in *Trivia*.

As to the second point mentioned above, there is a close identification in Johnson's argument between luxury products and waste. Both are treated as aspects of superfluity, but both are accommodated as beneficial factors in the account of the

71

providential organization of the economy. In one paragraph in particular, the distinctions between the two are broken down altogether, in a formulation which effectively does away with the category of redundant waste. Johnson writes:

> In the endless variety of tastes and circumstances that diversify mankind, nothing is so superfluous, but that some one desires it; or so common, but that some one is compelled to buy it. As nothing is useless but because it is in improper hands, what is thrown away by one is gathered up by another; and the refuse of part of mankind furnishes a subordinate class with the materials necessary to their support. (p. 385)

The physicality of the city's refuse which is dwelt on and celebrated in the passage of Mandeville is here minimized, as refuse itself is treated purely as an economic abstraction. Nevertheless, Johnson establishes just as firmly as does Mandeville that it is an essential and beneficial component in the city's economic life.

If we return to Gay's poem in the context of the points we have made about these passages, we will be able to see more clearly some of the problems that are involved in its representation of the social economy, as much by outlining the areas it avoids and the connections it does *not* make as by identifying the elements of a coherent and explicit presentation of society and its ethics. As we have already suggested, the whole poem is loosely motifal rather than closely argued in its organization, and its pointedly inconsequential structure serves to accommodate all sorts of contradictions in its representation of society. This structure allows it to skirt round or avoid having to articulate the economic considerations that underlie that representation—considerations such as those that are made explicit in the passages we have just examined. The poem thus includes representations of or tangential references to all three economic categories referred to in those passages, without ever elaborating on any connections between them. All three are problematic. With regard to the first, many of the descriptions of London life in each Book are couched in terms of the traditional and orthodox denunciation of luxury. In Book I, for instance, we are presented with the rather strange example of Venice as the model of an uncorrupted city, on the grounds of

72

the lack of wheeled transport there, and that example is set against London:

> Nor shall the Muse through narrow *Venice* stray,
> Where *Gondolas* their painted Oars display.
> O happy Streets to rumbling Wheels unknown,
> No Carts, no Coaches shake the floating Town!
> Thus was of old *Britannia's* City bless'd,
> E'er Pride and Luxury her Sons possess'd. (I, 97–102)

At other times the poem presents us with castigations of luxurious appetite in food, 'What will not Lux'ry taste? Earth, Sea, and Air/ Are daily ransack'd for the Bill of Fare' (III, 199–200), and in clothes and equipage: 'Let Beaus their Canes with Amber tipt produce,/ Be theirs for empty Show, but thine for Use' (I, 67–8). However, as John Chalker and others have pointed out, its catalogues of the material effects of that luxury are so glowingly enthusiastic as to counter any sense of sustained condemnation of it.[12] Similarly its reports of waste on every side do not produce the effect we might expect—of sustained offence or of satiric condemnation of the society that produces it, while its references to and mythologizations of labour and the rôle it plays in society are pervaded by ironic circumlocutions and qualifications, and by evasions of the implications of the subject-matter.

In all these areas we can best approach the poem by looking at the contradictions that run through the representation of the Walker/Poet himself. He is represented throughout as a figure who is both involved in and abstracted from the economy he describes. As Tom Woodman notes elsewhere in this volume (pp. 85–9), he walks for reasons of ideological purity rather than economic necessity, and is apparently qualified as a moral commentator purely by virtue of the fact that he is walking. This gives him a particular perspective on society, on its economy and on the luxury and waste which characterize it. For a start, it forms the basis of his sense of unity with the implied readership of fellow 'trudging Wits' that he addresses. These walkers are not naïve intruders into the urban environment, as the innocent milkmaid (II, 11–16) and gullible yokel (II, 77–82) mentioned in different parts of the poem are. They have unspecified 'Business' to attend to in the city. However they do not participate in the luxury economy that is emblematized in the carriages and sedan chairs of the riders, and in their ornamental, as opposed to functional, canes, shoes and clothes. As a result, they are presented as being fully aware of and vulnerable to the unpleasantness and danger of life in the streets, from which those of a more exalted station think themselves immune. Most obviously they are liable to be splashed as they go about while

> The tricking Gamester insolently rides,
> With *Loves* and *Graces* on his Chariot's Sides;
> In sawcy State the griping Broker sits,
> And laughs at Honesty, and trudging Wits. (I, 115–18)

Conversely, and as a corollary of that, they are morally and physically healthy, avoiding feebleness, corruption and the possibility of nemesis, all of which afflict the luxurious. Because of this they are taken to represent a positive standard at the centre of the passages of moral and satirical commentary on luxury that we have mentioned above. However, Gay's treatment of them ignores the fact that they are themselves firmly established as judicious consumers of luxury, and that a considerable amount of the poem reads as an elaborate consumer advice column for them. Despite this, it is implied in large parts of the poem that the walkers—and in particular the Walker himself—exist outside the realm of the commercial economy in all its aspects. This emerges in various ways. In one respect it informs the passage on Christmas in Book II (437–66), where the Walker is established morally as a proponent of the 'lib'ral' but 'judicious' charity which is conspicuously absent from the 'Proud Coaches' of the luxurious. Less than fifty lines later, he provides an encomium on 'The Happiness of Walkers', who are free from dependence on the labour of others for their means of transport and, at the end of the Book, sets the walkers' unconcern for 'mean Ambition' (569) in material things against a series of satiric emblems of the luxurious corruption indulged in by the occupants of 'Chariots' (573–90).

This exemplary lack of interest in material things on the part of the Walker is particularly clear in relation to his literary activities. In the invocation at the beginning of Book I, for example, his thoroughly laudable poetic ambitions are announced

74

as being entirely uncommercial, with a nice play on words in the process: '... my Country's Love demands the Lays,/ My Country's be the Profit, Mine the Praise' (I, 21–2). The suggestion here is echoed all through the poem. In Book II it emerges most strongly in the two ideal images of the contexts in which the Walker's work is produced and disseminated. The first comes in passing, in the description of Lord Burlington's patronage of the arts. For the Walker, Burlington's patronage takes the form of a privileged friendship outside the terms of any commercial exchange:

> Yet *Burlington's* fair Palace still remains;
> Beauty within, without Proportion reigns . . .
> There oft I enter (but with cleaner Shoes)
> For *Burlington's* belov'd by ev'ry Muse.
>
> (II, 493–94, 499–500)

The last couplet here is particularly interesting in its quiet refusal to acknowledge the poet's dependent position in relation to his patron. Instead of the reading we expect—that the Walker is in the palace because he is beloved by Burlington—we find a suggestion that the Walker's presence confers something on his patron, as it is a sign that Burlington himself is 'belov'd by ev'ry Muse'.[13]

At the description of the bookstall in the same Book (551–68), we find an alternative ideal, this time of an equally uncommercial dissemination of literature to a democratic audience of walkers:

> Volumes, on shelter'd Stalls, expanded lye,
> And various Science lures the learned Eye;
> The bending Shelves with pond'rous Scoliasts groan
> And deep Divines, to modern Shops unknown:
> Here, like the Bee, that on industrious Wing,
> Collects the various Odours of the Spring,
> Walkers, at leisure, Learning's Flow'rs may spoil,
> Nor watch the Wasting of the Midnight Oil,
> May Morals snatch from *Plutarch's* tatter'd Page,
> A mildew'd *Bacon*, or *Stagyra's* Sage.
> Here saunt'ring 'Prentices o'er *Otway* weep,
> O'er *Congreve* smile, or over D***[ennis] sleep;
> Pleas'd Sempstresses the *Lock's* fam'd *Rape* unfold,
> And *Squirts* read *Garth*, 'till *Apozems* grow cold.
>
> (II, 551–64)

and the poet exhorts his publisher:

> O *Lintott*, let my Labours obvious lie,
> Rang'd on thy Stall, for ev'ry curious Eye;
> So shall the Poor these Precepts *gratis* know,
> And to my Verse their future Safeties owe. (II, 565–68)

The passage is interestingly ambiguous in its representation of this ideal. The walkers scan the books while they are 'at leisure', and pick up knowledge without needing to waste the 'Midnight Oil' in acquiring it. Yet they are likened to 'the Bee that on industrious Wing/ Collects the various Odours of the Spring'— except that their activities 'spoil' 'Learning's Flow'rs' and 'snatch Morals' from the 'tatter'd Page'. Further, the audience before which the books are displayed seems to encompass both the exclusive group of 'walkers' who are described elsewhere in the poem, and far less laudable figures such as the 'saunt'ring 'Prentices', a phrase that is redolent with disparaging iconic associations. The passage thus seems to blur a distinction that is important elsewhere in the poem between culpable idleness such as that traditionally shown by ''Prentices' and the privileged leisure necessary for the consumption of literature.

In the last lines quoted, the Walker/Poet's elevation of the importance of the 'Labours' involved in the pursuit of his artistic task, and representation of himself as a dispenser of useful social precepts for the public good, reinforce a motif that is echoed in various other parts of the poem. In both aspects of his claim he allies himself firmly with the moral stance and seriousness of the Georgic poet. The ironies that play around this identification have been well described by Tom Woodman and John Chalker. The latter writes that:

> The reader is aware of a continuous irony in Gay's presentation of the walker, the 'speaker' in the poem. He is full both of practical good sense and also of moral earnestness, convinced of the utility of his work to all 'honest men' and with a strong feeling of superiority to those who 'laugh at honesty and trudging wits'. He feels, in fact, that he embodies the kind of active virtue which is Virgil's ideal in the *Georgics*—simple, rugged, hard-working. But the reader knows that this idealised view is a little spurious. The walker's constant activity conceals a real idleness in which . . . all the genuine activities of the town become the object of his contemplation and take on the quality of a ballet or a pageant. (pp. 177–78)

76

We can generalize from these observations, suggesting that the poem's ironies continually undermine the terms in which the production of 'art' traditionally transcends the category of 'luxury'. In its organization through the persona of the Walker, the poem ironically concedes the marginality of its own didactic utterances. Despite its claims, it does not offer Georgic instruction on an economically useful and morally admirable life, or engage the large civic and public issues that are raised in the *Georgics* itself, although those issues hover at its edges as implicit points of reference all through. Instead it elaborates on its own conspicuous redundancy, providing only mock-Georgic advice on points of personal comfort and convenience, parading the superfluousness of that advice, and interspersing it both with burlesque digressions and with the diversions of 'trivial Song' and 'amusing Lay'. Implicitly and explicitly, it acknowledges its own status as a luxury commodity in the economy it describes. The Walker himself does not succeed in eschewing luxury, but is at various times a consumer and a eulogist of it. Dianne Ames has shown how his poetic 'Labours' do not serve to teach anything, but only translate the labours of others into decorative spectacle for the entertainment of his readers.[14] In line with this his 'Precepts' are not distributed *gratis* to the poor, but are incorporated into an 'amusing' literary text which is every bit as much a commercial commodity as are the debased productions of Ned Ward and Charles Gildon to which it is compared. In the final paragraph of the poem he claims a literary immortality that will outlive the 'mighty Names' of 'W** and G**':

And now compleat my gen'rous Labours lye,
Finish'd and ripe for Immortality.
Death shall entomb in Dust this mould'ring Frame
But never reach th'eternal Part, my Fame. (III, 407–10)

However, his claims collapse bathetically as we realize that his 'Fame' will only be perpetuated by the prominence of the bookseller's commercial advertisements for his work:

When Criticks crazy Bandboxes repair,
And Tragedies, turn'd Rockets, bounce in Air;
High-rais'd on *Fleetstreet* Posts, consign'd to Fame,
This work shall shine, and Walkers bless my name.
(III, 413–16)

This then is the paradoxical context in which we must examine the poem's representation of economic matters. We can follow through some of its consequences by having a final look at some details from a passage to which we have already referred on several occasions—the Cloacina episode in Book II (107–216). In the case of each of these details, we can identify various strands of suggestion and implication, which may not be developed fully at any stage of the poem, but which build up in the course of it into cumulative patterns of motifal association, and which colour our reading of it throughout. The episode begins with a couplet that seems to invite a large emblematic reading, suggesting exactly the economic connections that we have said are lacking in the poem: 'What though the gath'ring Mire thy Feet besmear,/ The Voice of Industry is always near' (II, 99–100). However, those possibilities are not taken up, and instead the couplet is developed literally in the 'mythological' account of the origins of the bootblack boy. This begins with a passage in which we can find details that relate to several leading motifs of the poem:

> Hark! the Boy calls thee to his destin'd Stand,
> And the Shoe shines beneath his oily Hand.
> Here let the Muse, fatigu'd amid the Throng,
> Adorn her Precepts with digressive Song;
> Of shirtless Youths the secret Rise to trace
> And show the Parent of the sable Race. (II, 101–6)

There are several interesting points here in the representation of the Boy's industry and the Walker's apparent—if momentary—idleness. We have already mentioned the ironies that surround the latter's claims for the seriousness of his own didactic purposes. The apology here for his moment of relaxation and digression from them is echoed at the end of the episode:

> Like the sweet Ballad, this amusing Lay
> Too long detains the Walker on his Way;
> While he attends, new Dangers round him throng;
> The busy City asks instructive Song. (II, 217–20)

Both apologies contrast interestingly with the passage in Book III where we are warned:

> Where the Mob gathers, swiftly shoot along,
> Nor idly mingle in the noisy Throng.

> Lur'd by the Silver Hilt, amid the Swarm,
> The subtil Artist will thy Side disarm. . . . (III, 51–4)

and slightly later:

> Let not the Ballad-Singer's shrilling Strain
> Amid the Swarm thy list'ning Ear detain:
> Guard well thy Pocket; for these *Syrens* stand,
> To aid the Labours of the diving Hand. (III, 77–80)

Both of these incorporate ironic applications of terms that might otherwise be used to describe the Walker's own activities and address to his readers. Here, for example, the 'subtil Artist' and 'Ballad-Singer' are seen as employing their 'Labours'— but only to take advantage of the idleness of the vulgar 'Swarm'. The ironic echo of the poet's own remarks about himself serves to reinforce our sense of the distance between the Walker and the crowd that surrounds him, and highlights the poem's repeated implication that we are peculiarly privileged in our literary idleness as we read it—a point that is reinforced throughout by the treatment of those not fated to share that privilege.

The bootblack boy is one of these. His occupation of his 'Stand' is literally 'destin'd' by the Gods, as part of the providentially designed economy. His only moment of real unhappiness occurs when he is not fulfilling his rôle in that economy and working, but is 'pensive through Idleness' as he stands 'musing' on the banks of Fleet Ditch; and this is speedily relieved by the 'Gifts' of the Gods, which at once secure his release from beggary and provide an added convenience for the walkers he serves. Every aspect of this outcome has echoes and ramifications in the poem. The intervention of the Gods is a reassuring demonstration of charity, as 'Each Power contributes to relieve the Poor' (II, 157), and so relieves us of the necessity of doing so—not that we are led to feel an undue desire to do so in the first place, as we have been told that when the Boy was a 'Beggar's Brat', 'His Infant Tongue soon learnt the canting Art,/ Knew all the Pray'rs and Whines to touch the Heart' (II, 143–44), and we are consoled with the knowledge that anyway he did not suffer as a rich child might have done:

O happy unown'd Youths, your Limbs can bear
The scorching Dog-star, and the Winter's Air,
While the rich Infant, nurs'd with Care and Pain,
Thirsts with each Heat, and coughs with ev'ry Rain!
(II, 145–48)

The passage stands in interesting contrast to the ideal passages on charity elsewhere in the poem.

At the same time we can set the 'Gifts' of the Gods among a series of 'gifts' that appear in the economy in the course of the poem, without any need for productive human labour to manufacture them. Patty's Pattens, described at the end of Book I (223–82), provide the other long and fancifully mythologized example of these gifts, and various others are mentioned in passing. An interesting and typical one, also from Book I, occurs when the Walker writes:

Rosie-complexion'd Health thy Steps attends,
And Exercise thy lasting Youth defends.
Imprudent Men Heav'ns choicest Gifts prophane.
Thus some beneath their Arm support the Cane. (I, 73–6)

Here, 'Heav'ns choicest Gifts' refers back to 'Health' and 'Youth', but also forward to the 'Cane', reinforcing our sense of the distinctions to be made between the Walkers, for whom a cane is a natural aid rather than a commodity, and the Beaus, for whom it is an item of luxury. The repeated suggestion in the poem that there is a large element of extra-economic spontaneous generation of commodities within the economy is an important factor in its refusal to represent the economic relations we have seen discussed elsewhere.

This leaves us with Fleet Ditch, the filth in the streets and the Boy's employment. All the potential is there for satiric emblems or for Mandevillian economic exposition. Elsewhere in the poem filth often seems to be about to acquire emblematic status—as when the pride of a Beau is humbled as he is tipped into it (II, 523); or more loosely, when two coachmen fight in the street and are likened to 'Boars' who 'dispute the Reign of some luxurious Mire' (III, 48). However, the suggestiveness of individual phrases and references is never quite followed through. Similarly with Fleet Ditch. We can recognize that in the passage on Cloacina the Ditch is primarily the site of a burlesque parody of the Aristaeus episode in the Fourth Book of the *Georgics*.[15] We can accept John Chalker's claim that the tone of the passage embraces more than simple burlesque, and that it 'hints . . . at dimensions beyond the one that is immediately dominant', particularly in the 'potentially serious sensuous appeal' of the Goddess herself (p. 176). We can also agree with Pat Rogers's more general suggestion about the poem's 'inchoate' inferences that the city's filth is somehow 'energetic' and 'life-giving', but what we cannot do is develop those inferences beyond the point of generalized suggestiveness, as the poem repeatedly shies away from the domain of economic discourse in which those suggestions might be made concrete, and implicitly announces to us that such matters are no concern of 'polite' light verse.

NOTES

1. References to *Trivia* are to the text of *PP*, I, 134–81.
2. T. F. Reddaway, *The Rebuilding of London after the Great Fire* (London, 1940), pp. 201–15; Pat Rogers, *Grub Street: Studies in a Subculture* (London, 1972), pp. 145–48. Subsequent references to Rogers are recorded in the text.
3. 'Due Preparation for the Plague As Well For Soul As Body', in G. H. M[aynadier], *The Works of Daniel Defoe*, 16 vols. (Boston, 1903–4), XV, 29.
4. *Works*, XV, 24.
5. *The Parliamentary History of England, from the Earliest Period to the Year 1803*, 36 vols. (London, 1812), XI (1739–41), col. 1011.
6. *London Transformed* (New Haven, 1978), p. 62. See also Peter Stallybrass and Allen White's discussion of City Fairs in *The Politics and Poetics of Transgression* (London, 1986), pp. 100–24, and David Nokes's analysis of financial metaphors in *The Beggar's Opera* in *Raillery and Rage: A Study of Eighteenth Century Satire* (Brighton, 1987), pp. 122–35.
7. See Rogers, pp. 159–66; Dianne S. Ames, 'Gay's *Trivia* and the Art of Allusion', *SP*, 75 (1978), 199–222; Sven M. Armens, *John Gay: Social Critic* (New York, 1954), pp. 72–95; Martin C. Battestin, *The Providence of Wit* (Oxford, 1974), pp. 127–40; John Chalker, *The English Georgic: A Study in the Development of a Form* (London, 1969), pp. 165–69.
8. 'Swift's Fallen City: *A Description of the Morning*', in Brian Vickers (ed.), *The World of Jonathan Swift* (Oxford, 1968), pp. 171–94.
9. Battestin, pp. 126–31; Armens, pp. 72–3; Alvin B. Kernan, *The Plot of Satire* (New Haven, 1965), pp. 45–50; Chalker, pp. 177–78.

10. F. B. Kaye (ed.), *The Fable of the Bees*, 2 vols. (Oxford, 1924), I, 10–13.
11. W. J. Bate, J. M. Bullitt and L. F. Powell (eds.), *The Idler and The Adventurer* (New Haven, 1963), pp. 383–89. Subsequent references are recorded in the text.
12. Chalker, pp. 163–69. Subsequent references are recorded in the text.
13. For a fuller discussion of this passage, see Ames, pp. 207–8.
14. Ames, pp. 199–200.
15. See Chalker, pp. 174–77.

4

'Vulgar Circumstance' and 'Due Civilities': Gay's Art of Polite Living in Town

by TOM WOODMAN

The great influence of Virgil's *Georgics* on English poetry of the first half of the eighteenth century has often been commented on. The Latin poem gave a classical authority for the treatment of agricultural improvement and, by extension, industry, trade and commerce. Such topics could be elevated by the example of a poet who delivers, as Addison put it in his influential essay on the *Georgics* (1697), 'the meanest of his precepts with a kind of grandeur',[1] and who is able to suffuse the details of husbandry with a patriotic and religious enthusiasm. Yet the match with Virgil's poem could hardly be an exact one, as many examples unintentionally display, and various ideological tensions and paradoxes emerge. Virgil's poem of rural labour could not be translated without a certain awkwardness into the terms of an economic system increasingly dependent on capitalism and the city. Even with the topic of agricultural improvement as such, the dependence on capital meant that the Roman poet's sense of the dignity of labour could not apply unproblematically to a situation in which gentlemen did not work with their hands and where money bred money mysteriously and, it seemed, idly.

Relatively serious georgics like John Philips's *Cyder* (1708) thus seem partly the product of rural nostalgia rather than a full confrontation with the new realities, whilst Pope's *Windsor Forest*, as a recent critic has pointed out, ends with a panegyric on trade that deliberately ignores the actualities of London commercial life.[2] Gay himself reflects these problems in *Rural Sports*, which cannot decide whether it is about work or leisure pursuits and which tries to blur the distinction by calling the happy fields 'the kind rewarders of industrious life' (437) and contrasting them with the fruitless labours of the town. We notice, too, that Gay's sojourn in the country is a very brief one, despite his complaints: 'Farewel.—The city calls me from your bow'rs:/ Farewel amusing thoughts and peaceful hours' (442–43).[3] Gay's rural poem in fact testifies to its own marginality.

In classical literature city life had either been unreservedly satirized or else seen entirely from the perspective of a leisured class whose arts of civility—both politics and manners—were superior to unpolished nature. The growth of capitalism and the modification of the aristocratic ethos of leisure necessitated a different approach. Addison and Steele, in particular, unambiguously affirmed the centrality of commerce, capitalism and the city, and various *Tatler* and *Spectator* essays are prose city georgics, written with total seriousness in celebration of the hive of industry that is London. When Addison extravagantly praises the Royal Exchange in the *Spectator* 69 (19 May 1711) he is surrounding labour, as Virgil does, with a patriotic and quasi-religious enthusiasm.

The true georgic, however, succeeds in generalizing the significance of its central activity so that it becomes symbolic of an art of living as a whole. Gay's version of this in *Rural Sports* has to be a series of trite moralizations on fishing or hunting because of the peripheral nature of such activities in the modern world. Even Addison and Steele find it hard to imbue the actual details of urban commercial life with the kind of significance Virgil gave agriculture. The art of living motif enters instead with their great concern for manners. This theme was traditionally associated with court life and leisure, but new circumstances brought a new perspective. Manners had for some time now been losing any necessary connection with high birth as such. In Lord Chesterfield's view (16 May 1751), for example, even a ploughman could learn the graces.[4] The interest in politeness reflected the burgeoning consumerism and the new prosperity. In more conservative eyes it has become a veritable *'Genteel Mania'*,[5] but manners were at the heart of Addison and Steele's whole enterprise of reconciling the upper classes and the commercial interest. It was helpful for merchants and financiers, for example, to learn a certain style for their contacts with upper-class customers. Jebediah Strutt sent his son a copy of Chesterfield's letters and urged him: 'it is almost as necessary to learn a genteel behaviour, polite manner as it is to learn to speak, or read or write.'[6]

The very conditions of London life itself in the period necessitated an especial attention to manners. As Richard Sennet explains in *The Fall of Public Man*, new codes of behaviour that could no longer depend on the fixity of court or rural rôles were an urgent necessity 'in a populous environment filling and refilling with strangers'.[7] He points out that walking in the streets acquired an importance as a social activity in the eighteenth century that it had never had before.[8] The ability to respond appropriately to those one met became an important test of decorum. In an essay in this collection, Stephen Copley and Ian Haywood analyse the ambivalences and contradictions about commerce, labour and city life inscribed in *Trivia*. I want to look specifically in this essay at the associated matter of Gay's attitudes to that 'civility and politeness' for which London was also 'famous', according to Lord Tyrconnel.[9]

Gay's own city georgic could certainly not have been written without an awareness of the *Spectator*, but he significantly distances himself from the ideology of Whig panegyric. Praise of the Royal Exchange as one of the great achievements and attractions of London is conspicuous by its absence, and the only reference to merchants is the cynical advice to seek accurate directions from them, for a merchant will only deceive you when he 'profits by't' (II, 72).

On the other hand Gay's poem is not the product of what might be considered a Tory use of georgic either. It is not a condemnation of the corrupt upstarts of the town from the landed gentry's traditional perspective of the stability of rural order, although *Rural Sports* carries something of that weight. The primary implication of *Trivia* is surely not that of a terrible modern degeneration from the ethos of its classical prototype. If the poem shows the dirt and danger of London, it is also full of the attractive liveliness and variety of its sights and sounds. As William Bowman Piper points out, Gay's typical couplet is a brisk, 'short-winded' unit like Waller's, and it comes especially into its own here to represent the stops and starts of his own engaging curiosity, his short-lived, excited attention.[10] In a letter to Parnell (April–May 1714), Gay writes as follows:

> Ye Chariots rolling through the Street
> Ye Operas with voices Sweet
> Ye Ladies dress'd in rich array
> That walk the Park or grace the Play
> Ye Balls, Assemblees Tea & Ombre
> And other pleasures without *Nombre*

> Oh Dear Doctor Parnelle, whats all your Trees, your Meadows, your Streams & Plains to a walk in St James's Park, I hope you won't be so profane as to make any comparison of the sight of a Cow & a Calf to a Beau & a Belle? do you imagine a Place beneath a shady Back of equal value, to a Place at Court?[11]

The last phrase, of course, reverts to traditional anti-court satire and the letter is anti-pastoral parody, but the tone of the verses carries the same light-hearted but genuine sense of pleasure in the town as there is in *Trivia*.

Gay's mock-heroic tone therefore serves to distance him from the ideological seriousness of Addison and Steele, but it is certainly not condemnatory of the city like some other contemporary examples. Rather, the effect seems to be analogous to the treatment in *Wine*, a joke poem in which the description of familiar pursuits with constant reference to an older, elevated mode is humorous and affectionate. London was, after all, already familiar to most of Gay's original readers and the basic joke of the poem, as most of Gay's more solemn commentators have forgotten, is the idea that you should need instructions about how to walk through it at all. Gay plays cleverly with Praeteritio in this respect:

> Yet let me not descend to trivial Song;
> Nor vulgar Circumstance my Verse prolong;
> Why should I teach the Maid when Torrents pour,
> Her Head to shelter from the sudden Show'r?
> Nature will best her ready Hand inform,
> With her spread Petticoat to fence the Storm. . . .

. . . . Who knows not, that the Coachman lashing by,
Oft', with his Flourish, cuts the heedless Eye.

(II, 301–6, 311–12)

In keeping with the convention, he discourses on topics that he
says he will refrain from mentioning, but in this case, he is
inverting the effect of the traditional rhetorical device and using
it to highlight the fact that his instructions are literally unnecessary and redundant this time.

Similarly mock-heroic in its basic effect is the comparison of
London to exotic and dangerous foreign climes:

Thus the bold Traveller, (inur'd to Toil,
Whose Steps have printed *Asia*'s desert Soil,
The barb'rous *Arabs* Haunt; or shiv'ring crost
Dark *Greenland*'s Mountains of eternal Frost;
Whom Providence, in length of Years, restores
To the wish'd Harbour of his native Shores;)
Sets forth his Journals to the publick View,
To caution, by his Woes, the wandring Crew.

(III, 399–406)

The main effect here too is to emphasize the familiarity and
safety of London, though this is not, of course, to deny that
Gay's method also makes his readers think twice about the very
real dangers that London life did involve.

Gay's motif of walking is thus a mock-heroic joke and a
means for conveying enjoyment, a device, as in the *Spectator*, for
getting us through London. The walker is certainly a 'Mr.
Spectator' figure in this respect: 'Here I remark each Walker's
diff'rent Face./ And in their Look their various Business trace'
(II, 275–76), but because Gay has chosen the georgic mode he
has to give 'Walking' much greater significance than it has in
the *Spectator*. He does not wish to be identified with Addison's
ideological praise of commerce, nor can he make lower-class
urban work his main subject in a polite poem. 'Walking'
therefore becomes his great central activity, equivalent to agriculture in Virgil. He walks, he says, on 'bus'ness', though the
nature of that business is never specified. He also associates
walking as 'exercise' with the georgic theme of 'use', found in
the context of gardening and agriculture in Pope's *Epistle to
Burlington* (1731) but hardly convincing here. For 'Walking' in

this poem is actually the sign of a deliberate non-involvement in the economic system. It is a leisure pursuit as much as a form of labour. The walker has time to remark on all he sees, to stop and browse at bookstalls and to taste oysters. Walking thus has a fairly precise class orientation as a golden mean between *nouveau riche* selfishness and idleness and the vulgar labours of the lower classes. But it can hardly be taken seriously as a georgic activity. Gay cannot find a convincing form of work as the georgic art of living in his period, and it is for this reason that he needs the saving grace of mock georgic. Through the mock mode he expresses his ambivalent yet affectionate attitude to city life as a whole. He also evades the problems about labour he faced in *Rural Sports* and yet at the same time apparently masters them by a joke.

The activity of 'walking' does take on a certain symbolic rôle as an art of living however, in its undeniably close relationship to the theme of manners. To walk through London is quite literally for Gay an art of reading codes of dress and speech and learning to respond appropriately to strangers in the confusing new conditions. Affectation, social climbing, and even down-right impersonation and confidence trickery are a much more potent possibility now, as Gay makes clear. A certain know-how is genuinely required, despite the fact that many of the poem's instructions are unnecessary for the kind of people who would read it: 'Careful Observers, studious of the Town,/ Shun the Misfortunes that disgrace the Clown' (II, 285–86). The art of town living is not simply a matter of expertise, sophistication and prudence. Intelligence and moral discrimination are also required: 'Let the vain Virgin, lur'd by glaring Show,/ Sigh for the Liv'rys of th' embroider'd Beau' (II, 571–72). The theme produces an uncharacteristically sustained earnestness of tone in a well-known passage:

> Let due Civilities be strictly paid.
> The Wall surrender to the hooded Maid;
> Nor let thy sturdy Elbow's hasty Rage
> Jostle the feeble Steps of trembling Age:
> And when the Porter bends beneath his Load,
> And Pants for breath; clear thou the crouded Road.
> But above all, the groaping Blind direct,
> And from the pressing Throng the Lame protect.

You'll sometimes meet a Fop, of nicest Tread,
Whose mantling Peruke veils his empty Head,
At ev'ry Step he dreads the Wall to lose,
And risques, to save a Coach, his red-heel'd Shoes;
Him, like the *Miller*, pass with Caution by,
Lest from his Shoulder Clouds of Powder fly.
But when the Bully, with assuming Pace,
Cocks his broad Hat, edg'd round with tarnish'd Lace,
Yield not the Way; defie his strutting Pride,
And thrust him to the muddy Kennel's side;
He never turns again, nor dares oppose,
But mutters coward Curses as he goes. (II, 45–64)

This is both detailed and generalizing, with its personifications and generic phrases. The satire on dress gains real weight from the recognition that in a sense after all the clothes *are* the man. The matter of taking or ceding the wall becomes a test of intelligence, courage and even charity as well as of etiquette. In his *Present State of Wit* (1711) Gay had praised Addison and Steele warmly for their reconciliation of politeness and morality. This surely remains one of his own basic aims. He satirizes an excessive attention to fashion in the beaux and fops and anything that smacks of the 'genteel mania' of social climbing. On the other hand, a proper attention to clothes and manners is recommended, as Anne McWhir points out in a fine recent discussion, his own ideal is the mean between the two extremes of beau and clown.[12]

Nevertheless, it remains true that one of the most marked characteristics of all Gay's best work is his refusal to make a structured hierarchy of moral discourse. When in this poem he witnesses a funeral procession in London, he is led into the reflection, 'Contemplate, Mortal, on thy fleeting Years' (III, 225), and he goes on to remark, like his friend Parnell in 'A Night Piece on Death' (1722), on the futility of elaborate ceremonies: 'How short is Life! how frail is human Trust!/ Is all this pomp for laying Dust to Dust?' (III, 235–36). As with many of Gay's moral reflections this is so deliberately commonplace as to be arch; it verges on a parody of traditional *sententia*. The suspicion is confirmed by the fact that Gay's conventional generalization is immediately followed by the most prosaic of advice about avoiding paint:

89

Where the nail'd Hoop defends the painted Stall,
Brush not thy sweeping Skirt too near the Wall;
Thy heedless Sleeve will drink the colour'd Oil,
And Spot indelible thy Pocket soil. (III, 237–40)

Gay's remarkable command of tone enables him to indulge in sentiment at the same time as parodying it and to be both didactic and yet non-committal. He is serious about manners, but he refuses to make them or anything else for that matter an absolute. His intimacy with Pope and Swift reinforced a temperamental attraction to a Renaissance *sprezzatura* that rejected too much overt moralizing: 'What gain we by this solemn way of teaching?/ Our precepts mend your lives no more than preaching.'[13] But Gay does not have the assured and sanctioned position of the traditional commentator on *mores* anyway. No totally consistent class or moral perspective seems to emerge. There is some collusion on Gay's part in what conservative writers saw as the reprehensible and even threatening results of the growing consumerism, and his enjoyment of all the aberrant phenomena he describes is often evident.

Gay's city poem is secular and largely demystified. He alludes to all the rich traditional complexes about art and nature that are built into both georgics and discussions of politeness, but he does so very lightly and in deliberate juxtaposition with such matters as where best to urinate in the streets. He does not try to suffuse the details of London life with the religious significance Virgil gives agriculture, nor does he commit himself to quasi-religious panegyrics about commerce. Gay's 'walker' is indubitably himself a member of the polite world, who has led 'the Fair' from the 'crouded *Play*' (III, 256). Politeness is the art of modern living in town, and Gay is well aware of its importance. Yet he is also aware that, as William Empson points out, all politeness has an element of irony about it.[14] He knows that the polite world is not innocent, spontaneous and natural, though he is equally aware of the limitations of those who are not polite, and his questioning of polite values is carried out in a tone of teasing intimacy with his readers.

In the 'Preface' to *The What D'Ye Call It* Gay asserts that the

Sentiments of Princes and Clowns have not in reality that difference which they seem to have: their Thoughts are almost the same, and they only differ as the same Thought is attended with a Meanness or Pomp of Diction, or receive a different Light from the Circumstances each Character is conversant with.[15]

This is a traditional enough form of the pastoral identification of high and low, but various versions of it are at the heart of all Gay's best work. Its especial attraction for him and the way he elaborates upon it suggests his own and his age's uncertainties and anxieties about the traditional class and moral basis of manners, which was reasserted, modified and questioned all at the same time in the period. *The Beggar's Opera* is the most brilliant hall of mirrors of these complexities. The view that we are all the same beneath the skin does after all relativize manners somewhat. Yet, as we might expect from the traditional origins of the identification, its effects are only fleetingly radical in their implications. It intimates rather, as William Empson points out,[16] the possibility of a beautiful harmony between rich and poor. The differentiation of classes is not simply going to disappear. If manners are truly the main mark of differentiation, then their importance is affirmed at the same time as being relativized.

A special version of this device occurs in the identification of town ladies with birds and fawns in the attractive passage parodying the georgic signs of the seasons in *Trivia*:

> Nor do less certain Signs the Town advise,
> Of milder Weather, and serener Skies.
> The Ladies gayly dress'd, the *Mall* adorn
> With various Dyes, and paint the sunny Morn;
> The wanton Fawns with frisking Pleasure range,
> And chirping Sparrows greet the welcome Change;
> Not that their Minds with greater Skill are fraught,
> Endu'd by Instinct, or by Reason taught,
> The Seasons operate on every Breast;
> 'Tis hence that Fawns are brisk, and Ladies drest.
>
> (I, 143–52)

Virgil's great central theme has been described as the 'interrelationship and interdependence of all things natural and human'.[17] Gay can only make such a georgic affirmation fleetingly and ironically. An obvious gap in dignity is measured in the gap between the sparrows and Virgil's great agricultural rhythms. We notice that, like the ladies, the fawns are 'wanton' in the modern as well as in the Latinate sense and that sparrows are traditionally associated with lechery as well as with the town. Gay plays with poetic diction here, too, for it is conventionally birds not ladies whose plumage is of 'various Dyes' and who 'paint the sunny Morn' (I, 146). The town's pretensions to an art and a politeness above nature are gently punctured here. Yet nature too is largely demystified in Gay, and the town is certainly not condemned from that perspective in any simple sense. As well as having charms of its own, it is allowed to share in the brightness of spring. Town life is not in fact traumatically alienated from nature. The traditional hierarchical analogy between reason and nature is allowed to stand—'Endu'd by Instinct, or by Reason taught' (I, 150)—and the ladies are at least as pretty and as lively as fawns and birds. Gay's georgic identification is a brief one, but it very characteristically manages to be comically deflating and yet deeply reassuring at the same time.

NOTES

1. A. C. Guthkelch (ed.), *The Miscellaneous Works of Joseph Addison*, 2 vols. (London, 1914), II, 9.
2. John H. Johnston, *The Poet and the City: A Study in Urban Perspectives* (Athens, Ga., 1984), p. 41.
3. Line references are to the texts of Gay's poems in *PP*, from which all quotations are taken.
4. Bonamy Dobrée (ed.), *The Letters of Philip Dormer Stanhope, Fourth Earl of Chesterfield*, 6 vols. (New York, 1932; rept. 1968): 'I fear the want of that aimiable and engaging *je ne sais quoi*, which, as some philosophers have . . . said of the soul, is all in all, and all in every part. . . . All these engaging and endearing accomplishments are mechanical, and to be acquired by care and observation as easily as turning or any mechanical trade. A common country fellow taken from the plough, and enlisted on an old corps, soon lays aside his shambling gait, his slouching air, his clumsy and awkward motions, and acquires the martial air, the regular motions, and the whole exercise of the corps (pp. 1730–731).
5. *The World*, 199 (21 October 1756). See also Neil McKendrick, John Brewer and J. H. Plumb, *The Birth of a Consumer Society: The Commercialization of Eighteenth-Century England* (London, 1984), pp. 34–99.

6. Quoted in R. S. Fitton and A. P. Wadsworth, *The Strutts and the Arkwrights, 1758–1830: A Study of the Early Factory System* (Manchester, 1958), p. 145.
7. Sennet, *The Fall of Public Man* (Cambridge, 1977), p. 62.
8. See Sennet: 'By the middle of the 18th. Century walking in the street as a social activity acquired an importance which in Paris and London it had never had before. The promenade was at the time described as the advent of an Italian taste; . . . This sense of the monumental city, translated into the life of London or Paris a century later, became less a matter of seeing sights than seeing other people' (pp. 84–5).
9. See Copley and Haywood, this volume, note 4, p. 81.
10. *The Heroic Couplet* (Cleveland, Ohio, 1969), p. 375.
11. *Letters*, pp. 6–7.
12. 'The Wolf in the Fold: John Gay in *The Shepherd's Week* and *Trivia*', *Studies in English Literature*, 23 (1983), 413–23.
13. 'Prologue' (7–8), *The Captives*, *DW*, I, 345.
14. Empson, *Some Versions of Pastoral* (London, 1935), p. 236.
15. *DW*, I, 175.
16. Empson, p. 11.
17. Johnston, p. 7.

5

Gay and the Ironies of Rustic Simplicity

by NIGEL WOOD

1

In his *Letter to a Lady, Occasion'd by the Arrival of Her Royal Highness, the Princess of Wales* (1714), Gay seems to disown Arcadia:

> Once Ladies fair in homely Guise I sung,
> And with their Names wild Woods and Mountains rung.
> Oh, teach me now to strike a softer Strain!
> The Court refines the Language of the Plain.
>
> (107–10)[1]

The most crucial factor in any reading of this poem, and indeed of many of Gay's 'courtly' Epistles is quite how we judge the value and status of this softer and more refined idiom. The language, divested of its 'homely Guise' and with no sympathetic acoustics, does not flow easily. The whole poem portrays Gay's failure to write courtly panegyric on demand, even if preferment depends on it. Certain new tricks have to be learnt by the erstwhile pastoralist in order to get on and the poem provides no proof that Gay is willing to learn them. The epigraph from Juvenal's *Seventh Satire*: 'nam si Virgilio puer, & tolerabile desit/ Hospitium, caderunt omnes a crinibus Hydri' (69–70), emphasizes the need for a roof over one's head and the leisure-time to write poetry, otherwise there would have been no Virgilian epic. Rather than praise of Princess Caroline, it is this

94

dependence of Muse on Patron that forms the main nexus of interest in the poem: the situation's anxieties, inevitable conventionalities and, ultimately, its futility, when his 'sullen Muse' is crowded out by the mass of 'needy Courtiers' (153–54) who awaited the Princess on her arrival at Margate.

The poem is an exercise in poetic hesitancy and indecision. It commences with apologies for writing what 'should long since' have been written. 'Silence would be thought a Crime', so he has been constrained to leave 'trifling Themes' where he sports 'on Plains with rural Damsels'. However, Gay is at some pains to display how unfit he now feels himself to tackle much else. He cudgels the 'unwilling Muses' (2–10) and only as a 'last Resort' does he leave 'the Muses to frequent the Court' (89–90). 'Courtly Grace' accompanies those in place (101), the ease of address and ready flow of verses a direct corollary of ambition satisfied. Gay realizes he has to achieve such 'Grace' and yet, if anything, he delivers an Horatian familiarity, quite distinct from the formulaic afflatus he apes in the italicized passages. Characteristically, Gay sees himself as the neglected outsider, to the simple manner born and heir to no other.

This ironic distance not only from the natural, but rough, dialect of the plains but also from the artificial, but refined, courtly patois, is no isolated case in Gay's work. His letter to Parnell of April/May 1714 provides a clear example of such deep-seated anxiety. Trees and meadows are paltry compared 'to a walk in St. James's Park' and livestock provides a 'profane' comparison to 'a Beau & a Belle':

> . . . do you imagine a Place beneath a shady Back of equal value, to a Place at Court? no, no, good Doctor, our good & pious Friend Pope stands now at your Elbow ready to confute all these praises of the Country [both were working at Binfield on the *Iliad* translation], he knows you can speak as well in the praise of great Men as of great Trees, & that you would as soon go to a Minister of States Levee, as look on a Haycock, or walk in a Dale. . . .[2]

Gay's pursuit of a secure livelihood is no isolated biographical fact, as it structures his work deeply. We see it in various forms: the Beggar writing Newgate Operas, the 'epigrammatic' petitioner of Robert Harley ('One can live without Money on Plains,/ But never without it at Court. . .'), the virtuous Walker

of *Trivia* right through to the sagacious Shepherd from the
'Introduction' to the first series of his *Fables*, 'Unvex'd with all
the cares of gain. . .'. Gay's quest met with no small measure of
eventual success. In 1714, however, the Hanoverian succession
meant frustration and lingering disappointment for him.
Arbuthnot advised Gay to write a flattering *Letter* because, as he
pointed out to Swift (19 October 1714), he was 'in such a
groveling condition, as to the affairs of the world'. Even so, he
feared Gay's Muse 'would not stoop to visit him' in this matter.[3]
In one of the informal passages from the *Letter*, it is clear how
keenly the effect of being 'unplaced' was felt: 'Places I found,
were daily giv'n away,/ And yet no friendly Gazette mention'd
Gay' (95–6). Gay can celebrate the freedom of independence
and its moral clarity at the same time as rue its penury and
backwoods lack of 'refinement'. When Gay depicts this context
in the *Letter*, the result is a poem that expresses *and enacts*
dislocation:

> Still ev'ry one I met with in this agreed,
> That Writing was my Method to succeed;
> But now Preferments so possess'd my Brain,
> That scarce I could produce a single Strain:
> Indeed I sometimes hammer'd out a Line,
> Without Connection as without Design. . . .
>
> (125–30)

W. H. Irving's comment on the poem treats it as a symptom of
a wider poetic concern: 'Obviously he feels the need for a
pattern into which to fit his ideas, but for our part as readers we
are grateful for the lack of plan; . . .'[4] This 'lack of plan' is a
means by which convention and myth are exposed as fictions.
As to whether they are necessary fictions Gay seems radically
undecided.

This is nowhere more evident than in his more pastoral
references. *The Shepherd's Week* is often with good cause regarded
as a contribution to the Pope-Philips debate over the correct
bucolic style. We have Pope's testimony in his letter to John
Caryll (8 June 1714) that Gay wrote his 'Pastorals' because
Philips had withheld Homer subscription money, and this has
led critics such as Hoyt Trowbridge to seek traces of a
burlesque of Philips's *Pastorals*. William D. Ellis, Jr. reads

Thomas D'Urfey for Ambrose Philips; W. H. Irving sees more ridicule of Virgil.[5] It is the object of this essay to consider *The Shepherd's Week* as *sui generis*, generated as much by Gay's own preoccupations as by the suggestions of friends or the natural antipathy to certain enemies.

2

Towards the conclusion of his 'Proeme' to *The Shepherd's Week*, Gay seems comforted when he realizes that, when his 'Words in the course of transitory Things shall decay', there will arise 'some Lover of *Simplicity* . . . who shall have the Hardiness' to translate his inevitably archaic language 'into such more modern Dialect as shall be then understood'. It is for this reason that he has included 'Glosses and Explications of uncouth Pastoral Terms'. This bid for some measure of immortality depends on the recovery of the zero degree of 'Simplicity' as the correct contemporary idiom, one freed from meretricious Wit as well as rustic Barbarism. Irony inevitably surrounds any claim to Simplicity in the 'Proeme to the Courteous Reader', so much so that it has almost become axiomatic to regard Gay's 'true' meaning as radically indeterminate. We can be sure what Gay did *not* want his pastorals to be to the extent that what they end up being is at best a series of double negatives, at worst a Puckish *jeu d'esprit*. Simplicity 'after the true ancient guise of *Theocritus*' might well involve 'his Louts [giving] foul Language' and a peek at 'Goats at Rut',[6] as the 'Proeme' has it, but, *faut de mieux*, can also form the basis for whatever success we can claim for *The Shepherd's Week*, where irony is a weapon, not a mode of concealment, and its target the Courteous Reader, not a blundering Grubbinol or Sparabella.

William Empson characterized pastoral simplicity, its mocking realism, as a convenient idiom for the expression of 'a sense of social injustice. . . This is a source of irony both against [the writer] and against the society' from which he is exempting himself.[7] The criticism of 'complex' society cannot exonerate or even condone 'simplicity' unreservedly. This inescapable string of double meanings that attaches itself to pastoral writing stems from its defiant artificiality. Pastoral can be a way of *not* writing about the pastoral life outside literature. Theocritus's Doric, as

97

Spenser's, is a library invention not a Henry Higgins transcription. Virgil's Golden Age countrymen are passionate *ingenus*, piping woodnotes wild, yet as is obvious from *Eclogues* 1 and 10, answering an urban need rather than providing a corrective alternative. 'Simple people' are signifiers, not signifieds. Gay is not unaware of this. The language he provides for his shepherds 'is neither spoken by the country Maiden nor the courtly Dame', and is only timeless in that it can never actually be uttered; it is, in short, *written*, with all that that implies. This rootless rusticity is, surprisingly, illustrated by an analogy with the distinctly ephemeral self-seeking of town life:

> Granted also it is, that in this my Language, I seem unto my self, as a *London* Mason, who calculateth his Work for a Term of Years, when he buildeth with old Materials upon a Ground-rent that is not his own, which soon turneth to Rubbish and Ruins.

This opportunist fraud Gay's 'Shepherd-Poet' seems innocently to perpetuate. The writing here seems consistently aware of Modern presumption. The representation of 'higher' truths is jettisoned for a merely conventional realism, an investing in the fashion of the moment with as much foundation as a jerry-built town-house.

'E.K.'s apology for Spenser's Doric was based on its allegorical function, the unfolding 'great matter of argument covertly' rather than 'professing it'.[8] It was not self-evident in the period, however, that a decorative Doric was comic. Even if non-allegorical, the Doric could be appealing for its rugged simplicity. In Dryden's *Virgil* (1697), his 'Dedication of the *Pastorals*' dubs Spenser the Master of our 'Northern Dialect' who has

> so exactly imitated the *Doric* of *Theocritus*, that his Love is a perfect Image of that Passion which God infus'd into both Sexes, before it was corrupted with the Knowledge of Arts, and the Ceremonies of what we call good Manners.[9]

This primitivistic simplicity of character and prelapsarian instincts is thus exactly mirrored by a suitably artless roughness and lack of civilized cadence in the Doric. This veneration for Spenser's diction is repeated in his 'Preface' to *Fables Ancient and Modern* (1700) where he is hailed as one of the 'Great Masters in our Language . . .' who saw 'much farther into the Beauties of

our Numbers, than those who immediately followed' him.[10]
This northern simplicity demonstrates the Theocritean ideals of
uncivilized freedom with little of the emasculating pathos.

The contrast with Pope is striking. In his 'Discourse on
Pastoral Poetry' (1717), prefixed to the *Pastorals* in the *Works*,
Spenser is kin to Theocritus in 'manners, thoughts, and
characters', but also 'was certainly inferior in his Dialect', not
because of artistic incompetence but because the object of his
imitation is 'entirely obsolete, or spoken only by people of the
lowest condition'. The Doric of the *Idylls* had its own 'beauty
and propriety' on account of its currency 'in part of *Greece*' and
also its use by 'many of the greatest persons'. Dryden's relish at
a Golden Age libertinism is completely rejected here for a
censorship of 'low' life and its idioms. It is then that Pope
justifies this fastidiousness in terms that annex social assumptions to artistic ones:

> As there is a difference between simplicity and rusticity, so the
> expression of simple thoughts should be plain, but not clownish.
> The addition he has made of a Calendar to his Eclogues is very
> beautiful: since by this, besides the general moral of innocence
> and simplicity, which is common to other authors of pastoral, he
> has one peculiar to himself.[11]

This concurrence of 'simplicities' and the struggle to define the
term satisfactorily creates several problems in interpretation.
Initially, there is the clear parallel between simplicity/plainness
and rusticity/clownishness which already overlays aesthetic and
moral criteria as to mimetic truth. The waters get muddier
when Pope gets to the 'general moral', for here pastoral is
deemed to advocate both innocence (perhaps Dryden's primitivism) as well as this socio-aesthetic value of simplicity.

Pope, alternatively, could define Spenserian simplicity with a
quite different emphasis. In the heavily ironic *Guardian*, 40
(27 April 1713), his anonymous contribution to Thomas Tickell's
pastoral series, it proves to be a less enviable attribute. In
'praising' Ambrose Philips's '*Elegant Dialect*, which alone might
prove him the eldest born of *Spencer*, and our only true *Arcadian*',
Pope concludes that it might be as well if pastoralists confined
themselves to their own home dialect. The example quoted is
the opening of Spenser's 'September', which Pope believed was

set in Wales 'where with all the Simplicity natural to that Part of our Island, one Shepherd bids the other *Good-morrow* in an unusual and elegant Manner'.[12] Pope chooses a particularly convincing but unrepresentative example to denigrate Philips's colloquialisms, as 'E.K.', in his *'Glosse'* to the Eclogue admits that, even by Spenser's Doric standard, 'The Dialecte and phrase of speache in this Dialogue, seemeth somewhat to differ from the comen'.[13] The full force of the irony behind naming Philips 'our only true *Arcadian*' is thus obvious; by claiming to base his diction and characters on a Doric idyllic model, he is truly opposed to the self-conscious, highly-wrought artistry of Virgil and runs the danger of singularity, a travesty of the traditional esteem won by artful predecessors.

This sense of a canon of acceptable pastorals is crucial to a full comprehension of 'simplicity's' rhetorical force. A return to a native simplicity or a lost innocence is a pastoral gesture. Pope himself is not above invoking Spenser's ghost in his own pastorals. In 'Summer', Alexis uses a Flute

> . . . which *Colin's* tuneful Breath
> Inspir'd when living, and bequeath'd in Death;
> He said; *Alexis*, take this Pipe . . .
>
> (39–41)[14]

Presumably Pope wants to keep a memory of Spenser's mellifluousness not his low subject-matter. To Ambrose Philips, the attraction of Spenser lay immediately in other areas. In the 'Preface' (1710) to his own *Pastorals*, he feared lest the 'Innocency of the Subject' should make it so unappealing. His traditional models are Theocritus, Virgil and Spenser, the only writers 'to have hit upon the true Nature of *Pastoral* Poems'.[15] Pope had not accepted Theocritus or Spenser so unreservedly. It was perhaps Philips whose taste accorded with his own age. Henry Felton's *A Dissertation on Reading the Classics* (1713) gives Spenser the palm for pastoral poetry 'even with *Theocritus*, for I dare prefer him to *Virgil*'. In Felton's reading, 'the Sweetness and Rusticity of the *Doric Muse*' is a considerable bonus only recently imitated by his contemporaries, those who 'have assembled all the Beauties of Arcadian Poetry, and restored their Simplicity, Language, and Manners, to the Swains'.[16] This appropriation of Arcadia to a Spenserian model is the very opposite to Pope's attempt to keep the Virgilian ideal uncontaminated by the less ideal primitivisms of Philips.

'Clownish' or 'rustic', the Doric threatens several neo-classic premises. Strictly speaking, 'simple' mimesis, the inclusion of visceral details cheek-by-jowl with the 'literary', is exactly Gay's tactic in *The Shepherd's Week*. The possibilities of Arcadian transformation, the appeal to universal and non-topographical norms, are frequently alluded to whilst just as constantly denied. The Golden Age is also tacitly exposed as myth only, confronted as it is, in the 'Proeme' especially, by realistic country people. Given the suspiciously polite address to the 'gentle' or 'courteous' reader, the 'citizen-reader' becomes the 'shepherd-poet's' accomplice. The 'prudent Citizen journeying to his Country Farms' would be aghast to find his farms peopled by poetry's 'Court Clowns, or Clown Courtiers'. Instead, he would expect 'plain downright hearty cleanly Folk; such as be now Tenants to the Burgesses of this Realme'. The telling use of 'prudent' would seem to ensure that some of the mud thrown sticks to city clothes. Indeed, 'Gay' sets out to inform 'gentle' city-dwellers of rural conditions by setting before them 'a Picture, or rather, lively Landscape of thy own Country, just as thou mightest see it, didest thou take a Walk in the Fields at the proper Season'. Once again, the one adjective 'proper' provides some measure of commentary on the delicate choice of such pilgrimages. If this detail could be said to reflect as much on the visitor as the visited, then Gay's quotation from *Paradise Lost* (IX, 445–51) which immediately follows is unequivocal. The depiction of the 'Summer's Morn . . ./ Among the pleasant Villages and Farms' seems to support the Virgilian epigraph to the whole collection ('—*Libeat mihi sordida rura,/ Atque humiles habitare casas*—' (*Eclogue* 2, 28–9)),[17] and yet, in context, this forms part of the description of Satan viewing Eve and remaining for an instant, 'stupidly good' (465).[18] Satan, we must remember, lived as 'one who long in populous City pent,/ Where Houses thick and Sewers annoy the Aire. . .', a fact brought to our notice forcibly in Gay's own quotation in the 'Proeme'. Manna is about to be transubstantiated into gall.

Gay's 'Proeme' is as much amused at Spenserian Hobbinols as the patent absurdity as well as inutility of Arcadians:

Thou wilt not find my Shepherdesses idly piping on oaten Reeds, but milking the Kine, tying up the Sheaves, or if the Hogs are astray driving them to their Styes. My shepherd gathereth none other Nosegays but what are the growth of our own Fields, he sleepeth not under Myrtle Shades, but under a Hedge.

Pope envisaged, at the conclusion to *Guardian* 40, that one could describe '*something better*' than slumber under hedges,[19] where the comical bumpkin is barred from problematic depiction by stringent decorum. When confronted by the neo-classical pastoral it is tempting to rush for relief to a Stephen Duck or George Crabbe for a salutary grasp at mimetic truth. Gay's British rustic taps some of this energy—*not* just by acting contrary to some Virgilian norm, but also by being unliterary, and hence comic. Dryden had felt the same about the Doric pathos of the *Idylls*. In his 'Preface to *Sylvae*' (1685) the 'incomparable sweetness' of Theocritus's 'Clownishness' could be admired even if discounted as a model for his own translations. He also presumes that Virgil would have modelled his idiom on Theocritus's if the 'severity of the *Roman* Language' had not 'denied him that advantage'. The provincial and the dialectal were not only more accurate but also 'sweet'. He figures this marriage of melody and roughness in terms that are as geographically precise and particular as in Pope's abhorrence that a Spenserian Eclogue could have been set in Wales, the dialect resembling 'a fair Shepherdess in her Country Russet, talking in a *Yorkshire* Tone'.[20] Gay's Doric is not so much formal experimentation as the recovery of non-Virgilian style.

This revision of the pastoral canon is not just a matter of a few colloquialisms and native 'Nosegays'. For both René Rapin and Bernard le Bovier de Fontenelle, the pastoral theorists Pope cites as his main sources for the 'Discourse', a great distance from country people lent enchantment to the view. In Rapin's *Dissertatio de Carmine Pastorali* (1659), translated by Thomas Creech as 'A Treatise de Carmine Pastorali' (1684), shepherds became metaphors in 'a perfect image of the State of Innocence, of that golden Age, that blessed time, when Sincerity and Innocence, Peace, Ease, and Plenty inhabited the Plains'. One should not look through and beyond the image but find it, in itself, exemplary. The 'Shepherd' escapes the vices of the Court by being transplanted into country soil but, as his lineage is

noble, blood demands that he be free of his environment and
not do a hand's turn. Rapin cannot, however, be too confident
that literary 'Shepherds' are self-evidently distinct from real
ones, for although '*Nature* is chiefly to be lookt upon', it is also
not quite enough '(for nothing that is disagreeable to Nature
can please) yet that will hardly prevail naked, by it self, and
without the polishing of art'.[21] The qualifications are most
significant here. 'Nature' is only 'chiefly' the focus of attention
and the parenthesis claiming that pleasure derives only from
the portrayal of the 'naturally' agreeable or fitting marks a
thought that is indeed parenthetical to the main argument, but
also necessary in advancing the hypothesis that the 'nakedness'
of Nature as experienced is insufficient—not that it fails to
render a true image of life but that it is unpleasant and so will
not please. Fontenelle, although less inclined to Golden Age
abstraction, is similarly concerned that pastorals should please.
In the *Discours sur la Nature de l'Eglogue* (1688) he is most
concerned at the episodic structures in the *Idylls*, where the
country people are individualistic because not absorbed into the
landscape in some seamless emotive synthesis:

> But I don't know how *Theocritus* having sometimes rais'd his
> shepherds in so pleasing a manner above their native Genius,
> could let them so very often fall to it again: I wonder he did not
> perceive 'twas fit that a certain gross Clownishness, which is
> always very unbecoming, should be omitted.

Here, in William Motteux's translation (1695), this glaring
gaucherie of indecorous and uneven portrayal is censored because
it does not conform to a required level of abstraction. Theocritus
is the black sheep in the classical canon:

> If those who are resolved to find no faults in the Ancients, tell us
> that *Theocritus* had a mind to draw Nature just such as it is, I
> hope that, according to those principles, we shall have some
> *Idyllia* of Porters or Watermen discoursing together of their
> particular Concerns: Which will be every whit as good as some
> *Idyllia* of Shepherds speaking of nothing but their Goats or their
> Cows.[22]

Theocritus's rustics become as 'real' in the comparison, and
consequently as 'poetic' as London porters.

This distrust of realism might be neo-classical, but it is hardly true of earlier pastoral writing. In most pastorals the *topos* of leaving Arcadia is never far away. It is not only Death that surprises us, but the 'Real' too. Usually, this establishes Arcadia's fragility, as in Gallus's retreat there in Virgil's *Eclogue* 10 or its distinctive instances of pleasurable forgetfulness contained in the Harvest-Home at the conclusion to *Idyll* 7. This is, however, caught in time, a vale of retreat and solace. It cannot exist for long—hence the brevity of both Idyll and Eclogue. From Virgil's leave-taking in *Eclogue* 10 (70–2), to Spenser's weary Muse in 'December' (139–44) and Milton's striking out for 'fresh Woods, and Pastures new' (193) at the conclusion to *Lycidas*, there has always been a consciousness *within* the form that greater events beckon, and that sporting with Amaryllis in the shade provides no security. What is distinctive about pastoral references in Gay's work is how the outer world of courtly patronage and urban markets leads to purification of the dialect only. Rural Simplicity provides Gay with an opportunity for patronizing jests, an occasional complicity with the urbane and 'placed', at the same time as a sympathy with the unambitious license of a Bowzybeus. In exposing this dichotomy he casts a cold eye on the fictions of 'courtly Grace' and the 'courtly' Eclogues of both Philips *and* Pope.

3

Gay's pastoral 'simplicity' of *The Shepherd's Week* is most unlike that of any of his contemporaries, and its humour stems from his being Theocritean about the pastoral form. This is not to say that his eclogues are not allusive. 'Monday', the 'Squabble' between Lobbin Clout and Cuddy, is a burlesque of Virgil's *Eclogues* 3 and 7; 'Wednesday' is based on the first half of *Eclogue* 8 (with hints of 1 and 2), whilst 'Thursday' is based on the second half; 'Friday's' Bumkinet and Grubbinol are country cousins of Menalcas and Mopsus in *Eclogue* 5 and in 'Saturday' Gay registers the more epic pastoral voices of *Eclogues* 4 and 6. These Virgilian models are rendered in Doric abruptness with more than passing resemblances to several of Philips's *Pastorals*. The remaining eclogue, 'Tuesday', resembles the Modern 'Pastoral Ballad' described in Pope's *Guardian* 40. Each poem is accompanied by select annotation which supplies more comprehensible 'plain' translations of the 'Saxon' original interspersed with some parallel Virgilian details. On only three occasions are there references to Theocritean sources. Unlike Pope's extensive annotation to the 1736 edition of his *Pastorals*, this editorial commentary *denies* the poetry allusive range.

In 'Friday', the lament for Blouzelinda, Bumkinet and Grubbinol's naïve and plaintive anthems appear straitened and bathetic, given the more expansive gestures proffered in the annotation. At the climax to the amoebaean dialogue, the details are emphatically British:

> Lament, ye Fields, and rueful Symptoms show,
> Henceforth let not the smelling Primrose grow;
> Let Weeds instead of Butter-flow'rs appear,
> And Meads, instead of Daisies, Hemlock bear;
> For Cowslips sweet let Dandelions spread,
> For *Blouzelinda*, blithesome Maid, is dead!   (83–8)

Whilst the saxon nomenclature (and indeed the poem's conclusion) show obvious signs of burlesque, there are long periods when the Doric rejection of Virgilian euphony is unquestioned. The Virgilian parallel to the above is quoted as *Eclogue* 5, lines 38–9: '*pro molli viola, pro purpureo narcisso/ carduus et spinis surgit paliurus acutis*' ('In place of the soft violet, in place of the glistening narcissus, the thistle flourishes and the sharply-spiked thorn'). The violet, narcissus, thistle or thorn of the Latin are hardly more sounding than the English, which points to a deft imitation, not a burlesque.

Grubbinol's response attracts a longer quotation:

> Albeit thy Songs are sweeter to mine Ear,
> Than to the thirsty Cattle Rivers clear;
> Or Winter Porridge to the lab'ring Youth,
> Or Bunns and Sugar to the Damsel's Tooth;
> Yet *Blouzelinda*'s Name shall tune my Lay,
> Of her I'll sing for ever and for aye.   (93–8)

> *tale tuum carmen nobis, divine poeta,*
> *quale sopor fessis in gramine, quale per aestum*
> *dulcis aquae saliente sitim restinguere vivo . . .*
> *. . . nos tamen haec quocumque modo tibi nostra vicissim*
> *dicemus, Daphnimque tuum tollemus ad astra; . . .*
> (*Eclogue* 5, 45–7, 49–50)

Blouzelinda is a poor substitute for Daphnis, but then actuality, 'the Prospect of thine own Country', would be. The divinity of the poet in the Virgil that inspires a talent as soothing as sleep on grass to the weary or the assuaging of thirst in dancing water is rendered by similes of physical detail. Gay's rustics remain stubbornly British and untransportable by courtly manners or heroic diction. The 'editor' mentioned in the 'Proeme' who wishes to preserve the language of the poems and highlight some unimpeachable classical authorities is not to be confused with the 'Shepherd-Poet'. If the critical apparatus is overbearing and unjustified, that is to the detriment less of the naïve text than the editorial effort itself, the perhaps Ancient quoting of chapter and verse for every pastoral gesture. It is no accident that the potential bathos of 'failed' allusion fades after this point in the poem. There is no comment on the passage describing Blouzelinda's death, a passage where bumpkin simplicity is also held in abeyance:

> When *Blouzelind* expir'd, the Weather's Bell
> Before the drooping Flock toll'd forth her Knell;
> The solemn Death-watch click'd the Hour she dy'd,
> And shrilling Crickets in the Chimney cry'd; . . .
>
> (99–102)

Indeed, this is a prologue to the most unironic section of the poem: Blouzelinda's last words and distribution of possessions (113–38).

This alternation between bathos and sentiment contributes much to Gay's pose as a writer of bucolics. Philips had claimed that pastorals brought 'a sweet and gentle Composure to the Mind' by offering what the countryside effortlessly 'affords': 'the most entertaining Scenes and most delightful Prospects'.[23] The Scriblerian perspective on this 'simplicity' is best represented by the entry under 'The Infantine' in *Of the Art of Sinking in Poetry* (1727/28): 'This is when a Poet grows so very simple, as to think and talk like a Child.' The examples (all taken from Philips) do not just reflect the inanity to which such 'simplicity' directs us, as at least two examples tax Philips with not being rustic enough by granting courtly gestures to those whose behaviour in real life would give them the lie. When quoting

106

Hobbinol's 'Innocent' reasoning in love from Philips's *Pastoral* 6 (45–7) and Myco's plangent portrayal of Stella's wake (*Pastoral* 4, 63–6), the Scriblerians ridicule Philips's readiness to find lyricism and nobility everywhere:

> The Love of this Maiden to him appears by her allowing him the Reserve of one Night from her other Lovers; which you see he takes extreamly kindly.
> With no less Simplicity does he suppose that Shepherdesses tear their Hair and beat their Breasts, at their own Deaths: . . .[24]

Gay's pastorals are reminders that 'realism' emerges as much by subverting vulnerable literary conventions as by recording details with graphic faithfulness. In literature, the *literal* is always contained within agreed generic paradigms.

Gay's eclogues are quite distinct from those of both Pope and Philips in this. The neo-classical consensus that swains were simultaneously shepherds and noblemen relies on a lyric unity of melody. For Pope this meant elegies for lost innocence or the recognition that Time can even conquer Love. For Philips rusticity merely signals the prolongation of the nursery's cosy warmth. Both allude to the pastoral canon—but very selectively. As 'Friday' testifies, Gay's rusticity has more initial edge and bite, *and* can also deliver a cocksnooking pathos despite this. Lobbin Clout and Cuddy's 'Squabble' in 'Monday' seems to allude to similar dialogues in Pope's 'Spring' and Philips's *Pastoral* 6. Both of the latter conclude (in Philips's case, the conclusion of the whole collection) with both singers rewarded. Pope's Damon bids Strephon and Daphnis:

> Cease to contend, for (*Daphnis*) I decree
> The Bowl to *Strephon*, and the Lamb to thee:
> Blest Swains, whose Nymphs in ev'ry Grace excell;
> Blest Nymphs, whose Swains those Graces sing so well!
> (93–6)[25]

The 'contention' in *Pastoral* 6 is similarly quieted, not through reciprocity but through flaccid anti-climax. All is secure in Hobbinol and Lanquet's world. Even the judge of their efforts, Geron ('to both [an] equal friend' (14)), can take time off from work as his goats 'secure from Harm, no Tendance need' (3). The 'pleasing Strife' (109) is brought to an end with both singers as victors. As with 'Spring' the proceedings are less *interrupted* by a 'mizling Mist' (113) (in Pope it is 'fruitful Show'rs' (102)) than given a 'natural' full stop.[26] Flocks are driven to shelter and consequently work must cease. Cloddipole terminates 'Monday' thus:

> Forbear, contending Louts, give o'er your Strains,
> An *Oaken Staff* each merits for his Pains.
> But see the Sun-Beams bright to Labour warn,
> And gild the Thatch of Goodman *Hodges'* Barn.
> Your Herds for want of Water stand adry,
> They're weary of your Songs—and so am I.
>
> (119–24)

Work calls the singers away from songs as the world of the *Georgics* invades the pastoral idyll. Cloddipole's contempt is a new ingredient, but not an unclassical one. The Goatherd applauds Thysis's lament for Daphnis at the conclusion to *Idyll* 1, but the prize-giving is brief indeed. The last detail of the poem is the Goatherd's order to his flock to keep calm lest the ram get frisky. Palaemon declares the Damoetas/Menalcas contest of *Eclogue* 3 a draw and then refers the reader to matters that are more pressing: 'claudite iam rivos, pueri: sat prata biberunt' (111, 'shut off the irrigation now, lads; the meadows have had enough'). Even allowing for the possibility of allegory here (Servius agrees that there is, but then he sees it everywhere in Virgil), these discords are sufficient to limit lyricism and place it within a world where such preoccupations are not vital or even especially virtuous—the perfect antidote to the pathetic fallacy.

Gay is fascinated by such deconstruction. As John Irwin Fischer terms it, the effect is absurd[27]—from the assumption that Doric is really rural to the occasional overturning of alphabetical order in the 'Alphabetical Catalogue' to the omission of a Sunday in the collection. Marian's wailing, Sparabella's toying with suicide or Hobnelia's exotic spells each promise a lyrical climax, the tragic insights of artistic despair, but do not surface because material or everyday concerns intervene and pose their alternatives—much like the press of would-be courtiers greeting Princess Caroline and Gay's writer's block when writing to order. In *The Shepherd's Week* individual local effects resist an assimilation into some grand scheme. There is no figure in the carpet, pore over it how we will. This is not to say that there is no ideology at work in Gay's pastorals. If he finds both the allegorical and the lyrical transformation of rural life absurd, this could be because there are charms and lessons for the urbanite that elude such *artistic* methods of appropriation (and blindness), even if they render Londoners 'stupidly good'.

4

Swift, writing to Gay on 8 January 1722–23, looked back to the dedication of *The Shepherd's Week* and pointed out that such a move had placed him 'under originall Sin'.[28] The dedicatee, Henry St. John, Viscount Bolingbroke, was attainted of treason by the Whigs in 1715, and although pardoned in 1723, remained a rather maverick presence in the Tory opposition, often associated with Jacobitism.[29] Gay, in 1713–14, was no clairvoyant. The Bolingbroke of the 'Prologue' is the peacemaker of the Treaty of Utrecht and 'Full stedfast both to Church and Queen' (76), not the Deist of sensation and rumour. Indeed, Gay appears ready to present the Oxford ministry as one which had trading interests as a high priority, securing a freedom of trade for 'Shepherds' ('clip your fleecy Care' (69)), 'Maids' ('your Spinning-Wheels prepare' (70)), and, in far less conventional mode, 'Weavers' ('all your Shuttles throw,/ And bid broad Cloths and Serges grow' (71–2)). The Swain had been enfranchized by Bolingbroke's diplomacy, so that no longer need he be cowed by 'Leasings leud' (74, 'ignorant lies' in Dearing and Beckwith's explanation)[30] or the threat of War's anarchy. Gay, in his distinctive rôle as an uninitiated countryman, counts himself as one of their number, able to speed to court

> Of Soldier's Drum withouten Dreed;
> For Peace allays the Shepherd's Fear
> Of wearing Cap of Granadier.

> (45–7)

This direct conflict between Shepherd and Grenadier emerges a year later in *The What D'Ye Call It*, where the depiction of rural life is darker and correspondingly more didactic. Pastoral serenity

109

is rudely disrupted by the press-gang. Dorcas's speech on Thomas Filbert's enlistment illustrates its affective potential:

> Ah! why does Nature give us so much Cause
> To make kind-hearted Lasses break the Laws?
> Why should hard Laws kind-hearted Lasses bind,
> When too soft Nature draws us after Kind?
>
> (I, i, 94–7)[31]

Peascod's threatened execution provokes a distribution of possessions reminiscent of Blouzelinda's in 'Friday'. Her meagre legacy is a sentimental parody of Daphnis's leave-taking in *Idyll* 1. Peascod's confrontation is with a firing-squad:

> Say, is it fitting in this very Field,
> Where I so oft have reap'd, so oft have till'd;
> This Field, where from my Youth I've been a Carter,
> I, in this Field, should die for a Deserter?
>
> (II, v, 7–10)

The ritual leave-taking is in full view of Corporal and soldiers. In his 'Preface', the Soldier and the Swain form synecdoches for wider ideological exposition. In travestying Aristotelian purity of 'action', Gay finds he can deconstruct the social hierarchies as well. In replying to those who 'say the Sentiments are not Tragical, because they are those of the lowest Country People', he challenges normal aesthetic categories much in the same way that the Hero can be a Great Man and even a Thief in *The Beggar's Opera*. Although Justices of the Peace, Parish Clerks or Embryo Ghosts do not appear in any of the Ancients' plays as they do in this one, this is a mere nicety as Nurses often make their entrance. Besides,

> the Sentiments of Princes and Clowns have not in reality that difference which they seem to have: their Thoughts are almost the same, and they only differ as the same Thought is attended with a Meanness or Pomp of Diction.

Tragic grief, in the Horace quotation, can often be uttered in prose. The Shepherd garb that so seems to suit Gay, part Clown, part innocent outsider, has the power to incorporate the unofficial with the canonical, the mirthful bawdy of a D'Urfey with the melancholic insight of Virgil in Pastoral vein, and a sanguine expectation of the Tory peace with an anxious uncertainty about the hopes for any Swain under any government. Just as war's rapine accentuates the fragile well-being of peace in *Eclogues* 9 and 10, in 1715, Gay has it assume just as specific a political shape. The dating at the end of the 'Prologue' (April 1714), and the local historical issues it mentions imply not just simply a perennial pacifism on Gay's behalf, but a clear support for this particular Peace and a secure grasp of its implications for him. This is announced both by what it does mention as by what it does not.

We get no indication, for example, that the Commons had failed to ratify the eighth, ninth and tenth articles of the treaty the previous June, exactly those areas that dealt in detail with trade with France. Article nine proposed a reduction of the general tariff between the two countries to its 1664 level with several lucrative exceptions allowed the French. Bolingbroke envisaged little opposition to these concessions as the treaty as a whole promised far greater French trading opportunities. Its defeat only served to highlight the fragility of Tory support in what, on the face of it, seemed a safe majority in the Commons. Bolingbroke believed that countries which traded together did not fight together; freer trade meant a safer continent—exactly the sentiments of the 'Prologue'. The Peace also involved a reduction in the armed forces and the onerous Land Tax, again to the applause of the 'Prologue'. By April, however, the Peace was not a raging issue, and it is more likely that the 'Prologue', in context, looks fearfully forward much more than it looks back: to the fate of the Protestant Succession on the Queen's death (hence the opening solicitude at her illness the previous Christmas) and to the fractured Tories (Oxford versus Bolingbroke) who seemed unable to meet the situation with any consolidated policies free of political in-fighting (hence the rather inaccurate portrayal of *Oxford* as a prime mover in free trade and not, as Bolingbroke believed, the instigator of Tory revolt against the treaty). The 'Leasings leud' which 'affright the Swain' were as much *de haut en bas* satires of honest yeomen as the rumoured distrust between the two Tory leaders—worrying to simple 'Swains' like Gay who hoped to find their patrons in place after the Queen's death. Gay is in the process of forging an idiom for this anxiety and also a rhetorical means to overcome it. His letters exhibit a close acquaintance with Virgil's

Eclogue 1. Writing to Charles Ford from The Hague (6 July 1714) on the diplomatic mission to Hanover, he quotes two lines of Meliboeus's opening lament: '*nos patriae fines et dulcia linquimus arva/ nos patriam fugimus, tu Tityre lentus in umbra*'[32] ('We are leaving our country's frontiers and sweet fields. We are outcasts from our country; you, Tityrus, at your ease in the shade (teach the woods to re-echo "the fair Amaryllis")'). The context is not a melancholy one, as Gay is bemoaning the lack of Kensington *belles* in Holland and turning his hand to worldly wit. Once again, however, the grass seems always greener in Kensington Gardens or with Pope and Parnell at Binfield. When Gay returns to such sentiments in a letter to Parnell (26 March 1716), he is lamenting the sale of Binfield: '. . . the Trees of Windsor Forest shall no more listen to the tunefull reed of the [Popeian?] swain & no more Beeches shall be wounded with the names of Teresa & Patty'.[33] The choice of eclogue is telling. Meliboeus encounters Tityrus who is piping contentedly by the roadside. The two men's fortunes are dramatically opposed. Meliboeus has had his land confiscated as the result of political manoeuvring in far-off Rome, but Tityrus, by taking the bold initiative of accosting and winning the favour of an influential patron there, has saved his patrimony. Tityrus has cause for thankful celebration and indulges in a humble panegyric on the *iuvenis* (often identified as Octavian) whose chance intercession has prolonged his stay in Arcadia. Meliboeus, on the other hand, is a victim of the impersonal forces of politics and circumstance, and expresses this in a melancholic, even elegiac, voice which stands in bold contrast to Tityrus's complaisance. Ultimately, in a quieter *coda* to the piece, Tityrus offers Meliboeus food and shelter—for just one night, and directs his guest to the idyllic peace of their (Tityrus's?) immediate surroundings of which both singers have been unaware up until then. In short, the poem is about the vagaries and necessity of patronage.

It is not entirely fortuitous that the opening lines of the 'Prologue' bring Tityrus (and his good fortune) to mind—'Lo, I who erst beneath a Tree/ Sung *Bumkinet* and *Bowzybee*'—and just as swiftly locates the likeness in the past. Will Bolingbroke be Gay's *iuvenis*? The prognosis of *The Shepherd's Week* is finely balanced. Tityrus's optimism is hardly characteristic of either

Classical pastoral or Gay's reading of the form. The epigraph to the 1713 version of *Rural Sports* also alludes to *Eclogue* 1: 'agrestem tenui Musam meditabor Avena', a conflation of line 2 ('you woo the woodland muse on a slender reed') and line 8 of *Eclogue* 6 ('I will woo the rustic Muse on a slender reed'). The *tenui Avena*, the 'Verse of simple Swain' in the 'Prologue' (91), resists Art and also Bolingbroke's larger world of political and commercial negotiation. By 1716 and Gay's epigraph to *Trivia* from the first line of *Eclogue* 9 the voice resembles that of Meliboeus: 'quo te Moeri pedes? an, quo via ducit, in Urbem?' ('Where are you off to, Moeris? Following the path, to the city?'). Both Lycidas, the speaker here, and Moeris are dispossessed. Moeris's journey is in order to pay a rent of a flock of kids to its new possessor. Contrary to common belief, the songs of Menalcas had not prevented such confiscation. Indeed, Moeris is doubtful about the potential of Art to affect society at all:

> . . . *sed carmina tantum*
> *nostra valent, Lycida, tela inter Martia, quantum*
> *Chaonias dicunt aquila veniente columbas.*

(11–13)

(But amidst the weapons of war, Lycidas, our songs are as much help as, they say, the doves of Chaonia when the eagle comes)

Both travellers try to remember Menalcas's songs, but they can recall only snippets. The meeting subsides into the exchange of sad news and wistful memories celebrated unsuccessfully by fragments from the past.[34]

There is much of the eagle's flight about *Trivia*, from those who travel easily in 'gilded Chariots' and 'lazily insure a Life's Disease' (I, 69–70) to the 'griping Broker' who can laugh at 'Honesty, and trudging Wits' (I, 117–18) right through to the depredations of the Mob, pickpockets and apocalyptic inferno of Book III. The pun of the poem's title leads to the constant association of the apparently unremarkable and contemporary with the timeless classicism of a goddess of streets and highways.[35] Gay does not mention the darker possibilities of the title directly: references both to Hecate, the nightly haunter of cross-roads, attended by demons, or the junction where Oedipus killed his own father, but rather leads the reader to appreciate the press of devils and death in the London of the present. Neither Meliboeus and Tityrus from *Eclogue* 1 nor Lycidas and Moeris from *Eclogue* 9 imagine an Arcadia that can any longer be enjoyed in security. Even Tityrus's escape from *servitium* involves excursions to the city and the dissolution of his own community.

In the light of this range of allusions it is perhaps necessary to stress that *The Shepherd's Week* is a comic poem. This is after all what strikes us most forcibly about its bucolic figures: their refusal to be objects of urban sentiment. Sparabella proves herself a 'prudent Maiden' (119) in 'Wednesday' and Lubberkin *does* return to Hobnelia in 'Thursday'. We leave the poem whilst he is in the process of giving her a 'green Gown' (135). Marian has to dry her eyes in 'Tuesday' because her bull is required to cover Goody Dobbins's cow. This is not foreign to the pastoral. For example, Theocritus can mention frisky rams and even include Priapus's suggestion in *Idyll* 1 that the semi-divine Daphnis is declining because he is impotent (82–91). Indeed, we are only able to find the poems amusing because they transgress the selective *decora* of Rapin or Fontenelle. If they were just bucolic *bricolage*, however, Gay would not have needed the 'Proeme' or 'Prologue' and its public declarations of alignment. Besides, it would hardly do justice to Gay's Bowzybeus, the 'simple Swain' of his 'Prologue' (90–1).

5

Gay's self-portrayal as Bowzybeus in 'Saturday' is itself an allusion to *Eclogue* 6's Silenus, its drunken, yet possibly inspired, carouser. Criticism of the poem has been more taken up with its satirical targets than with the root cause for the attack. Adina Forsgren has demonstrated Gay's amusement at recent experimental philosophy, and John Robert Moore, back in 1951, noted both the burlesque of Mopas's song of creation in Sir Richard Blackmore's *Prince Arthur* (1695) and also the complacent Christian appropriation of Lucretius in his *Creation* (1712).[36] The result of such satire is not without political edge. Moore is surely correct in reading 'Saturday' as

> diametrically opposed to all that Blackmore stood for—zeal for
> the Hanoverian Succession . . . for the Whigs, for the reformation

of manners and morals, for poetry free from indecent innuendo and devoted to the sublime causes of patriotism and religion.[37]

Is the poem therefore irreligious? As Alan Downie points out,[38] Gay is rarely a true-blue Tory so much as an independent sympathizer. In placing Virgil's sublimer pastoral voice as the climax to his own 'simple' eclogues, however, he is giving particular form to such independence. Silenus's catalogue of Ovidian metamorphoses and Epicurean accounts of creation forms a variegated jumble of episodes. Robert Coleman, in his recent edition of the *Eclogues*, has noted the prevalent rustic imagery in these renditions, whilst also recognizing that 'it all has a localized significance within the tales where it occurs. It does not, as in the other Eclogues, cohere to form a single evocative landscape.'[39] Silenus is a visitor to Arcady, a bringer of sublimer conceptual knowledge than can be contained in the artlessness of swains or nymphs. Its lack of concerted attention to a coherent philosophy is, on the other hand, hardly an accident. Silenus is, after all, a drunk. The conclusion to the poem may end in the stars but it has never departed from the bucolic. Gay's restitution of this mode of pastoral ignores Dryden's more consistently honorific treatment in his Virgil translation (1697)[40] and has Bowzybeus indulge himself in specifically folkloric narratives of rural culture—a 'grounding' of the 'Flights' or 'Sublimer Strains' (1) in effect. He also weaves several hints in the opening of the Messianic *Eclogue* 4: the account of Astraea's disappearance—but without any consoling hope that Justice might return.

Eclogue 6 had long been a battleground for those critics for or against its non-pastoral sublimity. Fontenelle was amused at 'honest Silenus' and his 'hearty Carouse', but disturbed at the same time at the invasion of 'philosophical Notions', especially those of 'Epicurus's System'.[41] Gay's irony proceeds to recapture some of the binary attraction found in the original and which had been denied by neo-classic commentary. Indeed, Rapin's Arcadia excluded physical love altogether, 'for all sort of lewdness or debauchery are directly contrary to the Innocence of the *Golden* Age'.[42] Gay's poem is much too much given over to unironic rural descriptions and its alternative culture to stand Rapin's test. This is certainly true of 'Nature's Laws' (51), a conglomeration of the superstitious and proverbial 'knowledge' that provides an alternative to intellectual and accepted laws. Granted that the mode is comic, the sonority of the form rescues it. Bowzybeus sings of:

> How *Will-a-Wisp* mis-leads Night-faring Clowns,
> O'er Hills, and sinking Bogs, and pathless Downs.
> Of Stars he told that shoot with shining Trail,
> And of the Glow-worms Light that gilds his Tail.
>
> (57–60)

Gay obviously used to notice such things. This panorama of instinctive 'Laws' modulates into an account of the immense variety and particularity of 'Fairs and Shows' (71), an account of:

> How the tight Lass, Knives, Combs and Scissors spys,
> And looks on Thimbles with desiring Eyes.
> Of Lott'ries next with tuneful Note he told,
> Where silver Spoons are won and Rings of Gold.
> The Lads and Lasses trudge the Street along,
> And all the Fair is crowded in his Song.
>
> (77–82)

Virgil's 'Flights' had included the Epicurean explanation of Creation whereby the forms of things were a chance amalgam of disparate elements in the *inane coacta* (31).[42] The eclogue similarly includes most unRapinian bawdy when Silenus first sights Aegle (20–6). Both of these freedoms are included and indeed go unchallenged in 'Saturday'.

It is also of note that Virgil's drunken god becomes in Gay's version, a ballad-singer. Chromis and Mnasyllos of *Eclogue* 6 had demanded songs. Silenus had responded with all the songs of old Phoebus (82). Bowzybeus supplies songs comprehensible to shepherds, and for his necessary heightening of tone towards the end quotes both 'The Children in the Wood' (91) and 'Chevy-Chase' (102), the ballads recently lionized by Addison.[43] As the poem draws to a close, there is scanty annotation and few reminders of Virgilian precedent. This coincides with an attenuated mock-pastoral framework and more of the guarded delight at 'lower' details to be found in Book I of *Trivia*.

Gay throughout the main body of 'Saturday' sports with a ballad's freedom from Aristotelian high seriousness. Pedlars provide 'glitt'ring Toys' (73); mountebanks and pickpockets jostle '*Raree-Shows*' (89) and swallows, bats and dormice demonstrate Nature's mysteries (65–6) without thereby complimenting the citizen-reader's greater perspicacity at all. What is more, all of this contemporaneity is truer to Silenus's proverbial recounting of well-known myths than Dryden's more portentous version. By remaining exactly true to *Eclogue* 6's loose form and occasional bawdiness, Gay is demonstrating a point about urban presumption, and incidentally replacing the 'Clowns' of the mock-pastoral with the 'Lads and Lasses' of a pastoral ballad without any of the rough dialectal forms of Pope's Somersetshire doggerel from *Guardian* 40.

6

Bowzybeus's voice is an optimistic one. Virgil's inclusion of Epicurean material was itself a holiday from more mundane eulogies of Varus, enough to distinguish the poem's rustic simplicity from the formulaic tales of grim war (6–7). *De Rerum Natura* was after all a poem to dispel fear of the gods. By 1720 and Gay's *Poems on Several Occasions* the pastoral allusions have become more sharply satiric and, accompanying this change, festivity gives place to polemical distaste. At the head of the collection 'The *Birth* of the *Squire*. An *Eclogue*. In Imitation of the *Pollio* of *Virgil*'. returns to 'Saturday' but substitutes a genial, if loutish, Bowzybeus with a degenerate and altogether rebarbative Tunbelly Clumsy. John Sutherland is not alone in being shocked by such uncustomary distaste: 'Gay's tone is, for him, oddly uncompromising; it comes near to disgust.'[44] Virgil's august homage to Pollio, instigator of continuity and peace, confronts a most unworthy successor, war-like in his tastes (61–76) and equally disruptive in his affections (49–60). Whilst snoring away 'Debates in *Parliament*' (76), a diurnal rural round exists, unchecked and still abundant. The Squire is undone by strong ale 'Brew'd or when *Phoebus* warms the fleecy sign,/ Or when his languid rays in *Scorpio* shine' (91–2). This same liquid, 'Old *October*', has the power to redden 'ev'ry nose' (14) and provide cheer and comfort:

> With frothy ale to make his cup o'er-flow,
> Barley shall in paternal acres grow;

117

The bee shall sip the fragrant dew from flow'rs,
To give metheglin for his morning hours;
For him the clust'ring hop shall climb the poles,
And his own orchard sparkle in his bowles.

(19–24)

This natural pattern alludes to the mythical abundance of Pollio's new order. Characteristically, Gay here forsakes myth for less 'poetic' details, for his Squire is more manifest and disturbing: 'O where is wisdom, when by this o'erpower'd?/ the State is censur'd, and the maid deflower'd!' (97–8). Natural abundance still exists but is abused by those fittest to dispense it. The climax is the insidiously heroic timbre of the closing lines, a re-casting of Bowzybeus's drunkenness but in much darker colours reminiscent of Satan in Pandemonium:

Triumphant, o'er the prostrate brutes he stands,
The mighty bumper trembles in his hands;
Boldly he drinks, and like his glorious Sires,
In copious gulps of potent ale expires.

(105–8)

Tamburlaine-like, his triumph is a prelude to his extinction. This is Gay's glimpse into the future; there are no blithesome spirits now, just a mute 'attentive Swain' (5) or dutifully hopeful tenants (11–12), who appear disenfranchized and helpless. This is no isolated *topos*, for in his Town Eclogues there is not the sturdy poise of *The Shepherd's Week*, but rather a desperate pessimism at what urban opportunity entails. The pastoral accents of his rural simplicity in *Acis and Galatea* (1718) and *Dione* (1720) are laundered and effortlessly courtly. Melody and negligent ease are summoned for their lyrical patina.

Gay's distrust of the pastoral tradition is in part a comment on politeness and its fictions. In his epistle 'To the Right Honourable *WILLIAM PULTENEY* Esq.', the journey Gay took with the dedicatee in July 1717 provides plenty of vulnerable Fontenellian artifice to undermine. Pulteney had been Secretary of War, but had resigned with Walpole in April 1717. Although his years as founder-leader of the Whig opposition to Walpole, the 'Patriots', lay in the future, his 'retired' status associates him with such figures as Burlington and Bathurst. Gay's return to French haunts in 1719 reminds him of the pretences of 'polite' society. When 'sweet-breathing Spring unfolds the buds' (101), the 'natural' consequence is Chelsea meadows overhearing 'perfidious vows,/ And the prest grass defrauds the grazing cows' (105–6). 'Court ladies' thus can also sin 'in open air' (108): 'What Cit with a gallant would trust his spouse/ Beneath the tempting shade of *Greenwich* boughs?' (109–10). Damons and Chloes are Virgilian in origin, but crucially bear no relation to the present, save as faint reminders of an alternative: 'But since at Court the rural taste is lost,/ What mighty summs have velvet couches cost!' (131–32). Pope was confident that Virgil might live again on Windsor's plains. Gay demonstrates that by 1720 the only assertion possible was that this hope was futile.

NOTES

1. Line references are to the texts of Gay's poems in *PP*, from which all quotations are taken.
2. *Letters*, p. 7.
3. Harold Williams (ed.), *The Correspondence of Jonathan Swift*, 5 vols. (Oxford, 1963–65), II, 137.
4. *John Gay: Favorite of the Wits* (Durham, N.C., 1940), p. 107.
5. George Sherburn (ed.), *The Correspondence of Alexander Pope*, 5 vols. (Oxford, 1956), I, 229; 'Pope, Gay, and *The Shepherd's Week*', *Modern Language Quarterly*, 5 (1944), 79–88; 'Thomas D'Urfey, the Pope-Philips Quarrel, and *The Shepherd's Week*', *PMLA*, 74 (1959), 203–12; Irving, pp. 82–3.
6. The reference here is ascribed incorrectly by Gay's 'Editor'. The 'Proeme' identifies this 'low' rusticity as coming from *Idyll* V, which would have been unsurprising as Comatas and Lacon provide there several instances of coarse jests. Gay chooses instead to commit a profound mistake by including Priapus's taunt to the semi-divine Daphnis from *Idyll* I (87–8), thus highlighting how mixed the Classical bucolic mode could be. David M. Halperin has recently argued that Theocritus's 'Pastorals' are no such thing in *Before Pastoral: Theocritus and the Ancient Tradition of Bucolic Poetry* (New Haven, 1983), pp. 1–23.
7. *Some Versions of Pastoral* (London, 1950), p. 17.
8. J. C. Smith and E. de Selincourt (ed.), *Spenser: Poetical Works* (Oxford, 1970), p. 418.
9. James Kinsley (ed.), *The Poems of John Dryden*, 4 vols. (Oxford, 1958), II, 871–72.
10. Kinsley, IV, 1445.
11. E. Audra and Aubrey Williams (eds.), *Pastoral Poetry and An Essay on Criticism* (London and New Haven, 1961), pp. 31–2. Vol. I of the Twickenham Edition of *The Poems of Alexander Pope*.

12. Paul Hammond (ed.), *Selected Prose of Alexander Pope* (Cambridge, 1987), p. 44.
13. Smith and de Selincourt, p. 455.
14. Audra and Williams, p. 75.
15. M. G. Segar (ed.), *The Poems of Ambrose Philips* (Oxford, 1937), p. 3.
16. *A Dissertation on Reading the Classics* (London, 1713), p. 223.
17. 'Live with me in our rough fields and lowly dwellings.'
18. Alastair Fowler (ed.), *Milton: Paradise Lost* (London, 1971), p. 466.
19. Hammond, p. 45.
20. Kinsley, I, p. 399. Dryden considers Theocritus famous for the 'inimitable tenderness of his passions; and the natural expression of them. . .'. This constitutes a 'simplicity [which] shines through all he writes: he shows his Art and Learning by disguising both'. The biggest sin is indecorous rustic behaviour, that is, too gracious a demeanour. Virgil is guilty of providing his shepherds with too much knowledge of Epicurus and Plato (a reference to *Eclogue* 6), whereas Theocritus's 'Shepherds never rise above their Country Education' (Kinsley, I, 398).
21. René Rapin, 'A Treatise de Carmine Pastorali', in *Idylliums of Theocritus*, trans. Thomas Creech (Oxford, 1684), pp. 5, 44. Those topics 'disagreeable' to 'Nature' include the strife between Comatas and Lacon in *Idyll* 5, which appears as 'bitter as *Billingsgate*' and not suitable to those 'sedate times of the Happy Age' (p. 67).
22. Bernard le Bovier de Fontenelle, 'Of Pastorals', 'Englished by Mr. Motteux', published with René le Bossu's *Treatise of the Epick Poem* (London, 1695), pp. 278, 284–85.
23. Segar, p. 3.
24. Edna Leake Steeves (ed.), *The Art of Sinking in Poetry: Martinus Scriblerus's 'Peri Bathous'* (New York, 1952), pp. 55, 57. This quality was noted by Pope in *Guardian* 40: 'Mr. *Pope* hath fallen into the same Error with *Virgil*. His Clowns do not converse in all the Simplicity proper to the Country: His Names are borrow'd from *Theocritus* and *Virgil*, which are improper to the Scene of his Pastorals' (Hammond, p. 41).
25. Audra and Williams, p. 70.
26. Segar, pp. 32, 36.
27. 'Never on Sunday: John Gay's *The Shepherd's Week*', *Studies in Eighteenth-Century Culture*, 10 (1981), 191–203. 'Gay's poem is an unusually disordering performance; consequently, one result of most modern efforts to read the poem is that those efforts illustrate sharply the poem's radical alinearity' (p. 192). In this connection David Nokes has recently stressed the hybridity of Gay's pastoral writing. See his *Raillery and Rage: A Study of Eighteenth Century Satire* (Brighton, 1987), pp. 122–35.
28. Williams, II, 443.
29. The best account of Bolingbroke's break with Oxford and his Utrecht negotiations is H. T. Dickinson's *Bolingbroke* (London, 1970), pp. 93–133. For his early career and 'Country' Toryism, see Isaac Kramnick, *Bolingbroke and his Circle: The Politics of Nostalgia in the Age of Walpole* (Cambridge, Mass., 1968), pp. 56–65.
30. *PP*, II, 521.

31. Act, scene and line references are to the texts of Gay's plays in *DW*, from which all quotations are taken.
32. *Letters*, p. 11.
33. *Letters*, p. 29.
34. It is clear that Gay realizes this, for in the 'Advertisement' to *Trivia* a Menalcan 'fragment' is included: '-Non tu, in *Triviis*, Indocte, solebas/ Stridenti, miserum, stipula, disperdere Carmen?' (*Eclogue* 3, 26–7), his riposte to Damoetas's boasting: 'Wasn't it you, thickie, who used to murder a poor tune on a screeching reed at the cross-roads [*Triviis*]?' The whole point about positioning oneself at a cross-roads was to busk more successfully.
35. Dearing is premature in discounting Gay's meaning of *Trivia* as approximate to ours, i.e. matters of little consequence. Sense *Trivial*, II, 5 in the *O.E.D.*, 'Such as may be met with anywhere; common, commonplace, ordinary, everyday, familiar, trite' is illustrated by quotations from 1589, 1620, 1665 and 1704. II, 6 ('Of small account, little esteemed, paltry, poor . . .') is represented by quotations from as far back as 1593 and 1655. It certainly cannot be held that 'The use of trivia to mean "things of little consequence", is too modern' and that the *primary* sense is 'streets' (*PP*, II, 549). Johnson includes *Trivial* in the 4th edn. of the *Dictionary* (1773) and sense 2, 'Light; trifling; unimportant. . .', attracts quotations from Shakespeare (*Richard III*), Dryden and Pope.
36. Adina Forsgren, *John Gay: Poet 'Of a Lower Order'*, 2 vols. (Stockholm, 1964), I, 135–40; John Robert Moore, 'Gay's Burlesque of Sir Richard Blackmore's Poetry', *JEGP*, 50 (1951), 83–9.
37. Moore, p. 85.
38. This volume, pp. 44–61.
39. *Virgil: Eclogues* (Cambridge, 1977), p. 203.
40. Kinsley, II, 894–97, e.g. see 'My Past'ral Muse her humble Tribute brings;/ And yet not wholly uninspir'd she sings' (9–10) cf. *Eclogue* 6, 9–11.
41. 'Of Pastorals', pp. 286–87.
42. *Treatise*, p. 67.
43. The particular passage Virgil appropriates can be found at Book V. 449–85 of *De Rerum Natura*. For its doubtful reception from the Restoration onwards, see T. J. B. Spencer, 'Lucretius and the Scientific Poem in English', in D. R. Dudley (ed.), *Lucretius* (London, 1965), pp. 131–64.
44. *Spectators* 70, 74 and 85 (21 May, 25 May and 7 June 1711). Addison appreciates these ballads as a challenge to received ideas of 'high' art. In the place of skill, he promotes a taste for the 'simple': 'The Song [*Two Children in the Wood*] is a plain Simple Copy of Nature, destitute of all the Helps and Ornaments of Art . . . There is even a despicable Simplicity in the Verse; and yet, because the Sentiments appear genuine and unaffected, they are able to move the Mind of the most polite Reader' (Donald Bond (ed.), *The Spectator*, 5 vols. (Oxford, 1965), I, 362).
45. 'John Gay', in *Pope and his Contemporaries: Essays Presented To George Sherburn* (London, 1949), p. 211.

6

The Beggar's Rags to Rich's and Other Dramatic Transformations

by PETER LEWIS

The chiastic quip, so well-expressed and so oft-repeated, about *The Beggar's Opera* making Gay rich and Rich gay suggests that, in a show-biz sense, these two Johns were made for each other: perfect complements. However, the mutual satisfaction they achieved from the play's unprecedented success during its first season in 1728 was more a case of the conjunction of the stars and the opposition of the mind than the Marvellian reverse. Rich was a darling of the town but hardly a favourite of the Scriblerian wits, and his theatre in Lincoln's Inn Fields was not Gay's first choice for the première of what proved to be his masterpiece. Even so, there was a certain appropriateness in their collaborative venture. The most intricate and original experiment in dramatic transformation by a writer who specialized in deliberate generic confusion, sporting with conventions and turning one form into another, was staged by the actor-manager whose expertise in theatrical transformation was second to none.

In 1728 the linking of 'opera' with 'beggar's' was so paradoxical as virtually to amount to an oxymoron. Opera was synonymous with Italian opera and was the preserve of the Opera House, which paid imported Italian singers superstarmegasalaries, provided lavish spectacle with no expense spared, and focused on the lives and loves of great figures from classical antiquity, mythology and romance literature. The last thing opera attempted to do was to reflect the realities of London life in the streets outside the Opera House itself, including prostitutes, thieves and ballad singers. An opera associated with beggars and highwaymen, holding a mirror up to the world of Jonathan Wild, was almost unthinkable, as indeed was an opera at Lincoln's Inn Fields. Yet presenting the unthinkable on stage was all in an evening's work for Rich, whose *commedia*-based pantomimic afterpieces known as 'entertainments', in which as a master of mime he usually played Harlequin using his stage name of Lun, were renowned for their startling transformation scenes—a bed-chamber into a garden, a tavern into a church, a tree into a house, a temple into a cottage, and a man into a wheelbarrow at a wave of Harlequin's wand-like bat. Harlequin even changed himself into various animals.

Although Gay's transformation of high Italian opera into low English ballad opera is analogous to Rich's spectacular visual 'magic' only in a very loose way, the artistically snobbish disapproval meted out to Rich by self-professed Augustan intellectuals, including the Scriblerians, does seem excessive. In no other period of English literary history were writers so self-consciously preoccupied with literary and dramatic transformation. Postmodernists today, who often sound as though they invented parody, pastiche and self-reflexivity, pale in comparison. As an antidote to the burlesque debasement of Greek and Latin texts in the manner of Scarron, popular in England after the Restoration, came the alternative mode of classical transformation advocated by Boileau, the mock heroic, which avoided doing dirt on the ancients. Epic could be reconstituted as mock epic, tragedy as mock tragedy: the two highest forms in Aristotle's classification of genres resurfaced much lower down the scale as satire and burlesque. Pope, whose genius is at full stretch in his mock epics, also mastered another type of Augustan literary transformation, the imitation—of a modern (Donne) as well as an ancient (Horace). Fielding excelled at mock tragedy (*Tom Thumb* (1730), *The Covent-Garden Tragedy* (1732)) and presented his first novel, *Joseph Andrews* (1742), as a species of literary transformation, 'a comic Epic-Poem in Prose'.[1] In *The Shepherd's Week* Gay himself deconstructed classical pastoral, simultaneously burlesquing Ambrose 'Namby-Pamby' Philips's anti-Arcadian *Pastorals* (1709) and regenerating the conventions of the genre in an individual way. Gay also squared city content with traditionally rural forms, the eclogue and the georgic, creating 'town' versions of these: in effect, examples of the anti-eclogue and the anti-georgic. Yet another of his achievements in adapting classical models was the revitalizing of the Aesopian fable.

Unlike these literary transformations, Rich's theatrical transformations were aesthetically disreputable in the eyes of the intelligentsia because they were thought to debase rather than, yes, enrich the English dramatic tradition. Such accusations, paralleling similar ones against Italian opera, which was particularly exposed to xenophobic attack by little-Englanders who prided themselves on being true-born Englishmen, increased when Rich's popularity forced the somewhat more intellectually respectable Drury Lane theatre into open competition. Strictly speaking, Rich was not the originator of English pantomime, which was developed by the dancing master John Weaver, a great advocate of dance and mime in the theatre during the first two decades of the eighteenth century. But after 1720, Rich quickly made the form his own, being acknowledged as its unrivalled exponent, and Lincoln's Inn Fields became the home of English pantomime, even though Weaver's productions in 1717 of the seminal dance plays, *The Loves of Mars and Venus* and *The Shipwreck; or, Perseus and Andromeda*, were at Drury Lane. An early example of the hostile reception to the form is the anonymous and unperformed satirical play, *The British Stage; or, The Exploits of Harlequin* (1724), which ridicules the two Faust entertainments staged at the end of 1723: first, John Thurmond's *Harlequin Doctor Faustus; with The Masque of the Deities* at Drury Lane in November, the success of which stimulated Rich to reply in December with the even more successful *The Necromancer; or, Harlequin Doctor Faustus*. Indeed, Rich's pantomime remained in the repertory for about fifty years and illustrates the theatrical development of the 1720s that probably worried the self-styled upholders of artistic standards more than any other: afterpieces, especially pantomimes, began to have long runs with the main-pieces being changed frequently, sometimes nightly, so that what was thought to be the normal pattern was inverted.

Hell hath few furies like bigoted and self-righteous intellectuals rankled as their hobby-horses and sacred cows are slaughtered in public, and the prospect of audiences attending the theatre for the entertainment rather than the play must have caused more than a few fits of apoplexy as indignant neoclassicists reached for their copies of the *Poetics* like drowning men clutching at elusive lifebelts. Offence was taken and displeasure expressed by a number of literati, perhaps most famously by Pope in the 'Whales sport in woods, and dolphins in the skies' passage in Book III of *The Dunciad* (1728),[2] but also in other poems including James Miller's anonymously published *Harlequin-Horace* (1731), and in several dramatic satires such as three plays staged in 1730, Fielding's *The Author's Farce*, Gabriel Odingsells's *Bays's Opera*, and James Ralph's *The Fashionable Lady; or, Harlequin's Opera*, and above all in Fielding's later *Tumble-Down Dick* (1736), with its three-pronged attack on Rich as Machine, Harlequin and the Covent-Garden Manager. In the case of *The Author's Farce*, Fielding was wearing his Scriblerian mask as Scriblerus Secundus, although this did not endear him to the original members of the Club. Fielding sustained his offensive in *Joseph Andrews* ('Not the Great *Rich*, who turns Men into Monkeys, Wheelbarrows, and whatever else best humours his Fancy, hath so strangely metamorphosed the human Shape')[3] and *Tom Jones* (1749)—the famous 'duller' and 'dullest' passage in the first chapter of Book V.

What is ironic is that some of this hostility to departures from orthodoxy in the theatre of the type being promoted by Rich should have emanated from writers who, however committed in theory to resisting change (like the Scriblerians), were themselves engaged in and encouraging far-reaching literary and dramatic changes. Fielding, for example, defended George Lillo's innovatory 'bourgeois' tragedy, which conspicuously breached the 'rules' concerning the status of tragic protagonists. He also pushed comedy quite close to tragedy in defiance of accepted convention to produce problem plays or *drames* such as *The Modern Husband* (1732), and transformed the stage into a platform for witty anti-government polemic during 1736 and 1737, when his 'Great Mogul's Company of English Comedians' performed at the Little Theatre in the Haymarket, unintentionally precipitating Walpole's major transformation of English drama in the form of the long-lived Licensing Act of 1737. From a literary rather than theatrical viewpoint, what Rich was doing inevitably appeared to debase and vulgarize drama, but he was not competing with literary drama (even though it seemed that way to some); he was extending and exploring the nature of theatricality. In his own way, not that of 'regular' drama but of mime and spectacle, Rich was extraordinarily inventive and original, an actor-manager of enormous talent though not perhaps of genius, like Garrick. The charge of debasement stems from applying a narrow definition of drama to work that manifestly falls outside it. Had Aristotle written a study of entertainments to complement the *Poetics*, as Fielding's ridiculous Machine in *Tumble-Down Dick* suggests he did, Rich would have been revered rather than reviled by neoclassical theorists. Ironically, Fielding laid claim to a hypothetical classical precedent for *Joseph Andrews*, the *Margites*, a non-extant and perhaps non-existent comic epic attributed to Homer and mentioned by Zeno and Aristotle. Fielding argues in his Preface that his 'comic Epic-Poem in Prose' is highly original ('this kind of Writing, which I do not remember to have seen hitherto attempted in our Language') and artistically reputable because rooted in the ancients and belonging to a tradition of unwritten comic epics descending from the *Margites* ('that we have no more Instances of it among the Writers of Antiquity, is owing to the Loss of this great Pattern, which, had it survived, would have found its Imitators equally with the other Poems of this great Original').[4]

Beginning with a narrow definition of poetry and literature, some of the best work of the major Augustans, including Gay, could be construed as 'debasement'. Why did Pope not devote his abundant creative energy to writing true epics instead of 'debasing' the genre in *The Rape of the Lock* (1714) and *The Dunciad*? Why did Fielding not turn his hand to tragedy, a form he never attempted despite his advocacy of Lillo, rather than 'debase' the form with his mock tragedies, in which he deliberately set out to debase what he saw as contemporary debasements of the genre. As the author of a Tragi-Comical Farce (*The Mohocks*), a Tragi-Comi-Pastoral Farce (*The What D'Ye Call It*), a classical travesty in the tradition of Scarron (*Achilles*), and pastorals that are far from orthodox even though they attack

Philips for departing from orthodoxy (*The Shepherd's Week*)—to name but a few generic oddities—Gay would seem to be in the forefront of Augustan 'debasers'. *The Beggar's Opera* itself involves a systematic 'debasement' of Italian opera. The escape clause for the literary Augustans is that, unlike Rich's, their 'debasement' is that of satire, parody and burlesque, carrying the imprimatur of Aristotle himself since satire, necessarily of a lower order than epic and tragedy, is permitted to employ methods and techniques impermissible in higher genres. Yet there is a resemblance too. If Rich's 'debasements' resulted in opening up new theatrical possibilities, the literary 'debasements' of the Scriblerians and other Augustans led to new expressive possibilities in poetry, prose, and drama—indeed, to a veritable expansion, 'like gold to airy thinness beat'.

Most of Gay's 'irregular' work for the theatre is far more rewarding than his 'regular' plays, in which his imagination seems to be operating well below full pressure. The same is broadly true of Fielding, whose dramatic satires and burlesques stand apart from the bulk of his considerable output for the stage, despite the historical importance of his 'problem' comedies, which appealed so much to Shaw. Gay's best work usually arises from paradox, from a clash or contradiction of some kind, between form and content (a beggar's opera) or generic incompatibilities (tragi-comi-pastoral farce), and the orthodoxy of plain tragedy and comedy proved to be something of a straitjacket for him. Of the six plays (counting the 1713 and 1730 versions of *The Wife of Bath* separately) to which Gay attached the label 'Tragedy' or 'Comedy', the most interesting by a long way is the most unorthodox, *Three Hours after Marriage*, a genuinely Scriblerian work—the only theatrical one—in that Pope and Arbuthnot collaborated in its creation, although Gay was the prime mover and principal contributor. So unorthodox is it that it is cast in the 'irregular' form of three acts, not the five acts of 'regular' comedy, a point Gay emphasizes in the short Advertisement included in the first edition of 1717, where he explains that 'the Players in Compliance with the Taste of the Town, broke it into five Parts in the Representation'.[5] A five-act version eventually appeared in 1758 in the Dublin *Supplement to the Works of Alexander Pope, Esq.*, but there is nothing to suggest that this was the authors' preferred version, despite John

Harrington Smith's ingenious arguments in his edition of the play for the Augustan Reprint Society (Los Angeles, 1961), arguments convincingly rebutted by John Fuller in his recent edition of Gay's *Dramatic Works*.

While *Three Hours after Marriage* is technically a comedy, and generates humour as such, it is also an anti-comedy in that it makes fun of the routine devices and conventions of contemporary intrigue comedy by 'over the top' exaggeration; it is therefore doubly funny, as a farcical comedy and a send-up of this type of play. In their edition of *Three Hours after Marriage* for the Lake Erie College series (Painesville, Ohio, 1961), Richard Morton and William M. Peterson draw attention to resemblances between it and four late seventeenth-century comedies by Shadwell, D'Urfey, Behn and Ravenscroft, notably the latter's *The Anatomist* (1696), which was on the boards in 1716 and therefore fresh in theatrical memory; but the Scriblerian trio are burlesquing this kind of elaborately plotted comedy, as the names Plotwell and Underplot, two of the major characters, indicate. Parallels to other plays, and even borrowings from them, must be interpreted not as plagiarism but as a parodic strategy. The burlesque is located almost entirely in the situations and action of the play rather than its language, and consequently differs from most Restoration and Augustan dramatic burlesques, in which stylistic parody and close verbal imitation dominate. The blend of this unorthodox burlesque technique with zany farce and abusive caricature, especially of the physician John Woodward as Fossile and the critic John Dennis as Sir Tremendous (one of his favourite words), results in a most eccentric play, characteristically Scriblerian in its assault on misplaced scientific curiosity, bogus intellectuality, and bad writing. The brief extracts from a tragedy by Fossile's niece, Phoebe Clinket, possibly modelled to some extent on Lady Winchelsea, exemplify what the Scriblerians were to call 'the art of sinking in poetry'.

The transformation of comedy into burlesque by stretching its devices to breaking point and beyond is mainly embodied in the attempts by both Plotwell and Underplot to cuckold Fossile during the three hours after his marriage to Susanna Townley, an extremely promiscuous young woman already married to a sailor and the mother of at least one illegitimate child, although

Fossile believes her to be an unspotted virgin. The two competing lovers resort to a series of disguises, subterfuges and
deceptions in order to outwit Fossile and reach the ever-ready
Townley in his house. During their adventurous pursuit of her,
both experience hair's-breadth escapes from injury and perhaps
even death. Transformation is *le mot juste* for what these
determined rivals for Townley's post-nuptial, extra-marital
favours do to themselves to achieve their end, but in a sense
they are only following her example since she is plainly not what
she appears to be, a pure and innocent newly-wed. Fossile, too,
indulges in a little transformation when he dresses as his own
footman and intercepts a number of letters to Townley at his
front door after becoming suspicious that she is secretly com-
municating with an admirer. Plotwell's first transformation,
derived from *The Anatomist*, is into a Polish scientist, Cornelius
Lubomirski, who speaks fluent but ungrammatical, uncolloquial,
heavily accented, and badly pronounced English. As such, he is
able to gain access to the house, but his scheme is thwarted by
Underplot's arrival in the guise of a sick man urgently in need of
Fossile's medical care.

Further attempts to penetrate Fossile's home and 'wife',
including Plotwell's successful entry of the first concealed in a
large chest but failure to achieve the second when Fossile
arrives unexpectedly, forcing Townley to conceal her beau very
intimately beneath her domed petticoats, culminate in the
grotesque, almost surreal museum scene in the final act. Until
this point, the would-be cuckolders have retained human form,
but now they ludicrously resort to the tactic of metamorphosis
employed by some of the classical deities when lusting after a
bit of Greek skirt. At the beginning of the play, Fossile himself
alludes to one story of divine metamorphosis—Jove adopting
the form of Amphitryon in order to seduce his wife Alcmena—
when he ironically contemplates his own January-and-May
situation as an old man with a young wife: 'She may be an
Alcmena, but alas! I am no Thunderer' (I, 42–3).[6] But it is the
two lovers who, for their final attempt, follow the example of the
deities in having themselves delivered to Fossile's house as new
specimens for his private museum, Plotwell as an Egyptian
mummy and Underplot as an alligator or crocodile (both words
are used). Although not magically induced by Harlequin's bat,

these transformations are as bizarre as anything later perpetrated by Rich. In an attempt to secure Townley from amorous approaches, Fossile shuts her in the museum, where she is first wooed by the mummy, who cites mythological precedent for his appearance ('Thus *Jove* within the Milk-white Swan compress'd his *Leda*', III, 51–2), and then by the alligator as well in what she calls 'a Contest of Beauty' (III, 95). Before Fossile makes another unexpected return, this time with his fellow-scientists Nautilus and Possum to examine the two 'specimens', the absurd love scene becomes an amalgam of bawdy and goonery, with the mummy Plotwell inviting Townley to consider 'how I am embroider'd with Hieroglyphicks . . . My Balmy Breath . . . My erect Stature' (III, 88–9, 91, 93) and the alligator Underplot recommending 'my beautiful Row of Teeth . . . The strong Joints of my Back . . . My long Tail' (III, 90, 92, 94).

Having resurrected themselves in order to seduce Townley, Plotwell and Underplot have to act the parts of museum specimens to deceive Fossile, but the prospect of being probed with a sword and a rusty knife is too much for the two lovers who reveal themselves to be alive. On cue, as it were, Clinket comes to the rescue of both Townley's image and the lovers' skins by pretending that the two oddities are really actors in one of her dramatic masquerades, not Fossile's museum pieces: they experience yet another transformation. This comic lunacy finally dissolves in a burlesque denouement involving a rapid concatenation of false allegations, confusions, revelations, and a few ambiguous red herrings thrown in for good measure. *Three Hours after Marriage* is a comedy of intrigue that succeeds in exploding the conventions of intrigue comedy by systematic burlesque exaggeration, 'paradoxing them into derealization', to quote Jayne Morgan's unforgettable though seemingly impenetrable phrase about a different but not dissimilar example of literary transformation. Appropriately, the dramatist in the play, Clinket, adds a self-reflexive gloss in the penultimate speech when she informs Fossile that what she has got 'by this Day's Adventure' is 'a Plot for a Comedy' (III, 546, 548).

The process of dramatic transformation in *Three Hours after Marriage* raises an important question: for an audience in a theatre as opposed to a reader in a study, especially in a fast-moving production with one laugh rapidly following another, would the burlesque properly register as such, or be subsumed into the total comic effect of what might appear to be a particularly crazy example of farcical comedy? Burlesque functions by imitative mockery, and if the target is serious (tragedy, tragicomedy, heroic play, English dramatic opera, Italian opera), there is no mistaking the intention. Comedy—laughing comedy, at any rate—is much more resistant to burlesque, partly because it is without the pretensions, even sublime aspirations, of more elevated genres, and partly because it uses the same weapon and provokes the same response as burlesque—humour. Since burlesque is a comic mode, the distinction between what is burlesqued and the burlesque imitation is much less obvious when the former is comic rather than tragic or operatic. Indeed, despite the growth of burlesque in the theatre after the Restoration, comic drama was only rarely subjected to this treatment, and it was its 'sentimental', not its farcical intrigue, qualities that usually drew satirical fire. Whereas such terms as 'mock heroic', 'mock epic', and 'mock tragedy' have entered the critical vocabulary, 'mock comedy' has not. Even after coining playfully ironic labels for two earlier plays, *The Mohocks* and *The What D'Ye Call It*, Gay (or the authorial triumvirate) was content with Clinket's word 'Comedy' as a description of the idiosyncratic *Three Hours after Marriage*, which hovers between being a highly irregular 'regular' play and the most regular of Gay's 'irregular' dramas.

It is among the undisputed 'irregular' ones that Gay's dramatic transformations, usually involving burlesque manipulation, are most conspicuous, especially in *The Mohocks*, *The What D'Ye Call It*, *The Beggar's Opera* and *Achilles*, but not, surprisingly enough, in *Polly*. As the sequel to *The Beggar's Opera* (though not staged until 1777 because of the government ban on the planned production in 1729), *Polly* might be thought to reproduce the operatic transformations of its pioneering predecessor. The ridicule of ultra-sensitive Italian singers in the Introduction promises another anti-opera, as does the Fourth Player's determination to follow the example of the previous year's 'Opera without singers' (97), *The Beggar's Opera* itself, but *Polly* is largely devoid of burlesque. With *The Beggar's Opera*, Gay achieved a genuine anti-opera and simultaneously created

131

a completely new and 'irregular' genre, the ballad opera, which could then be adopted without necessarily repeating his burlesque inversion of Italian opera. Gay arrived at ballad opera by means of burlesque, but, once created, the form immediately became independent of its burlesque origins, except in the very broad sense that it continued as an English antidote to Italian opera, an alternative mode of music drama. Even in Gay's two subsequent ballad operas, *Polly* and *Achilles*, there is little trace of the systematic ironic displacement of Italian opera characteristic of *The Beggar's Opera*. Polly, in fact, exhibits Gay's distinctly 'sentimental' tendencies when his Scriblerian side, favouring irony and satire, is held in check or even suppressed—tendencies also evident in his sententious 'Pastoral Tragedy' *Dione*, unperformed but published in *Poems on Several Occasions* in 1720, and his more orthodox, heroic-pathetic tragedy *The Captives*, which did reach the stage in 1724. Whereas the central character in *The Beggar's Opera*, Macheath, is an ambivalent anti-hero, both romantic and anti-romantic, the equivalent figure in the 'Opera' described as 'The Second Part of *The Beggar's Opera*', Polly herself, is a straightforward heroine, despite spending part of the play in breeches; Macheath, in disguise as a black, is reduced to a minor rôle. Gay's finest dramatic achievements, *The What D'Ye Call It* and *The Beggar's Opera*, embody his unique blend of the satirical and the emotional, detached amusement and involved feeling. There is no shortage of social satire in *Polly*, but Gay's emotional spree in idealized noble savagery is too unqualified for comfort.

Posthumously produced in 1733, *Achilles* differs substantially from *Polly* in that it does involve transformation, but this is more of content than of form: a comic travesty of a classical story rather than a satirical send-up of Italian opera. *Achilles* nevertheless alludes obliquely to Italian opera, which so often draws on classical mythology and history for its subject matter. Gay retells the story of Achilles's life disguised as a girl, Pyrrha, at the court of Lycomedes on Scyros, where his goddess-mother Thetis conceals him from the Greek leaders during the Trojan War, knowing that if he is discovered he is destined to die young after achieving the glory of a great hero at Troy. Following in the wake of Scarron and his English imitators, though without descending to the deliberate crudity and coarseness that disfigure a number of earlier literary and dramatic travesties of both ancients and moderns (such as Thomas Duffett's *The Empress of Morocco* (1673), *The Mock-Tempest* (1674) and *Psyche Debauch'd* (1675), John Wright's *Mock-Thyestes* (1674), and Colley Cibber's *The Rival Queans* (1710)), Gay belittles the 'great' men (or supermen) of Greek legend by making them all too human, so that they behave like characters in a comedy of contemporary life. Lycomedes and his wife Theaspe, for example, are locked in marital combat like many bickering and squabbling married couples in Restoration and Augustan comedy, and the lecherous husband most certainly would if he could, except that he misguidedly aims his lust at 'Pyrrha', whose physical rather than moral strength quickly defeats the would-be rapist. In the cases of both Achilles and Ajax, who is presented as an over-grown bully verging on the mentally retarded, Gay has considerable fun at the expense of the male predilection for so-called military virtues, including valour, glory, heroism and honour. A conventional notion of 'greatness', based on power (Alexander the Great), is ironically deflated by the opposite mechanism to that used in *The Beggar's Opera*. There, a highwayman is elevated to the status of a 'great man' (a phrase applied at the time to Robert Walpole, not always ironically), whereas in *Achilles* the heroic world of classical epic is humanized and shown to be subhuman (Ajax) or dehumanized (Achilles responding to the martial trumpet calls in III, x, like Pavlov's dog salivating at the sound of a bell). Are the most valiant warriors no more than robots?

Pursued by three prominent Greeks, Ulysses, Diomedes and Agyrtes, themselves in disguise as merchants, Achilles finds himself facing the same dilemma as so many male protagonists in post-1660 heroic and pathetic drama, the choice between love and honour, between Lycomedes's daughter Deidamia, whom he has made pregnant, and the prospect of 'fame' at Troy. Yet Gay brilliantly burlesques the popular and supposedly heart-rending versions of this crisis in contemporary drama by subjecting what Empson called 'the structure of complex words', especially 'fame' and 'honour', to ironic scrutiny. By drawing attention to her own 'fame' and 'honour', which are in direct competition with what Ulysses calls 'the Honour of *Greece*' (III, xi, 19) and what Agyrtes means by 'fame' in Air

133

XLVII ('Fame shall our Deeds requite', III, x, 107 and 115), Deidamia completely undercuts the emotive power they possess in an all-male context of military conquest. The ease with which Achilles is swayed by the three Greeks establishes his school-boyish immaturity, not his much-vaunted heroic greatness (Ulysses says, 'now, *Achilles*, the House of *Priam* shakes', III, x, 90–1), but Gay's point is that these are two sides of the same coin. Ulysses's grandiloquent rhetoric and nationalistic fervour mask an appeal to personal aggrandizement, to an ego-trip based on violence; Achilles joins the other three in an air, singing: 'Now great *Hector* shall bleed. . . . How I pant! How I burn for the Fight!' (III, x, 106, 113). However, because the ballad opera is a comedy and therefore requires a conven-tionally happy ending, Achilles achieves a resolution of sorts by marrying Deidamia before leaving for Troy. Comparisons may be odorous but they are inevitable, and *Achilles* has always suffered from comparisons with *The Beggar's Opera*, as has *Polly*. Of Gay's two 'inferior' ballad operas, *Achilles* is undoubtedly the more engaging, partly because its ironic transformation of a classical legend teasingly subverts and challenges stock responses in Gay's typically light-fingered way. Elsewhere in this book, *Achilles* receives the sympathetic and detailed treatment it merits but is usually denied, so here consideration should now be given to Gay's subversive transformations of genres and styles, as opposed to a pre-existing story, in three earlier plays.

Despite being extremely topical when it was written early in 1712, Gay's first attempt at playwriting, *The Mohocks*, failed to reach the stage, although it did find its way into print. The activities of gangs of London rakehells, currently known as Mohocks following the visit by four Mohawk Indian chiefs from North America in 1710, were causing concern, and Gay's comic afterpiece is about a Mohock adventure in which the gang seize members of the City Watch and accuse them in front of magistrates of being Mohocks, before being exposed at the very end. According to the Mohocks, ''twas only an innocent Frolick' (iii, 159–60), but they are threatened 'with the utmost Severity' (iii, 179), which they quietly accept ('We'll submit, ask Pardon, or do any thing' (iii, 180)), and the work ends cheerfully enough with a celebratory song and dance by the released watchmen. The topsy-turvy 'Frolick' is cast in three

scenes, but only in the first, devoted solely to the Mohocks, is
the style also topsy-turvy. It is this opening scene that justifies
Gay's deliberately anomalous designation of the play as 'a tragi-
comical farce'. With the introduction of the quasi-Shakespearean
watchmen in the second scene, the idiom changes from blank
verse to prose, and on their subsequent appearance the Mohocks
adopt the same linguistic register as their victims, rather than
the elevated rant of their initiation ceremony in the first scene.
Burlesque transformation is therefore limited to this episode.

In his heavily ironic dedication 'To Mr. *D****' (John Dennis),
a few years later to suffer the indignity of a Scriblerian broadside in *Three Hours after Marriage*, Gay claims to have slavishly
followed the critic's dogmatic neoclassical prescriptions concerning the writing of plays ('the exactest Rules of Dramatick
Poetry')[7] and to have modelled his own work on Dennis's recent
tragedy, *Appius and Virginia* (1709). Although this is manifestly
not the case, Gay opens his farcical play with a mock-heroic
conversion of both the high-flown idiom of contemporary
tragedy, including Dennis's, and a dramatic incident fairly
common in plays of the preceding forty years and occurring in
Appius and Virginia: the swearing of oaths and allegiances, or
avowals of commitment to a course of action, most famously by
the conspirators in Otway's *Venice Preserv'd* (1682) but also by
Lucius Icilius's faction in Dennis's tragedy. Before Gay, writers
of dramatic burlesque rarely exploited the potential of mock
heroic, choosing instead to use exaggeration within a framing
structure (*The Rehearsal* (1671) provided this model although
Buckingham does not completely eschew mock heroic) or
Scarron-like debasement (high subject, low style), as in the first
example of burlesque drama after the Restoration, the playlet
about Caesar, Ptolemy, Antony and Cleopatra in the fifth act of
Davenant's *The Playhouse to be Let* (1663). The first scene of *The
Mohocks*, on the other hand, is shaped on the genuinely mock-
heroic principle of applying a high style to a low subject. The
Mohocks' 'Rites' (i, 38), in which they 'Renounce Humanity,
defie Religion' (i, 47), provide a mock heroic analogue to those
in serious plays, making fun of the intense solemnity and
emotionalism of such scenes. As in the speech of the New
Mohock to his Emperor, the discrepancy between the inflated
rhetoric and what is being referred to, the criminal activities of

hoodlums, makes the style itself, with its tropes and euphemistic circumlocutions, appear absurdly artificial and mannered:

> Great Potentate, who leadst the *Mohock* Squadrons
> To nightly Expeditions, whose dread Nod
> Gives Law to those, lawless to all besides:
> To thee I come—to serve beneath thy Banner.
> Mischief has long lain dormant in my Bosom
> Like smother'd Fire, which now shall blaze abroad
> In glorious Enterprize—
>
> (i, 29–35)

By making the Mohocks sound like figures in high tragedy, Gay pokes fun at the stilted pretentiousness of contemporary dramatic poetry, but his ironic inversions, which lend the gang an unexpected dignity, also suggest another form of transformation. The effect of Gay's mock-heroic incongruity is to narrow, even close, the gap between the high and the low, thus creating an uneasy zone of indeterminacy. If the Mohock leader is a 'Great Potentate' and 'our most High and Mighty Emperor' (i, 44), are potentates and emperors necessarily all that different from Mohocks? Are the high really any higher than the low, and vice versa? In *The Mohocks*, Gay does not explore the implications of his mock-heroic burlesque, but here in embryo is the satirical method brought to full flower in *The Beggar's Opera*, which features an underworld gang with its potentate and emperor, Macheath the great.

The What D'Ye Call It was Gay's second play to be produced— the first version of *The Wife of Bath* was staged in 1713—and deserved the success it enjoyed as an afterpiece in 1715 and subsequent seasons. Gay now consolidates and refines his tentative exploration in *The Mohocks* of the potential of mock heroic in the theatre, adding pastoral to the generic mix of the earlier work to produce a much more accomplished 'tragi-comi-pastoral farce'. The Preface Gay wrote for the published version is a superb piece of Scriblerian irony, in which he makes fun of the unsmiling criticisms by such critics as Dennis of what is, at the most obvious level, a sophisticated burlesque play. Gay adopts the persona of a self-confident Modern, the supposed author, who offers his highly original 'Kind of Dramatick Entertainment' as a major advance in serious English drama because its art 'lies in interweaving the several Kinds of the Drama with each other, so that they cannot be distinguish'd or separated'. In his detailed refutation of any possible criticisms of the play as either tragedy, comedy, pastoral, or farce, Gay's mask claims that it is all four simultaneously and, even more surprisingly, that it conforms in many ways to the strict neoclassical orthodoxy found 'in the most perfect Pieces'. Gay uses the Preface to add insult to the injury caused to 'the graver sort of Wits' by the play, or mock play, itself.[8]

Strictly speaking, *The What D'Ye Call It* is a frame play, but one very different from *The Rehearsal* and plays written in imitation of Buckingham's seminal burlesque, in which the inner play is in rehearsal and is frequently interrupted by discussion between its foolish author, some questioning critics, and even the actors. Gay's inner play, which gives its name to the entire play, is an uninterrupted amateur performance, arranged as a Christmas entertainment by a country justice, Sir Roger, partly for the instruction of two fellow-justices who 'never saw a Play before' (Introductory Scene, 57). This is why Sir Roger is determined to 'shew them all sorts of Plays under one' (58)—'a Tragedy and a Comedy . . . a Pastoral too . . . a Farce . . . with a Spice of your Opera' (53–6). The frame consists of two brief scenes flanking the inner play, which includes bit parts for Sir Roger and his colleagues as themselves. In this way, the outer frame may be said to invade the inner play, but in a way totally different from that in rehearsal burlesques; likewise, the inner play invades the outer at the very end, dissolving the distinction between them. The concluding off-stage marriage between Thomas Filbert and Kitty Carrot is also the secret marriage between the actors who perform these two rôles, Sir Roger's son, Thomas, and his Steward's daughter, Kitty. By transforming some actors into their rôles and other rôles back into their actors, Gay tantalizingly touches on the dichotomies between art and nature and between illusion and reality, but the primary transformational process in *The What D'Ye Call It* is mock heroic, the conversion of aspects of Restoration and Augustan tragedy into parodic burlesque.

The inner play is an anti-pastoral mock tragedy with an appropriately happy ending, in which contemporary English peasants, not Golden Age Arcadians, incongruously speak

137

grandiloquent couplets as they undergo experiences comparable to those frequently endured by the heroes and heroines of 'pathetic' plays. Despite his use of rhyme, Gay is not aiming principally at Buckingham's target, the heroic play of the 1660s and 1670s, but at the type of blank-verse tragedy that became popular in the 1680s with Banks and Otway and remained so for many years: tragedy going for the heartstrings and the tear ducts. Gay employs rhyme for its comic potential in deflating sonorous rhetoric and creating deliberate bathos. *A Complete Key to the Last New Farce The What D'Ye Call It* (1715), published anonymously only five weeks after the first night (the authorship is still a contentious issue among scholars), is invaluable in identifying some of the passages from plays of the previous forty years alluded to by Gay, notably *Venice Preserv'd* and Banks's *The Unhappy Favourite* (1681) from the earlier part, and three of Rowe's 'she-tragedies' (particularly *Jane Shore* (1714)) and Philips's *The Distrest Mother* (1712) from the later part. For his long commentary on the play in his edition of the *Dramatic Works*, Fuller relies heavily on the *Complete Key*.

Nevertheless, *The What D'Ye Call It* does not contain as much direct burlesque imitation of specific lines and speeches as Fielding's first mock tragedy, *Tom Thumb* (revised in 1731 as *The Tragedy of Tragedies*). By concentrating on such stock situations as the forced parting of lovers, the preparation by doomed characters for death or execution, and the expression of remorse by those afflicted by guilt, Gay achieves a general burlesque of dramatic clichés while often having one or two particular scenes in mind. The first line of Kitty's appeal to the justices to take pity on her by not condemning her sweetheart to join the army, 'Behold how low you have reduc'd a Maid' (I, i, 53), is exactly the same as one of Andromache's lines in *The Distrest Mother* apart from the substitution of 'Maid' for 'Queen', but the speech does not develop as close parody, becoming instead a banter (to use a favourite word of the author of the *Complete Key*) on mawkish rhetoric in general. Kitty maintains a high idiom, with verbal repetitions and considerable departures from normal word order, but the rural content is low, with the result that the rhetorical tricks designed to provoke a powerful emotional response are made transparent and amusingly undermined:

138

> To Trade so barb'rous he was never bred,
> The Blood of Vermine all the Blood he shed:
> How should he, harmless Youth, how should he then
> Who kill'd but Poulcats, learn to murder Men?
>
> (I, i, 58–61)

Peascod, facing a military death sentence for desertion, launches into a long speech of penitence in which he acknowledges all his wrong-doing in the hope that others will learn from his fate 'to shun untimely Ends' (II, i, 6). However, the moralizing solemnity of his delivery is completely at odds with the trivial nature of what he calls his 'Evil Courses' (II, i, 7), and this glaring discrepancy again serves Gay's deconstructive purpose, subverting both the emotionalism and the stylistic pretensions of 'pathetic' tragedy:

> But I, sad Wretch, went on from Crime to Crime;
> I play'd at Nine-pins first in Sermon time:
> I rob'd the Parson's Orchard next; and then
> (For which I pray Forgiveness) stole—a Hen.
>
> (II, i, 11–14)

Throughout the inner play Gay maintains this technique, turning the high into the low while skilfully retaining the superficial appearance of the high. He transforms the (supposedly) tragic into comedy, sentiment into a source of humour, most memorably, perhaps, when the contrite Peascod weeps profusely over the title page of the eighth edition of 'this good Book' (II, i, 22), *The Pilgrim's Progress*: 'Oh! 'tis so moving, I can read no more' (II, i, 28).

The What D'Ye Call It places a Scriblerian fun-bomb under several aspects of contemporary drama, defining 'the art of sinking in poetry', but Gay's mock heroic is even more double-edged than in *The Mohocks*, as the Prologue to the inner play suggests:

> This Comick Story, or this Tragick Jest,
> May make you laugh, or cry, as you like best;
> May exercise your Good, or your Ill-nature,
> Move with Distress, or tickle you with Satyr. (5–8)

In a letter to Caryll (3 March 1715) shortly after the first production, in which the actors kept up the pretence of tragic seriousness, Pope notes that the less sophisticated members of the audience initially took the play at face value, responding 'with great gravity and sedateness, some few with tears'. Soon, however, audiences caught on to the irony of Gay's tragic jest, causing consternation to Pope's deaf friend Cromwell who, 'hearing none of the words and seeing the action to be tragical, was much astonished to find the audience laugh'.[9] Laughter is a right response to the play, but at times the laughter is close to tears, and those who were genuinely moved cannot be dismissed as naïve, easily deceived no-wits. A case has been made, notably by Allardyce Nicoll,[10] for linking *The What D'Ye Call It*, at least to some extent, with 'sentimental' developments in drama, even though it is ostensibly anti-sentimental. The ambiguity arises in the same way as in *The Mohocks*: lowering an elevated idiom by applying it to those at the bottom of the social scale has the effect of raising the humble characters themselves to a more serious status than the traditional one of country bumpkins and comic yokels. The transformation operates in two ways, and if burlesque is one side of Gay's mock heroic, social satire is the other.

Gay establishes the hardships and sufferings of a rural peasantry, largely at the mercy of their social superiors and a ruthless legal system, both of which are frequently characterized by corruption, officiousness, and inhumanity. The first act of the inner play incorporates an attack on the three country justices who are present throughout. Their treatment of the innocent lovers, Kitty and Filbert, is heartless as well as completely unjust, and they are eventually harangued and threatened by the ghosts of five previous victims of their cruelty, including an embryo, whose mother miscarried after being sentenced to a severe whipping. The embryo ghost sums up the ambivalence: it is both ludicrous and genuinely pathetic. At one level, this ghost scene is a mockery of those in such tragedies as *Venice Preserv'd* and Lee's *The Rival Queens* (1677), but the burlesque humour does not obliterate the social criticism. Elsewhere, this can be most explicit, as in the reply made by Peascod's young daughter Joyce to her father when he assures her that after his execution (from which, like Macheath, he is unexpectedly reprieved) she will be safe in the care of the parish:

The Parish finds indeed—but our Church-Wardens
Feast on the Silver, and give us the Farthings.
Then my School-Mistress, like a Vixen *Turk*,
Maintains her lazy Husband by our Work:
Many long tedious Days I've Worsted spun;
She grudg'd me Victuals when my Task was done.

(II, iv, 13–18)

The Beggar's Opera is the naural successor to *The What D'Ye Call It*, containing a similar mixture of ingredients: burlesque of a theatrical genre; social and political satire; and a low-life, triangular love story involving a man and two women (Macheath, Polly, Lucy: Filbert, Kitty, Dorcas), which eventually reaches a satisfactory resolution after coming close to tragedy. The resemblance between Gay's method of transformation in the two plays, debasing the high and elevating the low, is strong. Why, then, is *The What D'Ye Call It* usually thought of as a dramatic burlesque containing incidental satire, while *The Beggar's Opera* is just as frequently considered to be the opposite? The substantially different natures of the two genres being burlesqued go a long way towards providing an answer. A burlesque of tragedy, whether closely parodic or not, must reproduce the verbal texture of the original, albeit in a comically lowered form. The inevitable proximity of burlesque to burlesqued means that the characters immediately register as burlesque antitypes, even if they possess a non-burlesque dimension. Despite the failure of some theatregoers to respond to the burlesque humour of *The What D'Ye Call It* during its first few nights in 1715, others did not find Gay's irony difficult to fathom, and 'after the third day', according to Pope, 'the common people of the pit and gallery . . . also took the hint, and have ever since been very loud in their clapps.'[11]

In burlesquing Italian opera, on the other hand, Gay found it easy to widen the gap between burlesque and burlesqued so that he could liberate his characters to a much greater extent from their rôles as antitypes, thus giving them dramatic independence. It is easy to see Polly Peachum as a character in her own right, whereas it is difficult to see Kitty without seeing through her to the tragic heroines behind her. The most important reason for this difference is obviously linguistic. Because Italian was not widely known in England and the

141

operas were always sung in Italian after the first decade of the eighteenth century, close parody and burlesque imitation of the language, as opposed to the music, of recitatives and arias was pointless and was not attempted, except in the most general of ways. In the Introduction to *The Beggar's Opera*, the Beggar proudly draws attention to his equivalents of the numerous simile arias in Italian opera, 'I have introduc'd the Similes that are in all your celebrated *Operas*: The *Swallow*, the *Moth*, the *Bee*, the *Ship*, the *Flower*, &c' (16–18), but the airs in which these appear have no specific operatic targets.

As a form of music theatre, not literary drama, Italian opera is arguably a more suitable burlesque target for a composer or composer-librettist partnership than for a poet. Genuine mock opera of this kind, with recitatives, arias, duets, choruses, and Italianate music, certainly exists, most famously in two collaborations by the writer Henry Carey, using the name Signior Carini, and the composer John Frederick Lampe, *The Dragon of Wantley* (1737) and its sequel *Margery* (1738). Carey's comic-nonsense texts involve a farcical transformation of standard plot elements in Italian opera, but they were sung in Lampe's particularly grand settings with hilarious results. Less well-known instances of this type of mock opera (high music accompanying low words) were performed before *The Beggar's Opera*, including the first burlesque of Italian opera, Richard Estcourt's *Prunella* (1708). This brief Interlude was incorporated in a production of *The Rehearsal*, with Estcourt himself playing Bayes; London grocers and tradesmen sing inconsequential and silly words to the music of the two Italian operas that achieved most success immediately after the introduction of the genre to England in 1705, *Arsinoe* and *Camilla*. Richard Leveridge's afterpiece *The Comick Masque of Pyramus and Thisbe* (1716) is a rehearsal play in which the Bayes figure is a ludicrous composer, Semibreve; the inner play is Semibreve's allegedly tragic opera derived from the mechanicals' would-be tragedy in *A Midsummer Night's Dream*. Leveridge hit on the clever idea of creating a mock opera by giving Shakespeare's burlesque playlet the full Italian treatment, generating the same incongruity between comic text and serious music as Estcourt before him and Carey and Lampe after him.

The Beggar's Opera is plainly not a mock opera in the sense that these burlesques are, even though Estcourt and his successors reveal even less interest in verbal burlesque than Gay, whose simile airs, for example, do allude to the rhetorical elaboration of Italian arias. In *The Beggar's Opera* and *Polly*, Gay borrows a few tunes from Italian operas, such as the March from Handel's *Rinaldo* (1711) for the highwaymen's song and chorus in the former work (Air XX), but Italianate music is conspicuous by its absence. This might suggest that in conceiving *The Beggar's Opera* Gay had Italian opera only tenuously in mind, but the internal evidence contradicts this. He planned his work carefully on the Italian model, demanding at the outset a full instrumental overture (composed by Pepusch) rather than a spoken prologue as in conventional drama, and adopting the three-act structure of operas, not the five acts expected in non-operatic mainpieces. In the Introduction before the Overture, the Beggar, who has 'consented to have neither Prologue nor Epilogue' (24–5), insists that his work 'must be allow'd an Opera in all its forms' (25–6) except in one respect: it contains 'no Recitative' (24). Gay substitutes speech for recitative, with the arguable exception of Macheath's sung soliloquy in the condemned cell (Airs LVIII-LXVII in III, xiii), but the alternation between speech and the many songs in *The Beggar's Opera* corresponds to that between recitative and arias in Italian opera.

The rivalry between Polly and Lucy over Macheath at the heart of *The Beggar's Opera* has many parallels in Italian opera (Rossane and Lisaura over the eponymous Alexander the Great in Handel's *Alessandro*, for example), and also refers to the personal animosity between the two Italian prima donnas in London at the time, Francesca Cuzzoni and Faustina Bordoni. In *Alessandro*, the opera he wrote for Faustina's London début in 1726, Handel tried to achieve what the Beggar claims to have accomplished: 'such a nice Impartiality to our two Ladies, that it is impossible for either of them to take Offence' (Introduction, 20–2). The Beggar also mentions his 'Prison Scene which the Ladies always reckon charmingly pathetick' (18–19), referring to the popularity of highly charged and tearful prison scenes in Italian opera; in these the heroine usually visits her true love, wrongly held captive and abused by the villain. Most of the second half of *The Beggar's Opera*, after Macheath's arrest by

Peachum, is set in Newgate Prison in the centre of London, where Macheath is visited by Polly, Lucy, and finally 'four Women more . . . with a Child a-peice' (III, xv, 23). Other resemblances to Italian opera include the episode in which Lucy plans and fails to poison Polly (III, vii-ix)—cups of poison, which are spilled or untouched, are not uncommon in the Italian form—and the obligatory happy ending in defiance of dramatic logic. The player interrupts the performance to demand a reversal of what would otherwise be 'a down-right deep Tragedy' (III, xvi, 8–9) and the Beggar complies, noting 'that in this kind of Drama, 'tis no matter how absurdly things are brought about' (III, xvi, 12–13).

Gay's approach differs fundamentally from those of Estcourt, Leveridge and Carey in that he debases not only the texts and stock situations of Italian opera, as indeed they do, but also the music. Like them, Gay provides a low equivalent of operatic narrative, but unlike them he also provides a low equivalent of operatic music. Instead of requesting a composer to add music for mock-Italian arias, Gay decided on the alternative approach of writing words for his airs after himself choosing the music from popular songs, especially broadside ballads. Because of this particularly drastic transformation of Italian opera, Gay created an anti-opera rather than a mock opera like other burlesquers, and by distancing his burlesque from Italian opera in this way he arrived at an alternative kind of opera: the thoroughly English form of music drama, mainly comic, which immediately became known as ballad opera. In a sense, Gay successfully emulated Rich's 'magical' ability to turn one thing into something completely different. A major consequence of pushing burlesque transformation to this extreme is that Gay's characters completely transcend their function as antitypes to emerge as figures in their own landscape. In comparison, even the characters in the ambiguous *The What D'Ye Call It* are shadows belonging to a landscape not their own.

Gay's transformation of tragedy in *The What D'Ye Call It* does not produce an alternative form of tragedy, a tragedy of low life, although it points tentatively in this direction. Even Lillo's pioneering tragedies were 'bourgeois', and in the early eighteenth century a tragedy of low life would have been so avant-garde a concept that it would have been out of sight. The artistic radicalism of Wordsworth in *Michael* or Büchner in *Woyzeck* was not a possibility for the Scriblerians. Yet working within comic conventions, Gay was able in *The Beggar's Opera* to write a play of very low life indeed (highwaymen, prostitutes, the London underworld, the condemned cell in Newgate) in which his characters are paradoxically raised to operatic status, 'Captain' Macheath being a romantic hero of sorts in his anti-romantic, anti-heroic world, and Polly the equivalent heroine. During his last-minute intervention to rewrite the denouement at the Player's request, the Beggar spells out the moral consequences of this equalizing of high and low:

> Through the whole Piece you may observe such a similitude of Manners in high and low Life, that it is difficult to determine whether (in the fashionable Vices) the fine Gentlemen imitate the Gentlemen of the Road, or the Gentlemen of the Road the fine Gentlemen. (III, xvi, 18–22)

An immediate consequence of the satirical power generated by Gay's ingenious irony was the banning of *Polly* in 1729, and *The Beggar's Opera* has lost little of its bite down the years, despite repeated English attempts to sanitize it by converting it into a charming period piece and a safe classic. Brecht honoured Gay exactly two hundred years after the first production of *The Beggar's Opera* with his Marxist transformation, *Die Dreigroschenoper* (1928), but for a work that was so topical in 1728 as to appear ephemeral, Gay's original has proved phoenix-like in its ability to make itself new. It remains as pertinent to Mrs. Thatcher's England, with its crooks in high places and get-rich-quick-at-any-price City yuppies, or yippies (young indictable professionals), as it did to Sir Robert Walpole's. Peachum lives O.K., and thrives. Gay thought so once, and now we know it.

NOTES

1. Martin C. Battestin (ed.), *Joseph Andrews* (Oxford, 1967), p. 4.
2. James Sutherland (ed.), *The Dunciad*, 3rd edn. (London and New Haven, 1963), p. 177 (1729 Variorum), p. 332 (1743 version). Vol. V of the Twickenham Edition of *The Poems of Alexander Pope*.
3. Battestin, p. 36.

4. Battestin, p. 3.
5. *DW*, I, 208.
6. Act, scene, and line references are to the texts of Gay's plays in *DW*, from which all quotations are taken (roman and italic reversed in predominantly italic passages such as Airs).
7. *DW*, I, 78.
8. Quotations from the Preface from *DW*, I, 174, 177 (italic).
9. George Sherburn (ed.), *The Correspondence of Alexander Pope* (Oxford, 1956), I, 283, 282.
10. *Early Eighteenth Century Drama*, 3rd edn. (Cambridge, 1952), pp. 197–98.
11. Sherburn, I, 283.

7

Gay and the World of Opera

by PAT ROGERS

1

If satirists do not precisely kill the thing they love, then at least some contributory negligence may be imputed when satire takes the form of parody. As Peter Lewis has remarked (in the best discussion immediately relevant to my theme),

> Gay aimed to create an original type of opera by turning the conventions of Italian opera upside down so that he was simultaneously poking fun at them. . . . *The Beggar's Opera* is much more than a mock-opera, but at one level that is what it is.

That is well said; and so is Lewis's concluding observation on this point, that the work owes its theatrical success to its artistic identity, that of 'a lively and unconventional musical comedy, a kind of opera'. Behind this comment lies Lewis's awareness that 'Gay himself was musical and did not dislike Italian opera in the way that his more doctrinaire neo-classical contemporaries did'. This might present an awkward contradiction for the critic, but Lewis has an apt analogy to hand:

> Just as Jane Austen objected much less to the Gothic novel *per se* than to the excessive seriousness with which it was taken by impressionable members of the reading public, Gay condemns not Italian opera but the completely uncritical theatregoers who had turned it into a fashionable cult.

On this reading, *The Beggar's Opera* becomes an insider-trading job, as Gay sets out 'to combine burlesque of Italian opera with the creation of a rival form, a comic and distinctly English form of opera that quickly became known as ballad opera'.[1] The apparent contradiction is thus happily resolved.

In outline Lewis seems to me to have justified his case, and one purpose of this essay will be to fill out some of the detail he did not have time to explore—that is, to establish in more detail Gay's absorption in the operatic world. There remains a little of a puzzle, as to why an admirer should burlesque and seek to rival a favourite form. But we can at least begin in a healthier state, thanks to the recognition of critics like Lewis, Bertrand Bronson and Yvonne Noble that Gay was far from sharing the cruder xenophobic distaste for opera prevalent in many corners of English culture. The hostile press which started with John Dennis, Addison and John Hughes remained alive for an astonishing length of time. Indeed, it has even now not entirely died out.

The tone and spirit of this tradition are represented in many of the standard accounts. Oliver Warner's rather inept treatment of Gay in the 'Writers and their Work' series, published in 1964 (thought it might as well have been 1864), contains the following:

> The public had grown sick of the fashionable Italian opera, sung by often unattractive people in the language the groundlings could not understand [three offensive references within a couple of lines]. Refreshingly, Gay's English was as clear as a stream, and although he employed a German, Dr. Pepusch, to write bases (*sic*), the tunes were familiar and beloved.[2]

Leaving aside the more obvious silliness here, there is a large question as to the current popularity of the Italian genre. According to Edgar V. Roberts,

> In 1728 . . . the Royal Academy of Music, which since 1720 had produced operas at the King's Theatre in the Haymarket, was undergoing a financial crisis and other internal difficulties. Gay's ridicule probably hurt attendance, and the Academy abandoned opera, and Handel, during the next season. For this reason, and also because Gay had proved that an English musical play could be popular, *The Beggar's Opera* may have influenced Handel's turning from Italian opera in the 1730s to dramatic oratorios for English libretti.[3]

Roberts does not seem as gleeful about this circumstance as some critics, but he does not evince much sense of loss.

The present generation of music lovers, who have so many opportunities to hear Handelian opera, live or on disc, are unlikely to take such a roseate view of the changes described here. After all, the vein of composition thus (ultimately) interrupted numbered among its triumphant masterpieces works such as *Giulio Cesare* and *Tamerlano*—not to mention some brilliantly innovatory operas still to come, in the decade following Gay's burlesque. Meanwhile editors continue to refer glibly to 'the formal, stylized Italian opera', and 'the extravagance and pretense of the Italian arias'. We are told of 'the basic incongruity of foreign-language opera on the English stage'; virtuoso arias are satirized by Gay to point up 'the absurdity of the Italian Opera's practice'.[4] This is hardly more enlightened than the tirades of Dennis, or of John Ireland in 1791 ('Gay must be allowd *the praise* of having attempted to stem *Italia's liquid stream*, which at that time *meandered* through every alley, street, and square, in the metropolis,—*the honour* of having almost silenced the effeminate song of that absurd exotic, *Italian opera*').[5] We cannot seriously uphold such a position today, in the light of operatic and musical history. The more important question is, would Gay have upheld it? The answer is surely no, and the reasons for such a judgement are worth exploring.

2

The biographical evidence assembled here to provide an operatic context for Gay's career is not recondite, but it seems never to have been brought together for this purpose. The standard life by William Henry Irving is in most respects still serviceable, although it needs updating after almost half a century. Irving clings to the older view; citing a famous letter to Swift on the 'reigning amusements of the town' (we shall return to this in more detail a little later), Irving asserts that 'in this matter of music, Gay—though familiar with the ways of the great and their curious aestheticisms—was at heart with the common man.' In *The Beggar's Opera* Gay 'at least knew how to win his confidence'.[6] He achieved this, we are to understand, by demonstrating his scorn for the modish Italianate entertainments. If this is indeed the case, then Gay must have reneged on many loyalties developed over the years.

Before he so much as left Barnstaple in his teens, Gay had encountered one significant rôle-model. This was his school-fellow Aaron Hill, best known today for his brushes with Pope and his friendship with Samuel Richardson. Hill was Gay's senior only by a matter of four months, but he was far quicker off the mark in the quest for artistic advancement. He became manager of Drury Lane in his early twenties and started publishing much sooner than his schoolfriend. By 1711 he had been employed to translate Giacomo Rossi's libretto for *Rinaldo*, Handel's first opera for the London stage. More than that, Hill tells us in his preface to the word-book that it was he who devised the scenario, derived from *Gerusalemme Liberata*, and gave it to Rossi. He tells us, in terms which deserve more respect than they traditionally receive, that his aim was 'to frame some Dramma, that, by different Incidents and Passions, might afford the Musick Scope to vary and display its Excellence'. Hill also signed the dedication to Queen Anne, emphasizing the point that 'this Opera is a Native of your Majesty's Dominions'[7]—true in an important sense, although the leading creative and executive figures were all from abroad. Hill had thus established major contacts in the world of opera, and crucially with Handel and J. J. Heidegger, the decisive infuences in the development of the genre in England.

Gay meanwhile had still not placed his first foot on the ladder of literary preferment. There is a good deal of evidence to show that it was Hill (perhaps by employing his friend as amanuensis) who more than anyone else oversaw his first ventures as a writer. As Irving puts it, 'Hill helped Gay publish his first poem, introduced him to his friends, employed him in his multifarious businesses, and doubtless gave him money for services rendered.'[8] When Richard Savage sought out the facts of Gay's earlier career after the dramatist's death, it was to Hill that he appealed for information. The interest for our present purposes lies in Hill's operatic associations; the friends to whom Gay was introduced would inevitably have included many persons from this walk of life. More broadly, we could assume that Hill's aesthetic experiments, in attempting to naturalize an Italian idiom to English stage conditions, would have excited Gay's imagination. It is entirely likely that Gay's earliest first-hand experience of the London theatre would have had its location in the Haymarket, rather than the 'legitimate' houses where straight drama was performed.

Nevertheless, Gay started off as what might be termed an orthodox man of letters with his plays and poetry. By 1711 he was acquainted with the leading authors of the day, Addison, Congreve, Pope and Arbuthnot; he joined the Scriblerian set, and appears to have shared in their less than reverential attitude towards fashionable operatic doings. In 1713 he went to Hanover as part of the Earl of Clarendon's unsuccessful mission: this was a highly musical court, although there was no opera, and Handel served nominally as Kapellmeister. For Gay this must have been an enlightening and even a liberating experience, freeing him from some of the native British prejudices, born of the eclipse of 'English' opera in the previous decade. It was here, too, that he first met Princess Caroline, who was to remain such an important figure in his life. To the Scriblerians she posed an ambiguous cluster of questions—her political stance, initially anti-Walpolian, would be comforting during the reign of George I, but her intellectualism ran in directions which the Tory satirists found disconcerting, not least her support for Samuel Clarke's freethinking brand of theology.

After his return to London, Gay moved more and more into the orbit of the great Apollo of the Arts, Lord Burlington. This was to be another long-lasting relationship, and one which carried with it important consequences for Gay's professional opportunities.[9] But again there was a significant strand of influence in a direction where we should perhaps not have expected it—in respect of music rather than architecture or the visual arts in general. James Lees-Milne and others have given a full account of Burlington's rôle in artistic patronage after his return from Italy, and the support which the Earl gave to musicians is a striking aspect of this activity. Most relevantly, Handel took up residence in Burlington House during 1713 or 1714, and passed at least three years there. He may have returned in 1718 and 1719; a letter from the composer dated 15 July 1719 testifies to the close association still apparent.[10]

From Gay's side we have the splendid *Epistle to the Earl of*

Burlington, which probably came out in early 1716, and describes a journey to Devon made possible by the Earl's generosity. Around the same time appeared one of Gay's most assured poetic achievements, *Trivia*. A celebrated passage links both Handel and the poet himself with the munificent patron; at the great mansion in Piccadilly, we are told,

> There *Hendel* strikes the Strings, the melting Strain
> Transports the Soul, and thrills through ev'ry Vein;
> There oft' I enter (but with cleaner Shoes)
> For *Burlington*'s belov'd by ev'ry Muse.
>
> (497–500)[11]

Five years later Gay could still write to a friend, 'I live almost altogether with my Lord Burlington and pass my time very agreeably.'[12] The recipient of this letter was Francis Colman (c. 1690–1733), recently appointed British envoy to Florence, where subsequently his son George Colman the elder, the well-known dramatist, was born in 1732. Colman *père* was an opera fanatic and kept a diary of performances now lodged in the British Museum.[13] It is not certain precisely when Gay made his acquaintance, but here was another personal link with the world of opera. It is worth adding that the Grand Duke of Tuscany, Prince Gian Gastone de' Medici (at the very end of that noble line of Florentine rulers), was himself a great devotee of music; he took a close interest in Handel's work from the time of an early visit to Hamburg in 1703, and later sponsored Vivaldi. Handel came to the court of Tuscany in 1706 and his early tutelage in Italian forms and styles owed much to the entrée afforded him by the Medici connection. For his part Colman continued to involve himself in operatic matters after he took up residence in Florence. As late as 1730 Handel and Owen Swiney were in regular contact with him in their quest for singers to augment the strength of the Haymarket personnel.[14]

By 1716 Handel was already deeply enmeshed with the famous impresario John Jacob Heidegger, who had succeeded Swiney as manager at the Haymarket some years earlier. For the next two decades the composer and the entrepreneur were to remain two key figures in London opera, either as colleagues or as rivals. As well as opera, the Haymarket staged masquerades regularly, and it is in this connection that we encounter Gay's main reference to Heidegger. This occurs in a poem dating from around the autumn of 1718, but which was published in full as recently as 1975, in a collection of literary autographs assembled by the late P. J. Croft.[15] 'A Strange and Wonderfull Relation how the Devill Appeared last night at the [Opera House *deleted*] in the Haymarket' is an amusing though heavily topical (and occasionally obscure) ballad in a vein much favoured by Pope at this juncture. Heidegger had started out translating libretti for the opera house, but was by now settled in his best-known rôle as theatrical manager. On the inception of the Royal Academy of Music in 1719, joint direction was allocated to Handel and Heidegger, respectively in connection with artistic and business matters. Again it is clear that Gay was very well acquainted with the leading figures long before this venture, a fact which could be obscured when we recall that Heidegger's name does not so much as appear once in the standard biography by Irving.

In 1717 Handel had left Burlington House to take up an appointment under the Duke of Chandos (as the Earl of Carnarvon shortly became). It was at Cannons that *Acis and Galatea* was first performed privately (the dating of this work has only recently been established with any certainty), a decade before its public début at Lincoln's Inn Fields in March 1731 and a well publicized revival at the Little Theatre in the Haymarket in 1732.[16] Gay was substantially responsible for the text, with small contributions by Pope, John Hughes and Dryden. According to Irving, Gay personally supervised the 1731 production.[17] It is worth adding in parenthesis that the master of music at Cannons when Handel joined the establishment was none other than Johann Christoph Pepusch, who was of course to provide the new setting for the airs in *The Beggar's Opera*.

The fortunes and misfortunes of the Royal Academy have been well chronicled, and there is no need to rehearse the story in any detail here.[18] It is enough for present purposes to observe that the sixty-plus subscribers to the new institution in May 1719 included many personages familiar to Gay, including Bathurst, Pulteney (recipient of Gay's epistle from Paris, and Francis Colman's uncle by marriage), James Craggs the younger and Dr. Arbuthnot. The two largest single contributions were those of Burlington and Chandos, £1,000 each. Arbuthnot was to take a leading share in the affairs of the Academy and indeed served on its court of directors at the outset. He was a regular subscriber to Handel's published scores, and partly as a consequence has been saddled with the authorship of a number of pamphlets dealing with things operatic—generally without much plausible evidence in support. For example, an attack on the popularity of *The Beggar's Opera* which appeared soon after the work's première has been improbably assigned to him; and Fielding's early satire *The Masquerade*, 'inscrib'd to C---t H-d-g-r', has even been associated with Arbuthnot.[19]

A few months later Gay himself had recourse to public subscription when his *Poems* were issued. As with the Royal Academy, the most conspicuous spenders were Burlington and Chandos, each of whom entered his name for fifty copies. Among the other multiple subscribers were Pulteney, Bathurst, Newcastle and Craggs. In all, one can trace exactly half (that is, thirty-one) of the Academy subscribers on Gay's list. It hardly needs saying that mere presence on such a register is no proof of close personal links, indeed of acquaintance on any degree of intimacy whatever. Nonetheless, the fact that six members of the current court of the Academy (again, almost a third of the number) were subscribers to the Gay collection is surely worth noting. At the moment when Italian opera appeared to be getting a firm institutional hold in England, the main promoters were people willing to espouse Gay's cause and in some cases people taking a particularly active interest in the progress of his venture.

The overlap is more striking than in the case of the two Homer subscriptions mounted by Pope. This may well reflect a closer relationship on the part of Gay to the world of opera supporters. It is true that Pope made efforts on behalf of Bononcini's subscription edition of *Cantate* a year later, with many of the same names involved, but this was a unique circumstance, not confirmed by any other comparable event in Pope's entire career. It looks as if, for some reason that is now obscure, Pope may have sided with Bononcini and against Handel when factious occasions were devised to create a rivalry between the two Academy composers.[20] Such competitive events as the joint setting of *Muzio Scevola* in March 1721 (when Handel, Bononcini and Filipo Amadei set one act each) must have contributed to the difficulties of having two considerable composers working in tandem. There could well be echoes of this situation in the Peachum-Lockit relationship in *The Beggar's Opera*, although this is generally connected with the disputes of the 'brother' politicians, Walpole and Townshend—brothers-in-law, literally. It may be added that *The Craftsman* in the 1730s sometimes alluded to operatic quarrels as a feint when political issues were at stake; the 'two late famous Antagonists' in a story run in 1732 appear to be Handel and Bononcini, but may also refer to rivalries at Westminster. At all events Handel came out decisively on top in any protracted competition; Lord Egmont actually wrote that 'after some years' struggle to retain his throne, Bononcini abdicated.'[21]

Gay appears always to have believed in the German composer's superiority. Handel had in fact subscribed to Gay's poems; Bononcini is not listed, but he did not arrive in England until the autumn of 1720, at the instance of Burlington, too late to be recruited for Gay's venture. We have this information thanks to one more crucial link in the chain of acquaintances, that is a letter by the librettist and poet Paolo Antonio Rolli. His importance owes most to his fluent command of Italian in a situation where most adherents of Italian opera had a sketchy hold on the language; Rolli taught Princess Caroline's children and may even have given Italian lessons to Burlington. It was Rolli who compiled the libretto for *Muzio Scevola*, upon which Gay wrote an epigram or 'motto': 'Who here blame's Words or Verses, Songs or Singers,/ Like *Mutius Scævola*, will burn his Fingers.'[22]

Rolli's central rôle in the Italian opera world has been fully explored by George E. Dorris in an interesting and absorbing study; indeed, this essay might be regarded as a pendant to Dorris, insofar as the cultural space occupied by Rolli is more or less identical with the area on which (in my submission) Gay intermittently trespassed in the two decades preceding the appearance of *The Beggar's Opera*. Broadly speaking, Rolli came to be identified chiefly with the Bononcini party, and Niccolò Haym with Handel; but the grounds of these demarcations are complex and hard to disentangle—Dorris indicates that nationalistic factors entered into the matter. One significant fact which does emerge is that the star castrato Senesino 'threw his weight on the Italian side, against Handel' (as Dorris puts it), which implies that the satirists' persistent baiting of Senesino could be in some measure a pro-Handel gesture.[23]

It is impossible to establish any personal contact between Rolli and Gay, something which would obviously strengthen the case under contention. The same reservation does not apply in the instances we must next examine, those of the singer Anastasia Robinson and her husband the Earl of Peterborough.[24] The Earl had long been a hero of the Tories, and more specifically a figure greatly admired by the Scriblerian group. In his enforced retirement Peterborough took up a number of new interests, not least the gardening passion he shared with Pope. In 1722 he contracted a secret marriage with Anastasia Robinson, who had been second woman in the London company for a number of years, and had sung many Handelian rôles. There were a number of other links to the Scriblerus set, including the marriage of Anastasia's sister Margaret (or Peg) to Dr. Arbuthnot's brother George, an event duly chronicled in Gay's own correspondence. The Robinsons were Catholics, and hence it was Pope who kept most closely in touch with them. But Gay was well acquainted with both the Earl and his wife; we need not take seriously the story that he composed love letters to Mrs. Howard in the Earl's name.

An episode from the winter of 1723–24 brought the relationship to public notice. That season the Academy's winter programme had opened with Bononcini's *Farnace*, dedicated on its publication to Peterborough. Soon afterwards an altercation erupted concerning an insult which Senesino had offered to Anastasia Robinson. According to Lady Mary Wortley Montagu, writing to her sister,

> The 2nd Heroine [Anastasia] has engag'd halfe the Town in Arms from the Nicety of her virtue, which was not able to bear the too near approach of Senesino in the Opera, and her Condescention in accepting of Lord Peterborrough for a Champion.[25]

Senesino, she went on to report, had been obliged to confess on his knees that Anastasia was a nonpareil of virtue and beauty. Swift received an account of the same episode in Dublin, presumably from Charles Ford. He wrote to Ford in February

1724, 'I do not understand as Raillery what you say upon the Court of the Musical Academy.'[26] This was a disclaimer Gay could not have made, after his long residence at the home of Burlington, the main promoter of things Italian in contemporary London. Moreover, as we have seen, the Academy court comprised many individuals who had taken an active part in supporting Gay's own work. It was only an augmentation of the existing state of affairs when Gay's personal acquaintances, Peterborough and his wife, became involved in one of the notorious personal feuds which were to plague Academy doings.

There is a particular reason why the ups and downs of the Academy should have had a weird familiarity at this juncture. The best known 'court' of directors was of course that of the South Sea Company, and the peccant members were even at this moment subject to prosecution and sequestration. The way in which the Academy obtained money it needed urgently—by a 'call' at intervals for further subscriptions—exactly matched the procedures of the South Sea Company in that baneful year of horrific memory, 1720.[27] Like everyone else, Gay had been a close observer of these happenings, not least because he himself had lost money in the fiasco—although even the diligent Irving was unable to put an exact figure on his losses.[28] Dorris has made the suggestive conjecture that the rapid change in personnel among the Academy court (only two of the peers elected in 1719 survived a year later) may have been connected with South Sea matters.[29] One of the two peers to be re-elected was Burlington, whilst survivors among the twelve gentlemen members included Bryan Fairfax, Thomas Coke, George Harrison, William Pulteney and Francis Whitworth, all subscribers to Gay's poems. New members listed are Brigadier-General Dormer and Brigadier-General Hunter, both men with durable links to the Scriblerian group; and several others listed in Gay's volume. Arbuthnot is a surprising omission from the new court.

Of all the new appointments, the most significant for Gay was emphatically that of the Duke of Queensberry. It is not necessary here to rehearse the important part played in Gay's career by Queensberry and his wife. More immediately relevant is the fact that both the Duke and the Duchess had entered their

157

names for twenty-five copies of Bononcini's *Cantate* in 1721. This was the subscription mounted whilst Bononcini was living at Twickenham, and one which Pope seems to have assisted. Dorris rightly observes that (despite a fulsome dedication to George I) it was the opposition nobility, pinning their reversionary hopes on the Prince of Wales, who showed their 'strong partisanship' in rallying to Bononcini's cause.[30] The Queensberry family were persistent in what might be called the oppositional rôle, most famously in the reign of George II at the time of Gay's suppressed ballad opera *Polly*. The point to stress here is that their leanings had drawn them into the politics of opera as early as 1721. The Duke had subscribed to the *Poems* in 1720, partly it is certain on behalf of his wife, but it was a few years before really close contact developed. Significantly, it is in respect of the period around 1725 that Irving notes Gay as 'at this time being more strongly drawn' into the 'orbit' of the Duchess.[31]

3

We have now reached a point where we can look more closely at the famous passage in Gay's letter to Swift of 3 February 1723. Usually this is cited as an isolated excerpt, as though it were the first time Gay had ever noticed Italian opera. In the light of the foregoing discussion, it may be possible to avoid the misconceptions which such an assumption would breed. It should be remembered that even as recently as 1966 the editor of Gay's letters did not know of his poem concerning Heidegger, and that when Irving cited the letter (adding the comments quoted at the beginning of the second section of this essay), he did not have available much of the relevant background information supplied by Dorris, not to mention modern Handel scholarship. The passage runs as follows:

> As for the reigning Amusement of the town, tis entirely Musick. real fiddles, Bass Viols and Hautboys not poetical Harps, Lyres, and reeds. Theres nobody allow'd to say I sing but an Eunuch or an Italian Woman. Every body is grown now as great a judge of Musick as they were in your time of Poetry. and folks that could not distinguish one tune from another now daily dispute about the different Styles of Hendel, Bononcini, and Attilliò. People

have now forgot Homer, and Virgil & Caesar, or at least they
have lost their ranks, for in London and Westminster in all polite
conversation's Senesino is daily voted to be the greatest man that
ever liv'd.[32]

It would be idle to deny that this echoes the most common
anti-operatic attitudes of the time; John Dennis could not have
expressed much more clearly the fear that serious 'high'
literature would be supplanted by popular 'low' entertainment
in the shape of opera. And it may well be that Gay was
beginning to have doubts concerning the form: the kind of
admiration for London opera (and especially the singing of
Anastasia Robinson), which he had expressed in his *Epistle to
Pulteney* (1717),[33] has been replaced by a conventionalized
jokiness at the expense of the dominance of Italianate music.
Nonetheless, it is not straining a point to observe that the scorn
is all directed at the cult of opera, rather than opera itself, much
as Peter Lewis suggests. Handel and his fellow composers
emerge relatively unscathed, even if the reference to Senesino is
unmistakably sneering. The force of the criticism is enhanced
by the fact that Gay—unlike Swift, for instance—had been
watching the progress of these cult figures ever since their
arrival in England.

It ought to be possible to apply some of the findings of this
enquiry, however tentatively, to *The Beggar's Opera* itself.
Clearly there is a limit to the critical relevance of any biographical synthesis along the lines I have attempted. At the
same time, the perception it may offer into Gay's relationship to
the world of opera need not be wholly discounted. If we
consider John Fuller's claim that 'Gay's parody of Italian opera
is not as central to the play as has sometimes been supposed,
and may represent comparatively late thoughts in his con-
ception of the piece',[34] then one can point out that Gay had
been witnessing operatic feuds long before the celebrated
quarrel on stage in 1727, when Faustina and Cuzzoni came to
blows in a manner foreshadowing Polly and Lucy.[35] Moreover,
Gay's joking suggestions in his correspondence that the success
of *The Beggar's Opera* was driving the Academy out of business
do confirm the impression that the satire *was* felt to aim directly
at highfalutin Italianate modes of theatrical expression.[36] We

159

know that Gay had at least some inklings of *The Beggar's Opera* germinating in his mind at least as early as 1723[37]; and, as we have seen, he was at that time seriously, if not in any sense obsessively, involved in the orbit of the Academy. Friendships do not guarantee shared patterns of interest, still less common affections, but they are in themselves a species of elective affinity. That Gay should have been drawn to so many in the penumbra of opera, and they to him, is surely a relevant circumstance.

There is another alternative. Perhaps, like much Augustan satire, *The Beggar's Opera* is to be viewed as a kind of Parthian riposte, a work of recantation which feeds upon lost loyalties and forsaken allegiances. The Scriblerian corpus often seems to contain a retrospective element of apologia, or even disguised palinode: does not even *The Dunciad* mock the decayed ideals of Pope's youth, lamenting the lost possibilities of scholarship as it flays the follies of contemporary book-making?

In any case, Gay was too intelligent to embrace all the narrow prejudices of anti-operatic polemic. If he was not, by the standards of men like Arbuthnot, especially musical, he was too close to the theatrical in his inmost being as a writer to miss the electric quality of the best Handelian opera, or to overlook its genuine roots in high artistic tradition. *The Beggar's Opera* subverts by loose associational and allusive means, not by minute line-by-line parody. Yet, the more closely one examines the record, the plainer it becomes that John Gay was making sport of a mode he knew well, whose rise and fall he had observed quite narrowly, and in whose early cult he had even taken some share.

NOTES

1. Quotations from Peter Lewis, *John Gay: The Beggar's Opera* (London, 1976), pp. 23, 10–11.
2. *John Gay* (London, 1964), p. 27.
3. Roberts (ed.), *The Beggar's Opera* (London, 1969), pp. xxii–xxiii.
4. C. F. Burgess (ed.), *The Beggar's Opera and Companion Pieces* (Arlington Heights, Ill., 1966), pp. xxii, xiv.
5. *Hogarth Illustrated*, 3 vols. (London, 1791–98), II, 575.

6. Irving, *John Gay: Favorite of the Wits* (Durham, N.C., 1940; reprinted New York, 1962), p. 251.
7. Quoted in Otto Erich Deutsch, *Handel: A Documentary Biography* (London, 1955), pp. 32–3.
8. Irving, p. 28.
9. See James Lees-Milne, *Earls of Creation* (London, 1962), pp. 103–69, especially p. 113; and Stanley Boorman, 'Burlington and Music', *Apollo of the Arts: Lord Burlington and his Circle* (Nottingham, 1973), pp. 16–18.
10. See Deutsch, p. 93.
11. *PP*, I, 157.
12. *Letters*, p. 39.
13. See Deutsch, p. 50, who expresses doubts about Colman's authorship of the opera diary; and George E. Dorris, *Paolo Rolli and the Italian Circle in London 1715–1744* (The Hague, 1967), p. 247.
14. See Deutsch, pp. 260–62; and Dorris, p. 248.
15. P. J. Croft (ed.), *Autograph Poetry in the English Language* (London, 1975), pp. 64–8.
16. See P. Rogers, 'Dating *Acis and Galatea*', *Musical Times*, 114 (1973), 792, where evidence is brought to locate the composition around May 1718.
17. See Irving, p. 283.
18. The story of the Academy can be followed in snatches in Deutsch; for a recent and more connected account, see H. C. Robbins Landon, *Handel and his World* (London, 1984), pp. 96–112.
19. For Arbuthnot's superior knowledge of music compared with the other Scriblerians, see the quotation from J. C. Smith's *Anecdotes* in Irving, p. 284. David Dalrymple, in a letter to the Earl of London in 1718, describes Arbuthnot as of the club of composers active in promoting *Acis and Galatea*: see Rogers, loc. cit.
20. See George Sherburn (ed.), *The Correspondence of Alexander Pope* (Oxford, 1956), II, 99. It is clear that the Bononcini subscription was in part an opposition gesture, but there are ramifications not yet fully explored.
21. Deutsch, pp. 124–25, 277, 295.
22. *PP*, I, 282.
23. Information in this paragraph is derived from Dorris, quotation from pp. 82–3. Dorris, p. 83, cites the famous epigram by John Byrom which 'crystallized' the rivalry between Handel and Bononcini. In addition Dorris, p. 139, stresses Rolli's close relations with Burlington and Bathurst, to whom Gay himself was so intimately linked. Finally, Dorris draws attention to other figures active in the Academy and close to Rolli, such as the Duke of Rutland, who supported Gay's *Poems*.
24. See William Stebbing, *Peterborough* (London, 1890), pp. 197–200. The closest to a first-hand account of these matters is provided by Mrs. Delany, as quoted by Charles Burney in his *General History of Music*, ed. Frank Mercer (reprinted New York, 1957), II, 712–13. For Hogarth's depiction of Peterborough as a supplicant of Cuzzoni in 'Masquerades and Operas', see Dorris, p. 85. He and his wife regularly entertained Giuseppe Riva, one of Rolli's closest friends (Dorris, p. 206).
25. Robert Halsband (ed.), *The Complete Letters of Lady Mary Wortley Montagu*

26. Harold Williams (ed.), *The Correspondence of Jonathan Swift* (Oxford, 1963–65), III, 6.
27. Boorman points out that satirists often proposed a comparison beween the Academy and the South Sea Company (p. 17).
28. See Irving, p. 186.
29. See Dorris, p. 79.
30. Dorris, p. 80.
31. Irving, p. 209. It has even been suggested that the Duchess aided Gay in the composition of *Polly* (the source is Anna Porter, daughter of the painter Allan Ramsay). See Alastair Smart, *The Life and Art of Allan Ramsay* (London, 1952), p. 9.
32. *Letters*, p. 43. Deutsch (p. 149) and Dorris (p. 84) are amongst others who quote the passage.
33. See *PP*, I, 213. The lines contrast stiff French opera productions with the thrilling immediacy of London offerings, in particular the emotional effect of Anastasia's voice.
34. 'Introduction', *DW*, I, 45. Cf. Bertrand Bronson, '*The Beggar's Opera*', *Studies in the Comic* (Berkeley and Los Angeles, 1941), p. 216.
35. There are many accounts of the Faustina-Cuzzoni quarrel; one of the best is to be found in Dorris, pp. 89–94 (followed by an immediate application of the contretemps to *The Beggar's Opera*), as 'one of a series of running allusions throughout the work, which makes good-natured fun of certain conventions in the opera, of particular operas, and of events in the operatic world' (p. 94). It is the last category of allusion which Fuller perhaps does not consider sufficiently.
36. See *Letters*, pp. 71–2.
37. See *Letters*, p. 45. It was in 1723 that Antonio Cocchi arrived in England, to establish immediate intimacy with the Italian opera circle, notably Rolli and Burlington (to which the very first edition of Benvenuto Cellini's autobiography was dedicated by Cocchi). Cocchi became friendly in due course with Francis Colman and Dr. Richard Mead, among Gay's acquaintance—not to mention Lord Hervey, Allan Ramsay, Joseph Spence, Lord Orrery and, most famously, Gray and Horace Walpole. See Dorris, pp. 240–68.

8

The Migrant Muses: A Study of Gay's Later Drama

by CAROLYN D. WILLIAMS

One of Pope's epitaphs on Gay tells only half the truth:

> Favourite of the muses,
> He was led by them to every elegant art:
> Refined in taste,
> And fraught with graces all his own:
> In various kinds of poetry
> Superior to many,
> Inferior to none.[1]

The muses were, in fact, cruelly capricious in their favours, alternately wafting Gay to pinnacles of brilliance and leaving him to flounder through a slough of well-intentioned tedium. They decreed that his masterpieces should be inimitable—even by Gay himself. Most exasperating of all was their habit of slipping away without letting him know they had gone: the man who could proudly offer *Polly* as a sequel to *The Beggar's Opera*, or follow *Fables I* with *Fables II*, clearly found it difficult to assess the quality of his own output.

The unevenness of Gay's work, combined with the apparently effortless elegance of his successes, gave the impression that everything came by chance. Dr. Johnson, doubtless perplexed by this haphazard performance and annoyed by the necessity of

163

reading (or finding excuses not to read) so much that was second-rate, treated Gay as a minor figure who happened to please the public taste from time to time. According to Johnson, the success of *The Shepherd's Week* was partly accidental: 'the effect of reality and truth became conspicuous, even when the intention was to shew them groveling and degraded.' He dismissed *The What D'Ye Call It* as beneath critical attention: 'Of this performance the value certainly is but little; but it was one of the lucky trifles that give pleasure by novelty.' Inevitably, *The Beggar's Opera* became 'this lucky piece'. *Trivia* confronted Johnson with a degree of excellence he was unable to ignore: 'To *Trivia* may be allowed all that it claims: it is spritely, various, and pleasant.' But Johnson still found a way to imply that Gay did not deserve all the credit: 'The subject is of that kind which Gay was by nature qualified to adorn.' In other words, Gay could not help writing *Trivia*, because that was what he was born for. Johnson gives the impression that he would have rated Gay more highly if he had been a more consistent writer, even if that consistency had been achieved at the expense of originality. He quoted with approval the female critic who relegated Gay to 'a lower order', but the real problem was Gay's inability to stay at one level long enough to be assigned to any order at all.[2]

Efforts to overthrow Johnson's verdict culminated fifty years ago with the publication of William Empson's *Some Versions of Pastoral* (1935), after which it has been possible to take Gay seriously without undue critical embarrassment. Some of his works, especially *The Beggar's Opera*, have received a great deal of respectful attention, and his tercentenary provided a welcome opportunity for making up deficiencies in other areas. However, a natural tendency to concentrate on Gay's best work has only increased general bewilderment at the muses' flighty conduct. In order to understand Gay properly, it is necessary to find out what he was trying to achieve when he was writing badly. 'Badly', of course, is a relative term when applied to Gay: even *Dione* displays some fugitive lyrical charm. Still, no one would attempt to deny that some of his works are better than others. The standard of his drama is particularly prone to fluctuation, exemplified most clearly by his failure to consolidate the position he gained by *The Beggar's Opera*. John Fuller sees Gay's later drama as the result of a pious but regrettable sacrifice of wit to responsibility:

> Like Pope, Gay 'stoop'd to Truth', but his growing preoccupation with sexual mores and with political corruption may seem at times a poor exchange for the imaginative riches of Scriblerian farce and burlesque.[3]

I should like to argue for a broader definition of 'Scriblerian' to encompass Gay's later drama, and help to account for its patchiness by showing that its faults and virtues owe just as much to Scriblerian influences as his earlier work. Gay's problems are a question of manner rather than matter: sexual mores, after all, loom large in such successes as *The What D'Ye Call It* and *Three Hours after Marriage*, and combine with political corruption to dominate *The Beggar's Opera*. Nor can it be reckoned an un-Scriblerian activity to follow Pope (not to mention Swift and Arbuthnot) into the realms of serious moral satire. Gay's troubles arose when he attempted to deal with common Scriblerian preoccupations in a way that was unsuited to his chosen form. An examination of *Polly*, *Achilles* and *The Distress'd Wife* will show where his difficulties lay.

Achilles, posthumously produced in February 1733, was condemned for tedium: an article in the *Daily Courant* (16 February 1733) charitably maintained that it was an unfinished piece, completed by a committee of Gay's friends, since 'Mr. *Gay* could not *deviate* into so much *Dulness*'.[4] Exception was also taken to the vulgarity (sometimes amounting to indecency) of the lyrics. This often caused more offence in the playhouse than in the closet, where readers could enjoy low humour without having their own virtue or gentility called into question. The most conspicuous deficiency of *The Distress'd Wife*, another posthumous production, is the character drawing. As a comedy of manners, it arouses expectations of realism and consistency that are disappointed in audience and readers alike. In a letter to Elizabeth Young (28 September 1743), James Thomson observed that Lady Willit's 'Affections are drawn so monstrous, they are not the Affectations of a Woman of Sense and Wit but of a Fool.' Miss Friendless's acceptance of the aging Lord Courtlove distressed Thomson who had 'expected, from her sensible and serious Turn, that she would have disdained the Proposal, and rather lived in a Cottage with some Person she loved'.[5] Fuller detects a 'touch of primitivism'[6] in these cavils, but even in these days of post-structuralist sophistication, traditional character criticism still haunts the theatre, refusing to be exorcized by repeated incantations that the text's the thing. However unscrupulously the dramatist uses a character as a moral exemplum or a convenient plot device, the actor insists on investing the part with a recognizable human identity, as does the theatrically minded reader of plays. *Polly* was a special case: it was banned before rehearsal in December 1728 and not performed until 1777. This may not have been an unqualified disaster for Gay. One can only imagine how an uninitiated first-night audience, all agog for the highly publicized sequel to the longest running show in history, would have responded to Macheath's impenetrable blackface disguise, Polly's transvestite heroics, and the interminably self-righteous noble savages. But one would much rather not.

In each instance, Gay required his cast to give bodily form to notions that were plausibly expressed in other Scriblerian texts (his own included) but which looked disconcertingly flimsy on stage. Idealistic moral, economic and political theory abounded; so did predictable diatribes on corrupt practice. Nominally happy endings were contrived by proposing impracticable solutions to insoluble problems. This made life awkward for the actors, and worse for the actresses, who carried the additional burden of exemplifying Scriblerian ideas about women. The Scriblerians were not conspicuously misogynist, by contemporary standards; they were capable of feeling, and expressing, genuine admiration for the virtues, charms and intellectual achievements of individual women. But they tended to view the sex as a whole with a mixture of suspicion and contempt that reflected the most drearily conservative doctrines of female inferiority—except for the occasions when they added a further twist of their own devising. And Gay, as usual, took his colour from his company.

However inadequate Pope's *Epistle to a Lady* (1735) may seem as an account of women in general, there is no disputing its accuracy as a survey of women in Gay's drama:

> In Men, we various Ruling Passions find,
> In Women, two almost divide the kind;

Those, only fix'd, they first or last obey,
The Love of Pleasure, and the Love of Sway.
    That, Nature gives; and where the lesson taught
Is but to please, can Pleasure seem a fault?
Experience, this; by Man's oppression curst,
They seek the second not to lose the first.

(207–14)[7]

Gay's women employ various subversive strategies to gain their ends; the most commonly effective is the cultivation of an attractive surface, as enjoined in *Achilles* by the court lady Artemona:

Think of Dress in ev'ry Light;
    'Tis Woman's chiefest Duty;
Neglecting that, our selves we slight
    And undervalue Beauty.
That allures the Lover's Eye,
    And graces every Action;
Besides, when not a Creature's by,
    'Tis inward Satisfaction.

(III, viii, 7–14)[8]

The end of the song suggests that most women are so consumed by vanity that beauty has ceased to be a means and become an end in itself.

Achilles provides a hospitable niche for this idea, since the plot hinges on the notion that preoccupation with finery is a distinguishing sexual characteristic. The young warrior prince Achilles, disguised as a girl at the behest of his mother, who wishes to keep him out of the Trojan War, is living at the court of Scyros. In order to expose him, Ulysses and Diomedes assume the rôle of merchants, peddling cloth, jewels, weapons and armour. The girls are fascinated by the adornments; the boy blows his cover by seizing a sword. If Achilles had shared his companions' concern with fashion, or any of the girls had been capable of taking an intelligent interest in Bronze Age metallurgy, the scheme would have misfired. An apparent exception to the feminine rule is Deidamia, Achilles's bedfellow, who is so worried by other matters that she pays hardly any attention to the merchants' wares. This anxiety, however, is still articulated in terms of dress; she is afraid that Achilles's indifference to clothes will betray his sex and consequently ruin

167

her reputation—which cannot, in any case, last much longer, since her pregnancy is becoming visible to observant eyes, despite her attempts to hide it under her gown.

Achilles and *The Distress'd Wife* show women attending to their chiefest duty in a woefully unbusinesslike manner. Lady Willit in the latter play runs up huge bills without caring that her husband will be unable to pay them: 'Was there ever a Man, who grew to be of any Consequence, who did not run out?—Would you have Credit, and not make use of it?' (I, ii, 58–61). Incurring debt was regarded as antisocial; George Lillo makes this point in *The London Merchant* (1731), when the exemplary Mr. Thorowgood instructs his apprentice

> to look carefully over the files to see whether there are any tradesmen's bills unpaid and, if there are, to send and discharge 'em. We must not let artificers lose their time, so useful to the public and their families, in unnecessary attendance. (I, i, 55–9)[9]

Prompt payment was not a virtue required only from the bourgeoisie; William Darrell, gentleman and Jesuit, inveighed against debtors in *The Gentleman Instructed* (1704), a conduct book ostensibly directed to the nobility:

> Now when a Creditor must be eternally upon the Trot to come up to his Debtor, and ply at all the *Coffee-houses* for Intelligence of his Haunts, the Irons cool at home, Trade sinks, Work is at a Stand, and a Bankrupt treads upon his Heels. For how shall a Merchant pay his Debts, who receives none? Now, Sir, here is *lucrum cessans* on the one hand, and *damnun emergens* on the other, and in the Sight of God you stand responsible for both: They will be put to your Accounts, and you must either repair 'em here, or suffer for 'em hereafter.[10]

Lillo and Darrell condemned debt as a general evil; the specific link between women and irresponsible expenditure appears more characteristic of Swift, who expresses his usual views with only a slight increase of his customary venom when he takes on the mask of the projector in *A Modest Proposal* (1729):

> ... the Body of a plump Girl of fifteen, who was crucified for an Attempt to poison the Emperor, was sold to his Imperial *Majesty's prime Minister of State*, and other great *Mandarins* of the Court, *in Joints from the Gibbet*, at Four hundred Crowns. Neither indeed can I deny, that if the same Use were made of several

plump young girls in this Town, who, without one single Groat to their Fortunes, cannot stir Abroad without a Chair, and appear at the *Play-house*, and *Assemblies* in foreign Fineries, which they never will pay for; the Kingdom would not be the worse.[11]

Scriblerian economics also underlie another constant in female consumerism as perceived by Gay: women prefer imported goods to native manufacture. As Artemona observes in *Achilles*: 'There must be something pretty in every thing that is foreign' (III, x, 64–5). In the same play, Philoe rejects a length of cloth, even though she likes the design, because it is locally made. She is like the women of quality in eighteenth-century Dublin 'who seldom wear any of our own Goods, Except impos'd on them under the Name of Foreign Works'.[12] The tastes of Artemona, Philoe and Lady Willit are typical of the female extravagance condemned by Swift in his *Answer to Several Letters from Unknown Persons* (1729):

> Is it not the highest Indignity to human nature, that men should be such poltrons as to suffer the Kingdom and themselves to be undone, by the Vanity, the Folly, the Pride, and Wantonness of their Wives, who under their present Corruptions seem to be a kind of animal suffered for our sins to be sent into the world for the Destruction of Familyes, Societyes, and Kingdoms; and whose whole study seems directed to be as expensive as they possibly can in every useless article of living, who by long practice can reconcile the most pernicious forein Drugs to their health and pleasure, provided they are but expensive; as Starlings grow fat with henbane: who contract a Robustness by meer practice of Sloth and Luxury: who can play deep severall hours after midnight, sleep beyond noon; revel upon Indian poisons, and spend the revenue of a moderate family to adorn a nauseous unwholesom living Carcase.[13]

Unfortunately for Gay, a playwright cannot indulge his imagination as freely as a pamphleteer; in bringing these creatures on stage, he did not realize that his audience expected to see women, and Swift had provided him with a formula for monsters.

Of course, the Scriblerians were not the first to take this view of women: it had long been proverbial that 'far fetched and dear bought is good for ladies.' Lady Dainty shows similar proclivities in Colley Cibber's comedy, *The Double Gallant* (1707), but she is provided with a discerning friend who refuses to share her perverse tastes:

> *Lady Dainty*. How came you, dear *Sylvia*, to be reconcil'd to any thing in an *India* House: You us'd to have a most barbarous inclination for our own odious Manufactures.
> *Sylvia*. Nay, Madam, I am only going to recruit my *Tea Table*: As to the rest of their Trumpery, I am as much out of humour with it as ever. . . .
> *Lady Dainty*. Well, thou art a pleasant Creature, thy distast is so diverting!
> *Sylvia*. And your Ladyship is so expensive, that really I am not able to come into it.
> *Lady Dainty*. Now, 'tis to me prodigious! how some Women can muddle away their Money upon Houswifry, Children, Books, and Charities, when there are so many well-bred Ways, and foreign Curiosities, that more elegantly require it—I have every Morning the Rarities of all Countries brought to me, and am in love with every New thing I see. (III)[14]

Cibber makes many of his most telling dramatic effects by juxtaposing different types of women; Scriblerian satire usually reaches the conclusion that all women are the same.

This is not to say that any one woman will be recognizably herself from one moment to the next: '*varium et mutabile semper/femina*' (Virgil's *Aeneid*, IV, 569–70). Pope's *Epistle to a Lady* expresses this paradox:

> Nothing so true as what you once let fall,
> 'Most Women have no Characters at all'.
> Matter too soft a lasting mark to bear,
> And best distinguish'd by black, brown, or fair. . . .
>   Come then, the colours and the ground prepare!
> Dip in the Rainbow, trick her off in Air,
> Chuse a firm Cloud, before it fall, and in it
> Catch, ere she change, the Cynthia of this minute.
>   (1–4, 17–20)[15]

If women are such shifting—not to say shifty—characters, how can their mental processes be recorded? *The Rape of the Lock* (1714) takes an appropriately indirect approach, working by allusion—almost by allegory. According to David Fairer, the poem 'is concerned with the imagination as a glorious, amoral, irresponsible and alluring thing, a paradoxical cluster of adjectives as apt for Belinda as for the sylphs'.[16] To say that the sylphs represent Belinda's imagination is not far from saying that they represent Belinda. Pope's language suggests that they are spectacular, impalpable, and not too reliable:

> Loose to the Wind their airy Garments flew,
> Thin glitt'ring Textures of the filmy Dew;
> Dipt in the richest Tincture of the Skies,
> Where Light disports in ever-mingling Dies,
> While ev'ry Beam new transient Colours flings,
> Colours that change whene'er they wave their Wings.
>
> (II, 63–8)[17]

Dramatists have made theatrical capital from female unpredictability for centuries, despite the danger that the 'infinite variety' which sounds so enchanting when Enobarbus describes its effect on Cleopatra's admirers might degenerate into maddening indecisiveness when it actually appears on stage. Forced to rely on the talents of a flesh-and-blood performer, unaided by a glamorizing aura of sylphs, they take certain precautions to ensure that their women do not appear merely demented. It is easy for narrative poets, such as Dryden in *Cymon and Iphigenia* (1700), to work on the assumption that it is a woman's privilege to change her mind:

> Then impotent of Mind, with alter'd Sense,
> She hugg'd th' Offender, and forgave th' Offence,
> Sex to the last. (366–68)[18]

Dramatists, however, have no opportunity for explaining developments with helpful asides *in propria persona*. They try to make sure that their characters' words and actions are self-explanatory, which accounts for their reluctance to show behaviour that has no apparent explanation at all. Women who vacillate on stage often do so on purpose, as a means of manipulating the men who are supposed—officially, at any rate—to control their destiny. Hippolita, in Wycherley's *The Gentleman Dancing-Master* (1672), pretends to change her mind in order to test her lover's sincerity. Millamant, the supreme exponent of inconsistency as sexual strategy, uses her lightning-swift changes of mood to keep Mirabel off balance, perplexed, and duly besotted in Congreve's *The Way of the World* (1700).

When a dramatist shows a woman who is genuinely unable to

make up her mind, her confusion often serves as a distress signal, to indicate an anxiety that she is unable to discuss with the other characters. The audience is usually put in possession of enough information to interpret her behaviour correctly, even when she does not appear to be aware of its significance herself. Lady Lurewell in Farquhar's *Sir Harry Wildair* (1701) is a typical case: exacting, capricious, and thoroughly unreasonable, she makes life miserable for herself and her entire household, but is unable to define the cause of her discontent:

> *Lady Lurewell.* Oh, Mr. Remnant! I don't know what ails these stays you have made me; but something is the matter, I don't like 'em.
> *Remnant.* I am very sorry for that, madam. But what fault does your ladyship find?
> *Lady Lurewell.* I don't know where the fault lies; but in short, I don't like 'em; I can't tell how; the things are well enough made, but I don't like 'em.
> *Remnant.* Are they too wide, madam?
> *Lady Lurewell.* No.
> *Remnant.* Too strait, perhaps?
> *Lady Lurewell.* Not at all! they fit me very well, but—Lard bless me! can't you tell where the fault lies? (II, i, 58–70)[19]

The fault lies with her recent marriage to Colonel Standard. The new stays, with their association of close restraint on the female physique, represent the marriage bond; her dislike shows that she has not yet reconciled herself to the adjustments she will have to make in her way of life. The stays do fit her, however, and there is no objective reason why she should not be perfectly comfortable: Colonel Standard is a good match and they are destined, after a few ups and downs, to live happily ever after. The audience might not be able to decode all these subtleties at first hearing, but they have certainly been fed enough data to be able to deduce that the lady's troubles are marital, not sartorial, in origin.

Lady Willit, on the other hand, produces virtuoso exhibitions of dithering for dithering's sake, as in a scene with her maid Fetch:

> *Lady Willit.* BLESS me!—How can any Mortal be so awkward! [Fetch *combing her Hair.*]—Dost think I have no Feeling?—Am I to be flea'd alive?—Go—begone. [*going.*] Come hither. [*returning.*]—

Who do you think is to dress me?—Tell 'em I'll have the Tea-kettle ready this Instant. [*going.*]—Is the Wench distracted?— What, am I to sit all Day long with my Hair about my Ears like a Mermaid? [*returning.*]—Now, I'll be sworn for't, thou hast not spoke for the Tea-water all this while, though I order'd it an Hour ago.

Fetch. Not by *me*, Madam.

Lady Willit. So you tell me I lye—that's all. [*going.*]—What is the blundering Fool a doing?—Am I to be dress'd to Day or no? [*returning.*]—Bid the Porter bring me up the Book of Visits.— Why don't you go? [*going.*]—Must I bid you do the same Thing a thousand Times over and over again?—I am to have no Breakfast to Day, that I find you are determin'd upon. (II, i, 1–17)

The first outbreak might be attributed to her natural agitation on learning that her husband means to take her back to the country, but Fetch's repeated protests imply that this is her normal *modus operandi*:

> If it be not an unreasonable Request from a Servant, I could wish your Ladyship would know your own Mind before you speak;— 'twould save you a great many Words, and me a great deal of Trouble. (IV, iv, 6–9)

A realistic interpretation might account for her behaviour by reference to various inner conflicts deducible from the text, such as the tension between her envy of Lady Frankair's flair for adultery and her fear of following her example. But Gay offers no explicit endorsement of this reading. Lady Willit's paranoid tone, if taken literally, could only issue from a neurotic state far too painful to be contained within the bounds of comedy. It is hard to resist the conclusion that Lady Willit dithers chiefly because Gay intends to make her a compendium of fashionable female failings.

This suspicion is confirmed by comparison with the girls in *Achilles*. The chief difference is that Lady Willit's condition is indistinguishable from mental illness, whereas Artemona and her companions appear to be labouring under some form of mental handicap. The moral is that all fine ladies are mad or stupid, as a just consequence of their selfishness, frivolity and affectation. Philoe suffers from the same sort of absent-minded-ness as Lady Willit:

Servant. The Anti-chamber, Madam, is crowded with Trades-People.

Philoe. Did not I tell you that I wou'd not be troubled with those impertinent Creatures?—But hold—I had forgot I sent for 'em.—Let 'em wait. (III, ix, 8–12)

When her mind is present, it serves her no better:

Ulysses. We have things of all kinds, Ladies.

Philoe. Of all kinds!—Now that is just what I wanted to see.
(III, x, 19–21)

The precision of 'just' is ridiculously nullified by the hopelessly vague 'all kinds', so that the two halves of her speech cancel each other out. Language is similarly mistreated by Lesbia: 'This very individual Pattern, in a blue Pink, had been infinitely charming' (III, x, 52–3). Her words are debased coinage. To provide an equivalent for her ideas, she either pays out too many (hence the tautology of 'this very individual') or chooses an inappropriately high denomination (the extravagance of 'infinitely'). As for the 'blue Pink', it has the same self-negating quality as Philoe's utterance, suggesting that there may not be an idea behind it at all. It might refer to a pink so deeply tinged with blue that it verges on mauve, but the overall satiric tendency of the dialogue suggests that Gay was endeavouring to create a touch of exuberant nonsense, analogous to the modern 'sky blue pink with orange spots on'. All in all, Gay's brand of girl talk is far from convincing.

This is disappointing because elsewhere he writes about women and their clothes with sympathy, precision and infectious delight. Even the notion that ladies are mindless creatures, activated by forces of nature, can appear charming in a descriptive passage that does not require the reader to think in terms of individual women:

> The Ladies gayly dress'd, the *Mall* adorn
> With various Dyes, and paint the sunny Morn;
> The wanton Fawns with frisking Pleasure range,
> And chirping Sparrows greet the welcome Change:
> Not that their Minds with greater Skill are fraught,
> Endu'd by Instinct, or by Reason taught,
> The Seasons operate on every Breast;
> 'Tis hence that Fawns are brisk, and Ladies drest.
> (*Trivia*, I, 145–52)[20]

A similar connection between female fashion and organic life appears in *The Fan*:

> Should you the rich Brocaded Suit unfold,
> Where rising Flow'rs grow stiff with frosted Gold;
> The dazled Muse would from her Subject stray,
> And in a Maze of Fashions lose her Way.

(I, 241–44)

The spontaneous vitality implied by 'unfold', 'rising' and 'grow', all associated with burgeoning vegetation, gives the impression that these flowers, worked to please the ladies, have been called into being by the natural laws that control the growth of real plants: not such an improbable hypothesis, if the same laws also govern the ladies' fancy. The use of 'frosted'— another natural process at work—strengthens the impression that fashion develops of its own accord without conscious human intervention, a phenomenon to be celebrated by the poet with the same respectful admiration as a sunset or a storm at sea. Then 'Gold' returns to the manufactured, inorganic reality, inviting the reader to participate with Gay in an ironic reappraisal of the relationship between nature and artifice.

If the poet handles his subject so felicitously, why does the dramatist blunder? Once more, the muses have been repelled by sound Scriblerian principles. 'Th'inconstant Equipage of Female Dress' (*The Fan*, I, 230) exemplifies the moral instability that Swift, Pope and Arbuthnot saw as a threat to civilization. Gay's court ladies are devoid of values; even aesthetic standards are unknown to them. 'Unless you have any thing that is absolutely new and very uncommon,' warns Artemona, 'you will give us and your selves, Gentlemen, but unnecessary Trouble' (III, x, 1–3). Taking novelty as a criterion of merit reduces every statement to nonsense sooner or later, as Swift demonstrates in *A Tale of a Tub*. He claims 'an absolute Authority in Right, as the *freshest Modern*, which gives me a Despotick Power over all Authors before me', but his work is avowedly 'calculated for this present Month of *August*, 1697',[21] and not published till 1704, which discredits it on its own terms. The quest for novelty was traditionally perceived as a symptom of political decadence as well as intellectual chaos. In *Catiline* (1611) Ben Jonson associated it with the fall of Rome:

> Can nothing great, and at the height
> Remaine so long? but it's owne weight
> Will ruine it? Or, is't blinde chance,
> That still desires new states t'advance,
> And quit the old? Else, why must *Rome*,
> Be by it selfe, now, over-come? . . .
> They hunt all grounds; and draw all seas;
> Foule every brooke, and bush; to please
> Their wanton tasts: and, in request
> Have new, and rare things; not the best!
>
> (I, 531–36, 569–72)[22]

Diomedes, playing up to the ladies in *Achilles*, declares that
'Novelty is the very Spirit of Dress' (III, x, 13) but this is a
contradiction in terms. 'Spirit' is a life-giving force, an eternal,
unchanging essence: novelty cannot be the spirit of anything. It
bestows an illusion of life that may keep the carcase twitching
for a little while, but cannot preserve it from corruption. And
the characters are as void of life as the ideas they represent.

Corruption—both sexual and political—is a key issue in
Gay's drama, and he often links them so closely that they
become indistinguishable. Women are potential bribes in political deals, such as Lady Willit's attempt to gain Lord Courtlove's
patronage by offering him the hand of Miss Sprightly. They are
also vulnerable to direct political manipulation. Some, like Miss
Friendless and Polly, are offered as instances of incorruptibility,
but doubts are raised by Miss Friendless's decision to secure
independence by marrying Lord Courtlove (marriage being the
only form of independence to which a woman of the period
could reasonably aspire) and the prudential thrust of Polly's
arguments in favour of virtue as a sound investment. They
suggest that it is woman's chiefest duty to keep an eye to the
main chance:

> Frail is ambition, how weak the foundation!
>   Riches have wings as inconstant as wind;
> My heart is proof against either temptation,
> Virtue, without them, contentment can find.
>
> (*Polly*, III, xv, 38–41)

Most women, like Mrs. Ducat, are blatantly out for whatever
they can get:

I will have my humours, I'll please all my senses,
I will not be stinted—in love or expences.
I'll dress with profusion, I'll game without measure;
You shall have the business, I will have the pleasure.

(Polly, I, viii, 9–12)

Her maid, Damaris, employs the language as well as the skills of the politician in the cause of female solidarity:

I am employ'd by my master to watch my mistress, and by my mistress to watch my master. Which party shall I espouse? To be sure my mistress's. For in hers, jurisdiction and power, the common cause of the whole sex, are at stake. (I, x, 3–7)

Women were commonly supposed to be natural Jacobites, but the Scriblerians appear to have believed that every woman was at heart a Whig: not an Old Whig, or an Opposition Whig, but an unscrupulous Walpolean Whig, venal from her laced shoes to her powdered hair. Women were ambitious and materialistic; money, power and influence at court lay in the gift of the Whig government. Another inducement to she-Whiggery was the widespread female tendency to prefer the town to the country. The expensive, glamorous amusements of London society were a dangerous distraction from the responsibilities of the landed gentry who were the natural upholders of the Tory interest. Only an exceptional woman, whose inborn proclivities were suppressed by common sense and a virtuous education, could be trusted. Dr. Arbuthnot showed the two types in action in *Law is a Bottomless-Pit*, one of the pamphlets constituting *The History of John Bull* (1712), where Bull's first wife (the Whig-influenced Godolphin ministry) is a precursor of Lady Willit, while her successor (Harley's Tory ministry) behaves more like Martha Blount. The first was 'an extravagant Bitch of a Wife . . . a luxurious Jade, lov'd splendid Equipages, Plays, Treats and Balls, differing very much from the sober Manners of her Ancestors, and by no means fit for a Tradesman's Wife'. The second was 'a sober Country Gentlewoman, of a good Family, and a plentiful Fortune; the reverse of the other in her Temper'.[23]

Gambling provided a powerful analogy between sexual and political temptation. Barter in *The Distress'd Wife* hints that Lady Willit's virtue is endangered by this pursuit:

Barter. Does she game as deep as ever?

Sir Thomas. You know she does.

Barter. And can you be so unreasonable as to put her out of the Way of so *innocent* an Amusement? (I, i, 61–4)

There is no need for more than a hint, when the danger is defined so clearly, time and again, in the literature of the period, a good example being the predicament of Lady Gentle in Cibber's *The Lady's Last Stake* (1707). A wife who lost heavily might be tempted to pay her debts of honour with her body rather than confess her extravagance to her husband. The masculine equivalent, endangering public virtue, was speculating on the stock market, according to George Berkeley in his *Essay Towards Preventing the Ruin of Great Britain* (1721):

> Money is so far useful to the public as it promoteth industry, and credit having the same effect is of the same value with money; but money or credit circulating through a nation from hand to hand without producing labour and industry in the inhabitants, is direct gaming.[24]

Barter rejects Lord Courtlove's offer of inside information from government sources with a crushing rebuke:

> But then one exorbitant Fortune of this sort hath made at least a thousand Beggars.—'Tis the most fraudulent, the most pernicious Gaming, under a more specious Denomination; and those who practise it, disgrace the Profession of a Merchant. (IV, xiv, 47–51)

It is unlikely that eighteenth-century merchants were quite so highly principled off stage, but Gay was prepared to sacrifice credibility, yet again, to moral edification.

Scriblerian ideals, however, were not always a deterrent to the muses. Even Gay's habitual hostility to Walpole, which slows down the action so badly in *Polly*, is turned to good theatrical account when government espionage is used to provide the catastrophe of *The Distress'd Wife*. Although the play opens with Sir Thomas Willit's resolution to give up his quest for a government employment and return to the country, he does not act on his decision until he accidentally reads a letter directed to Lady Willit, revealing that she has been getting money from his steward on the sly. A blunder by the Post Office brings about his enlightenment: the Clerk in the Inland Secretary's Private Office has opened the letter and neglected to seal it again. Intercepting the mail of suspected criminals and political opponents was longstanding government practice; according to Barter, ' 'Tis a Grievance that is become so general, that no Particular will take it upon him to complain' (V, iv, 27–8). Pope and Swift were both convinced that their correspondence was subjected to these flattering attentions and said so in their letters.[25] Dr. Johnson thought Pope was suffering from an inflated sense of his own importance: 'All this while it was likely that the clerks did not know his hand.'[26] Whatever the true state of affairs, it must have given the Scriblerians great satisfaction to envisage government policy defeated by its own weapons. It would have given them even greater satisfaction to know that John Lefebure, who became Foreign Secretary to the Post Office around 1718 and held that key post until his death in 1752, was a Jacobite mole.[27] This was one of many sardonic flourishes with which life has insisted on embellishing Scriblerian irony.

The Scriblerian attitude to humour was also a healthy influence on Gay's drama, encouraging him to uphold the tradition that comedy ought to be funny. The Scriblerian collaboration, *Three Hours after Marriage*, represents a reaction to the encroaching vogue for sentimentality: so do *Achilles*, *The Distress'd Wife* and even parts of *Polly*. Comparison between *The Distress'd Wife* and Cibber's *The Provoked Husband* (1728) shows Gay to advantage in this respect. Cibber based *The Provoked Husband* on Sir John Vanbrugh's unfinished *A Journey to London*. According to Robert D. Hume, *The Provoked Husband* is 'an important and undervalued play', which offers highly effective solutions to the marital problems under examination; Gay, on the other hand, 'was to end his *The Distress'd Wife* (1734) by having an extravagant wife hauled off to the country, an unsatisfying ending to a weak play'.[28] Cibber certainly treats his subject more seriously, in the main plot at least, attempting a convincing reconciliation between husband and wife, but not everyone was impressed. Henry Fielding gave his opinion in *Tom Jones* (1749):

> The Puppet-show was performed with great Regularity and Decency. It was called the fine and serious Part of the *Provok'd Husband*; and it was indeed a very grave and solemn Entertainment, without any low Wit or Humour, or Jests; or, to do it no more than Justice, without any thing which could provoke a

Laugh. The Audience were all highly pleased. A grave Matron told the Master she would bring her two Daughters the next Night, as he did not shew any Stuff; and an Attorney's Clerk, and an Exciseman, both declared, that the Characters of Lord and Lady *Townly* were well preserved, and highly in Nature. (XII, 5)[29]

Gay's comedy offers no obeisance to provincial respectability. He tries to maintain, and even intensify, the comic force of Vanbrugh's original sketch. Vanbrugh gives the town-loving wife, Arabella, a sensible friend who tries to persuade her that it is possible to enjoy both the town and the country, with due moderation:

> *Clarinda.* I would entertain my self in observing the new Fashions soberly, I would please my self in new Cloaths soberly, I would divert my self with agreeable Friends at Home and Abroad soberly. I would play at Quadrille soberly, I would go to Court soberly, I would go to some Plays soberly, I would go to Operas soberly, and I think I cou'd go once, or, if I lik'd my Company, twice to a Masquerade soberly.
>
> *Lady Arabella.* If it had not been for that last Piece of Sobriety, I was going to call for some Surfeit-water. (II, i, 167–74)[30]

Even with the surfeit-water to wash it down, Cibber found this dose of sobriety excessive, and reduced it drastically. Gay strikes a blow for laughter by removing the sensible friend altogether and substituting the effervescent Miss Sprightly, who has her own very strong reasons for preferring country life, but makes no attempt to confute Lady Willit. What the play loses in coherence it gains in vitality. James Thomson objected that 'Miss Sprightly's Wit is affected, and has not that amiable Softness and gentle Character which ought to recommend the Sprightliness of your Sex.'[31] This is high praise: a perusal of the sentimental melodrama *Edward and Eleanora* (1739), in which Thomson indulged to the full his taste for female softness, will confirm the reader's good opinion of Miss Sprightly.

The muses entertained no objection to morality, so long as it was compatible with good drama. It was when Gay forgot his need of them that they repaid his neglect by sneaking off. In an age of scholarly, cultivated gentleman dramatists, Gay had to remember how important it was to be a man of the theatre as well. He was always sure of attaining a reasonable degree of success when he kept established dramatic precedent in view; he achieved his masterpieces when he narrowed and sharpened his focus still further, to concentrate on the idea of theatre itself. Gay is at his best when he explores, and apparently defies, the nature of dramatic convention. *The What D'Ye Call It* and *The Beggar's Opera* engage the audience's emotions from within a framework that seems calculated to alienate them. He is not a conjuror, relying on concealment and illusions, but a magician, who can get his effect while leaving his apparatus in full view. This is a typically Scriblerian trick: *A Tale of a Tub* makes its point with a pyrotechnic display of controlled pointlessness; *The Dunciad* celebrates, in great poetry, the conditions that, according to its author, make great poetry impossible. Gay was the only Scriblerian to bring this technique to the stage, which explains the paradox that he was never more Scriblerian than when he was most himself. *Achilles* and *The Distress'd Wife* are, in structural terms, conventional dramas; even *Polly*, despite the promise of the Introduction, dwindles into a straightforward ballad opera, lacking the ironic complexities provided in *The Beggar's Opera* by the re-entry of the Beggar and the Player at the end. His later material was just as rich in Scriblerian associations, but he lacked the independent perspective that had previously enabled him to take command of his form. Christopher Smart understood the necessity, for all the Scriblerians, of the clear view that precedes the satiric kill. His observations would have made a more appropriate epitaph than Pope's:

> Let Eliada rejoice with the Gier-eagle who is swift and of great penetration.
> *For I bless the Lord Jesus for the memory of GAY, POPE and SWIFT.*[32]

NOTES

1. Quoted in *The Poetical Works of John Gay* (London, 1804 (C. Cooke)), I, 13. This inscription, although never finally used, was commonly quoted. See Theophilus Cibber, *The Lives of the Poets of Great Britain and Ireland*, 5 vols. (London, 1753), IV, 258.
2. Quotations from Johnson from George Birkbeck Hill (ed.), *Lives of the English Poets* (Oxford, 1905), II, 269, 271, 276, 283–84, 282.

3. 'Introduction', *DW*, I, 2.
4. Quoted in *DW*, I, 58.
5. Alan Dugald McKillop, *James Thomson: Letters and Documents* (Lawrence, Kansas, 1958), p. 168.
6. *DW*, I, 65.
7. F. W. Bateson (ed.), *Epistles to Several Persons (Moral Essays)*, 2nd edn. (London and New Haven, 1961), p. 67. Vol. III, ii of the Twickenham Edition of *The Poems of Alexander Pope*.
8. Act, scene, and line references are to the texts of Gay's plays in *DW*, from which all quotations are taken (roman for italics in Airs).
9. William H. McBurney (ed.), *The London Merchant* (London, 1965), p. 12.
10. *The Gentleman Instructed in the Conduct of a Virtuous and Happy Life*, 5th edn. (London, 1713), III, 374.
11. Herbert Davis (ed.), *The Prose Writings of Jonathan Swift* (Oxford, 1939–75), XII, 113–14.
12. *Dublin Intelligence*, 14 January 1729.
13. Davis, XII, p. 80.
14. *The Double Gallant; or, The Sick Lady's Cure*, 2nd edn. (London, 1707), pp. 27–8.
15. Bateson, pp. 46, 49–50.
16. 'Imagination in *The Rape of the Lock*', *EC*, 29 (1979), 54.
17. Geoffrey Tillotson (ed.), *The Rape of the Lock and Other Poems*, 3rd edn. (London and New Haven, 1962), pp. 163–64. Vol. II of the Twickenham Edition of *The Poems of Alexander Pope*.
18. James Kinsley (ed.), *The Poems of John Dryden* (Oxford, 1958), IV, 1750.
19. A. C. Ewald (ed.), *The Dramatic Works of George Farquhar* (London, 1892), I, 259.
20. Line references are to the texts of Gay's poems in *PP*, from which all quotations are taken.
21. Davis, I, 81, 26.
22. C. H. Herford and Percy Simpson (eds.), *Ben Jonson* (Oxford, 1925–52), V, 452–53.
23. Alan W. Bower and Robert A. Ericson (eds.), *The History of John Bull* (Oxford, 1976), pp. 12–13, 16.
24. A. A. Luce and T. E. Jessop (eds.), *The Works of George Berkeley Bishop of Cloyne* (London, 1948–57), VI, 71.
25. See George Sherburn (ed.), *The Correspondence of Alexander Pope* (Oxford, 1956), III, 431–32 (Pope and Bolingbroke to Swift, 15 September 1734); IV, 231–32 (Pope to the Earl of Orrery, 27 March 1740); and Harold Williams (ed.), *The Correspondence of Jonathan Swift* (Oxford, 1963–65), V, 119–20 (Swift to Pope and Bolingbroke, 8 August 1738).
26. Hill, III, 211.
27. See Eveline Cruickshanks, *Political Untouchables: The Tories and the '45* (London, 1979), p. 47. For details of Post Office procedure, see Kenneth Ellis, *The Post Office in the Eighteenth Century* (London, 1958), p. 64; for the official version of John Lefebure's career, see ibid., pp. 66–7.
28. 'Marital Discord in English Comedy from Dryden to Fielding', *MP*, 74 (1976–77), 263.

29. Martin C. Battestin and Fredson Bowers (eds.), *The History of Tom Jones* (Oxford, 1974), II, 637–38.
30. Bonamy Dobrée (ed.), *The Complete Works of Sir John Vanbrugh* (London, 1927), III, 150.
31. McKillop, p. 168.
32. Karina Williamson (ed.), *The Poetical Works of Christopher Smart*, I (*Jubilate Agno*) (Oxford, 1980), p. 26.

9

Sex and Gender in Gay's *Achilles*

by YVONNE NOBLE

At a time of unparalleled academic interest in the relationship (which is to say, discrepancy) between sex and gender, John Gay emerges as an extremely interesting writer, distinctively conscious and candid, able through his characteristic duple forms and modes to render the simultaneous state of authenticity and inauthenticity in which those who do not embody the norm are condemned to dwell. Little interested in party politics, uninterested in social theory, Gay was acutely aware of the transactions of oppression between individuals; he is able through these duple forms and modes to force those who would be intractable to preaching to take account of the unvoiced suffering even in their own circle. Gay's last work, the seemingly frivolous ballad opera *Achilles*, confronts in this way the serious issue of rape.

Achilles, which had just gone into rehearsal when Gay died, features its hero throughout dressed in the clothes of a girl. How is this figure to be read? Much current writing would presume that a figure like this, particularly in a work of burlesque, must at least trivialize its subject or at worst serve a retrograde and conservative function by embodying a mockery of woman to mollify the anxieties, and reinforce the prejudices, of men.[1] While by no means denying the applicability of such insightful analysis to the theatre of Gay's time—for indeed, the pronounced sexism of the period cries out for analysis of this sort[2]—I would nevertheless like to widen the realm of interpretation by suggesting quite a different possibility for Gay's travesty subject. I propose that Gay selected this Achilles as his subject precisely because the figure could open up interesting questions of gender-identity[3] and be used to undermine one of the key tenets of male dominance—the principle that women's sexual desire corresponds to men's—exactly at its most reinforcing point of textual authority in classical literature. My reading will locate an important significance of the figure of Achilles by reference to classical contexts it invokes, in a current of meaning flowing from Gay to those of his auditors who could recognize that context. This study will therefore also chart a little more of that relatively neglected side of Gay's artistry, his relation to and transformation of the literature of antiquity, through which he moves with grace, wit, fondness, and good acquaintance.[4]

Achilles is based upon the episode in which the hero, disguised as a girl, is concealed on the island of Scyros among the daughters of King Lycomedes. His mother, the sea-goddess Thetis, has learned by a prophecy that her son can have a long, uneventful life in obscurity or a short life of great glory if he joins the Trojan War; understandably Thetis seeks to preserve her son. The Greeks, on the other hand, discover that they cannot win without Achilles and therefore mount an expedition to find him. Ulysses, in the guise of a merchant, prepares a stock of women's gear amid which he places a suit of armour together with arms. When Ulysses displays these wares to the maidens of Scyros, Achilles is found out, tricked by the lure of the arms into revealing himself.

One epigraph to the printed *Achilles* (1733) directs us to Ovid's *Metamorphoses* for the classical source being represented or evoked. The passage occurs in Book XIII, as a part of a speech by Ulysses, debating against Ajax after Achilles's death in order to claim the hero's armour. Ulysses brings up the episode in order to demonstrate that the Greeks would not have had the services of Achilles except for Ulysses's cleverness— and he includes the gibe that his opponent Ajax was completely taken in by Achilles's disguise. (Gay alludes to this point in

making Ajax avid to duel for 'Pyrrha' in Act III.[5]) Besides
schoolboy exposure to Ovid's poem, Gay would have encountered the passage as one of Dryden's *Fables* (1700, reprinted
1713, 1721), an excerpt later collected into Garth's edition of
the *Metamorphoses Englished* (1717, 1720, 1727) to which Gay also
contributed work; this translation obtained new currency in
1732—the year *Achilles* was written—as the English part of a
sumptuous illustrated Latin-English folio of Ovid's poem, containing a visual representation of the disguised Achilles in the
recognition scene.[6] Accompanying other work by Gay, the
passage appears as translated by Theobald in the rival English
Metamorphoses edited by Sewell (1717 [1716], 1724 (reissued
1726)). Such repeated editions and reprintings imply a wide
public thoroughly familiar with the stories, whom a writer like
Gay could assume he was addressing. Book XIII—the pair of
speeches—was also often translated by itself, and Gay would
have had particular reason to notice two of these versions: one
in 1708 with Ulysses's speech translated by his schoolfriend and
early London mentor Aaron Hill[7], and a modernized burlesque
version in 1719 put out by his pseudonymous namesake and
bane, 'Joseph Gay' (later to be immortalized as a pursuable
phantom by Pope in the *Dunciad* games).[8] Of course, it would
not have taken someone else's work to put John Gay's mind
running on burlesque, and the low-life treatment by 'Joseph
Gay' is rather coarse, but certain features might have stimulated
his imagination, particularly the wife supplied for the first time
for Lycomedes and the garb and kit of a Scottish peddler that
Ulysses assumes.[9]

Gay incorporates into his ballad opera, however, many
aspects of the legend that were well-known in antiquity but do
not figure in the *Metamorphoses*, with its focus upon concealment
and disclosure.[10] These include such memorable features as the
clandestine amour with King Lycomedes's daughter Deidamia,
Achilles's engagement in women's work (spinning), the presence
of a group of daughters (or court maidens), the use of a trumpet
call as part of Ulysses's ruse, and Achilles's adoption of the
name 'Pyrrha'. The first two can be found elsewhere in Ovid
(*Ars Amatoria*), in Statius, and in (pseudo-)Bion. Lycomedes's
daughters are in Statius and in Bion, as well as in a number of
minor writers, and the trumpet call occurs in Statius and

others. From Statius, Gay could draw the psychology of awareness: 'Conscious of her and Achilles's concealed guilt, Deidamia is tormented with anxiety and thinks her sisters are aware but not mentioning what they suspect or know.'[11] The idea that the intrigue began as a result of the couple's having been assigned the same bed or bedchamber derives, by contrast, not from Statius but from Bion and Ovid (*Ars Amatoria*). To know that Achilles was called 'Pyrrha', Gay must have had first-hand or at least indirect access to the less familiar writers, Apollodorus, Hyginus and Sidonius.[12]

But as my review of the English versions of the *Metamorphoses* tale suggests, Gay could draw upon not only his own familiarity with the classical story, but also that of his readers, even the unlearned. Thus it is important to review, with the content of his likeliest sources, how widely they could have been known. Of the Bion—the fragmentary *Epithalamius of Achilles and Deidameia*—I have found no translation into English until long after Gay's death.[13] I believe, nevertheless, that Gay must have known this fragment, which occurs among a group of idylls often associated with those of Theocritus, of whom he composed a full-scale imitation in *The Shepherd's Week* and whom he cites there many times by name. In the Bion fragment the story of the love affair is told in the same Doric style that Theocritus uses and that Gay approximates with clattering rhymes, low country lore, and archaisms. In Bion such a version answers the call made by a rustic for 'a pretty (Sicilian) love-song such as Polyphemus sang to Galatea'; Gay's mind would have seized on this text, for he wrote exactly that song himself—'O ruddier than the Cherry!' for Handel's *Acis and Galatea* (II, 17–27).[14] Treating Achilles, Bion's singer stresses the clear male selfhood within the ostensibly feminine beauty, then paints in detail the lover's conduct in the early stages of courtship:

> Achilles alone hid among the girls, the daughters of Lycomedes, and he learned woolworking instead of arms, and with white arm he sustained a maiden's task, and he appeared like a girl; for he actually became girlish like them, and just such a blossom blushed on his snowy cheeks, and he walked with the walk of a girl, and he covered his hair with a veil. But still he had the heart of a man and the passion of a man, and from dawn to night he sat beside Deidamia, and sometimes he kissed her hand, and many a

time he raised up her fair weaving and he praised her patterned web; and he did not eat with any other companion, and he did everything in his eagerness to share her bed; and he even spoke a word to her: 'The other sisters sleep with one another, but I sleep alone and you girl sleep alone, we two maiden companions, we two fair; but we sleep alone in our separate beds; but that wicked crafty Nysaia cruelly separates me from you. For I do not you. . . .'[15]

As for Statius's version of the story, it was certainly known by part of Gay's audience, for one critic, 'Atex' Burnet, writing before the printed edition of *Achilles* (with its Ovid epigraph) was published, unhesitatingly declared Statius—that is, his *Achilleid*—to be Gay's source.[16] This work had been published in an English translation by Sir Robert Howard among his *Poems* in 1660. Many common details—for example, Achilles's insisting upon a ceremony to confirm his marriage to Deidamia— make it clear that Gay knew Statius's poem. The general currency of this classical author may be indicated by recalling the place of translations from his earlier epic, the *Thebaid*, among Pope's juvenilia and earliest publications. In Book I of the *Achilleid* Statius treats Achilles's time in Scyros at length. Here, Achilles agrees to put on the woman's garment only after he has been kindled by the sight of Deidamia. The poet slowly builds with psychosomatic details—tightenings of the scalp, flushes of the skin, impulsive movements checked by bash- fulness—the representation of the force of sexual feeling within an inexperienced adolescent boy. Achilles constantly hovers near Deidamia, keeping his presence known by little gaucheries. In Deidamia, similarly, Statius depicts the special psychological state of a nubile virgin, who encourages Achilles's courtship without allowing herself consciously to know the circumstances in which she is placed; whenever Achilles tries to explain his deception, she will not allow him opportunity to do so. After many days of restraint, combined with the loss of his old male activities and the frustrations of his new rôle, finding himself near the girl in the dark one night in a sacred grove, 'He gains by force his desire, and with all his vigour strains her in a real embrace.'[17] Statius conveys that this act, while not wholly unpremeditated, largely flows from a compulsion more power- ful than the lad at his stage of understanding and of physical development can control. Deidamia, who has had no idea that there was a man nearby, is of course frantic and terrified. When these stresses have abated, however, their mutual attraction draws them to continue a secret liaison as lovers and to protect each other. Deidamia achieves considerable mastery over her circumstances, for, with the assistance of her nurse, she manages to conceal her pregnancy, her lying-in, and her growing child, and to prevent Achilles impetuously giving himself away many times to Ulysses's searching eyes; Achilles, in turn, immediately his identity is revealed, also confesses their situation and asks (successfully) to marry her. In short, while Statius does not condemn the rape, and even uses it in his narrative as an index of his hero's masculinity, he also presents it as an index of his hero's immaturity.

Sustaining the sexual dynamic I have already described, Statius renders the disclosure of Achilles's true self at the sound of the alarm as the unleashing of even more irresistible natural power concentrated within the taut form: standing motionless amid the panic, Achilles simply grows huge and dominant: as his womanly garments fall away, *he* (his whole body) erects:

> *illius intactae cecidere a pectore vestes,*
> *iam clipeus breviorque manu consumitur hasta,*
> *—mira fides!—Ithacumque umeris excedere visus*
> *Aetolumque ducem: . . .*
> *immanisque gradu, ceu protinus Hectora poscens,*
> *stat medius trepidante domo: Peleaque virgo*
> *quaeritur.*
>
> (I, 878–81, 883–85)

From his breast the garments fall away untouched, now the shield and puny spear are swallowed up by his hands—marvellous to believe!—his head and shoulders loom up above those of Ulysses and Diomede: . . .

Mighty of limb, in combat stance, as if he could summon Hector, he stands amid the panic-stricken house: and the girl-that-was for whom they search [they will never find].[18]

Achilles in legend enacts the tragic impossibility of escaping one's destiny. At the moment Statius treats in this passage, the ties of life—the long life Thetis has sought for him, the inane alternative symbolized in his inappropriate raiment—are sloughed away by the true heroic reality that declares itself. Not accidentally is this heroic manifestation expressed by likeness to

189

the declaration one part of a man's body can make of exemption from qualifying circumstance and personal uncertainty. Throughout the Scyros episode Statius makes plain, both explicitly and symbolically, the relationship between male sexual, and heroic military, potency, and grounds them both in irresistible nature. Gay takes over Statius's themes, but recasts into questions his certainties.

Of all the classical treatments of Achilles and Deidamia, however, Ovid's *Ars Amatoria* would have been the most familiar and most influential. Throughout the history of secular classical education, the confident, urbane advice to men by the writer of the *Ars Amatoria* on how to obtain and retain women's love must have been devoured by schoolboys after hours when it failed to find a place in the formal curriculum. Since Gay's time, bowdlerism has successfully prevented many readers from becoming aware of Ovid's full text.[19] Gay's contemporaries, by contrast, could choose among many candid translations of Book I by Thomas Heywood (1650, 1662, 1672, 1677, 1682, 1684), Francis Wolferston (1661), Thomas Hoy (1682, 1692), or Dryden (1709, 1712, 1716, 1719). They could also read the advice applied to modern times—in the coarse anonymous *Art of Love* (1701, reissued slightly revised in 1702 as *The Poet Banter'd*) or in William King's elaborate adaptation (1708, reissued 1712), where quite witty burlesque elements sometimes conceal the onset of the bowdlerizing impulse.[20]

It was Ovid in the *Ars Amatoria* who introduced the idea that Achilles raped Deidamia (setting for his successor Statius the problem he so brilliantly solved of accounting for the rape).[21] The story is brought in as an illustration in a context I shall describe later. Ovid's narrator is a bully, interested in understanding others' psychology only in order to achieve an ascendancy: he therefore mocks Achilles for dressing as a woman and for spinning. But, for him, Achilles asserts his true nature not as a hero in warfare but as a man in rape. Manliness is staked upon sexual conquest.

Thus, while the account in the *Metamorphoses* focuses on Achilles as an object of concealment and disclosure, other sources concentrate upon the significance of the figure while in disguise, as he shares the education, occupations, indeed one of the beds, of the daughters of Lycomedes. Achilles's love affair with Deidamia, confirmed in her pregnancy,[22] testifies to the hero's genuine manliness despite his appearance. The figure—or idea—of the disguised Achilles spinning doubles with that of Hercules in similar garments engaged at the same task, and therefore indicates that what is represented is not man, or mere man, but hero, in displacement. Depending on the treatment, the image could suggest a wide range of possible values, from debasement through latent power to the enhancement of one's power by encompassing the attributes of the Other. These parts of the legend share an interest in the question of gender-identity and its relation to 'true' identity and to the ability to act effectively in the world.

The Achilles-in-Scyros story therefore held many interesting themes for Gay to explore. He would have met the figure of Achilles in petticoats early in his studies and had reason to be reminded of the figure over and over in the intervening years. Furthermore, the figure would in itself have appealed to Gay, whose imagination repeatedly created figures in cross-gendered disguise. In his plays such figures partly reflect common theatre conventions, but for Gay they also reflect his wider imaginative habitation in double forms—burlesque- or mock-modes—and his fascination with duple or liminal figures, such as pregnant maidens or castrati. Gender disguise can be found also in his poetry and translations. Particularly striking is the early passage in his *Epistle to Burlington* (circulating in manuscript in 1717, printed 1720) in which he candidly and without any suggestion of oddity describes his pleasure in finding himself in women's clothes. He and his squires have ridden four days on horseback; at an inn they have the chance to strip to the skin, and have all their clothes laundered; the maid gives them women's night-gowns to sleep in:

> The Maid, subdu'd by Fees, her Trunk unlocks,
> And gives the cleanly Aid of Dowlas Smocks.
> Mean time our Shirts her busy Fingers rub,
> While the Soap lathers o'er the foaming Tub.
> If Women's Geer such pleasing Dreams incite,
> Lend us your Smocks, ye Damsels, ev'ry Night!
>
> (103–8)

The idea of fingers touching the clothes from the outside combines with the reverie induced by comfort, relaxation, passivity, the sensation of unfamiliar but agreeable garments felt from the inside, and the strange but not unpleasant disruption of the attributes of sexual identity. Day returns the dreamers to the certainty of their masculinity, 'We rise; our Beards demand the Barber's art' (109), but allows them to reassume their reverie with all the elements I have mentioned—the stroking fingers, the sensation to the skin, the comfort, relaxation, passivity, the pleasing disruption of sexual norms:

> A Female enters, and performs the part. . . . .
> Smooth o'er our Chin her easy Fingers move,
> Soft as when *Venus* stroak'd the Beard of *Jove*.
> (110, 113–14)[23]

The composition of the immediate predecessor to *Achilles* among Gay's ballad operas may help to explain why Gay thought later of Achilles as a subject. In that work, *Polly*, Gay had put his heroine into breeches. Quite apart from any imaginative predispositions, Gay would have arrived at this feature by the same process that led him to write *Polly* in the first place: to follow up on the unprecedented success of *The Beggar's Opera*. Polly Peachum had become a celebrity—there were 'biographies' of her, books of her sayings, engraved portraits, her face on screens and fans—and the actress who embodied her had capped the glamour with a flourish by setting up with a duke. How natural to feature Polly in a sequel and to put her into disguise as a man, at once greatly extending the character's scope for action and the actress's scope for display.

For his next ballad opera Gay would easily think of reviving the travesty in reverse, and Achilles-in-Scyros would readily follow to mind—already associated, furthermore, with modernization and with burlesque. For Polly-in-breeches Gay had written a scene based upon the story of Potiphar's wife. As *Polly* had not been performed, Gay carried the idea over to his new piece and rewrote the scene with the sexes reversed. Adding a jealous wife for Lycomedes and taking over the two elements—love affair and disclosure—from the classical story, Gay had the material for his text. This material he then structured to raise questions about the relation of gender to personal identity.

A noticeable feature of his structure is that during the greater part of *Achilles* no other character present is aware that the person called Pyrrha is anything but the young woman she seems. The exposition is set out for the audience in dialogue between Achilles, already disguised, and Thetis, who then departs. Until II, x, the drama then deals with the feminine-gendered Pyrrha, whose treatment and circumstances the audience must evaluate in terms of the smouldering male consciousness that must endure them. The nature of what Gay achieves here can be made clearer by comparing his plotting with that of Paolo Rolli for Handel's last opera, *Deidamia* (1741). As soon as possible in Act I, Rolli establishes that both Lycomedes and Deidamia are aware that their guest Pyrrha is Achilles—Lycomedes has promised his friend Peleus, Achilles's father, that he will conceal his son. Without my delaying to set out the obvious male ruling-class affiliation of the heroic mode, we might notice that the goddess Thetis, whom antique plots were able to tolerate, if only to thwart, is obliterated in Rolli's heroic plot in favour of her mortal, but male, spouse: Lycomedes can be bound, against the claims of Ulysses, by an oath to Peleus, as he cannot by a promise to a female, a mother. Rolli can concentrate the action of his drama upon the efforts of his principal, Ulysses (for Ulysses, not Achilles, was *primo uomo*), to discern the evidences of heroic manliness in the lineaments of a nymph who hunts exceptionally well, and who fails to respond to the gestures of courtship, but who, in the end, cannot resist a helmet and shield.[24] Ulysses, the 'subject', or viewing mind, achieves mastery over the 'object', which has an existence and a true nature independent of him that can be 'dis-covered', and that, by the right test, he can force it to disclose. In this ontology, a person's nature inheres in his or her sexual identity, which informs all aspects of behaviour and taste; it therefore cannot be long concealed from the discerning eye. Rolli's position is precisely Ovid's: 'She, not discover'd by her Mien or Voice,/ Betray'd her Manhood by her manly Choice' (*Metamorphoses*, translated by Dryden).[25] With Ulysses as subject, Achilles does not simply *manifest* himself like Statius's hero; not self-directed and irresistibly powerful, he is beckonable, controlled.

Unlike Rolli, Gay holds off till the last moment—the tenth scene of the final act—before allowing Ulysses's configuration of reality to take hold of his play. Ulysses, observing the discernible behaviour of '*Achilles* . . . handling and poising the Armour', sees in it first the outward manifestations of the hero's nature—'That intrepid Air! That Godlike Look!'—then the heroic nature itself—'His Nature, his Disposition shews him through the Disguise.' 'Son of *Thetis*, I know thee', he declares, and Achilles acknowledges himself (III, x, 81–90). But the finale, which Gay gives to Ulysses and his point of view, in fact undercuts the value, and the grounds, of the discovery:

> Nature breaks forth at the Moment unguarded;
>   Through all Disguise she her self must betray. . . .
>
> Thus when the Cat had once all Woman's Graces;
>   Courtship, Marriage won her Embraces:
> Forth lept a Mouse; she, forgetting Enjoyment,
>   Quits her fond Spouse for her former Employment.
>
> Nature breaks forth at the Moment unguarded;
>   Through all Disguise she herself must betray.
>   (III, xii, 80–1, 84–9)

Here is a reality, a 'something' that can 'break forth', as the essence of 'catness' leaps out of the woman's clothes to pursue the mouse, when stressed by the irresistible temptation specific to its nature, which for the hero is the armour. Yet the 'something' is controlled neither by its own integrity (it can 'betray' itself), nor by its male master; it responds no more readily to guile than to random contingency. The hierarchical status of what Ulysses has discovered—the heroic male warrior—is discredited by his being equated with a female domestic beast in pursuit of her 'former Employment', while man-the-subject-discerner is left embarrassed at not being able to discriminate at all, even in the intimacy of marriage, between the image of woman concealing the nature of cat, the image of woman concealing the nature of hero, and the image of woman concealing the nature of woman (if, for such subjects, the latter distinction can be known).

Following *Achilles* backwards from this final wobbly affirmation of a knowable inner essence to its beginning, we find a series of progressively external definitions of identity that occupy more and more of the play time (or text) the earlier, and more external, they are. The speech preceding the finale, 'We may for a while put on a feign'd Character, but Nature is so often unguarded that it will shew itself.—'Tis to the Armour we owe *Achilles'* (III, xii, 77–9), suggests in its last phrase that the heroism lodges not in the man but in the armour. In one sense, Ulysses's clothing-trick brings out a distinction between Achilles and the maidens, but in another sense it is a distinction without a difference: some are attracted by costumes of one sort, some by costumes of another sort, but all are the same in being attracted by costumes. Rather than there being an innate, hierarchical difference, there may be no meaningful difference at all—Gay's irreverent presentation certainly supports the latter notion. His point is explored in the Prologue 'Written by Mr. *GAY*' (nevertheless attributed by some to Pope):[26]

> To Buskins, Plumes and Helmets what Pretence,
> If mighty Chiefs must speak but common Sense? . . .
> And whatsoever Criticks may suppose,
> Our Author holds, that what He [Achilles] spoke was Prose.
>   (17–18, 23–4)

The questions of diction and criticism—particularly if they are raised by the translator of the *Iliad* and the *Odyssey*—invoke the debate between Ancients and Moderns, with the indication that if Gay's Achilles 'speaks prose',[27] as he does (even while the Prologue 'speaks couplets'), correspondingly what is *embodied* or *dressed* in the epic verse will be absent, too. Once, 'Buskins, Plumes and Helmets' were put on by real warriors and corresponded to real danger, real courage: they signified grandeur and magnanimity as opposed to triviality and mean-spiritedness. Now they have no function except as costumes put on by actors or opera singers. But the first line hints by its metonymy that, even in the past, heroes—'Buskins, Plumes and Helmets'— were no more than their costumes and that their virtue had no more existence than now. Thus can be read Ulysses's summation: ' 'Tis to the Armour we owe *Achilles'* (III, xii, 79).

Institutionalized distinctions in virtually all cultures testify that for most people the essence of personal identity lodges in the sex organs and in their expression of fertility and potency. Gay uses the Deidamia plot to set forth sexuality's claim to be the lodgment of true identity. For him love-making—sex—is naturally a matter of mutual pleasure and desire understood to lead to pregnancy, Gay's copied Nature, making the Youths Amorous before Wedlock, and the Damsels Complying and Fruitful' (Preface, *The What D'Ye Call It*, 90–1). In the verse of Air III of *Achilles*—with a hint of Statius's outlook—Gay suggests the danger of attempting to repress the power of sexual energy in the metaphor of a foolish shepherd who would pen up a hungry wolf within the fold, while the tune Gay chooses for this air reinforces the theme by recalling that paragon of vainly-pent sexual energy, Macheath, in the condemned cell of Newgate Prison singing Air LXV to the same strains, 'But can I leave my pretty Hussies,/ Without one Tear, or tender Sigh?' (*The Beggar's Opera*, III, xiii, 18–19).

There are a few jokes that play upon the sense of the hidden male organ, particularly when Lycomedes's guards begin to search Pyrrha for a 'Dagger . . . You will find . . . some where or other conceal'd' (II, v, 9–10), but direct references like these to Achilles's sex are few. Gay is far more interested in the question of how sexual identity can be known indirectly: he sets up the Achilles-Deidamia plot as flowing from Theaspe's incorrect judgement about Achilles's sexual identity. This has induced her to demand that her daughter be 'scarce ever from her [Pyrrha]; they have one and the same Bed-Chamber' (I, viii, 83–4). Other lines in Theaspe's same speech indicate further ways of knowing on this plane of identity—direct verification of the organ (Deidamia 'insists upon it that I have nothing to fear from *Pyrrha*; and is . . . positive in this Opinion' [I, viii, 76–8], recalling Thetis's fear 'that when you are among the Ladies you shou'd be so little Master of your Passions as to find your self a Man' (I, i, 85–7)), and indirect indication through the symptoms of pregnancy, here morning sickness ('There must be some Reason that *Deidamia* hath not been with me this Morning' (I, viii, 86–7)).

In Gay's original text the subplot that presents this plane of the question of identity may have been introduced directly in dialogue between the two lovers[28]; even so, there, as in the published version, this subplot (and the plane it presents) are set aside until very late in the play (the last scene of Act II or, in Burnet, several scenes into Act III), where they occupy a brief, discreet segment of the text. It is important to notice that Gay, utterly in contrast to Statius, does not dramatize the love-making. Nor does he exploit the long-standing analogy of penis to weapon of warfare or conquest, hero to sexual conqueror, even disregarding Statius's striking represe̶n̶t̶ation of this theme. What interests him principally is the ̶e̶loquence of indirect testimony, as expressed in the shape of not the man's but the woman's body, which makes the male presence 'monstrously evident' (III, vii, 56–7)[29]: 'That she [Deidamia] hath all the outward Marks of Female Frailty must be visible to all Woman-kind' (III, vii, 65–6), say her sisters. Sexed—female—body here speaks to sexed (or gendered?) female eye.

Deidamia is defined by, and defines Achilles by, his sex, but he defines manhood by behaving publicly—and being recognized—as manly:

> *Achilles.* When shall I behave my self as a Man!
> *Deidamia.* Wou'd you had never behav'd yourself as one!
>
> (II, x, 9–10)

A whole repertory of gestures—long strides, swearing, 'aukward Behaviour'—define men as different from women (II, x, 72, 85–6; I, i, 75). Air XXXVI captures the process of rationalization by a man, Achilles, who finds it difficult to behave as women so easily do: soon the impossible attainment begins to be disqualified as merely a manifestation of a 'natural various-ness'; then that nature begins to be disqualified as one that a man, with his integrity of being, would not wish to have:

> Your Dress, your Conversations,
>   Your Airs of Joy and Pain,
> All these are Affectations
>   We never can attain.
> The Sex so often varies,
>   'Tis Nature more than Art:
> To play their whole Vagaries
>   We must have Woman's Heart.
>
> (II, x, 76–83)

In the first act the difference between men and women is asserted over and over in the dialogue between Thetis and Achilles, not precisely themselves a woman and a man but very conscious of their several natures—divine and heroic—that they feel they debase by pretending to be women (I, i, 30–2, 67–8). Here Gay approaches the issue at the heart of the old legend about the heroic destiny that cannot be gainsaid. Manliness longs to define itself as an immutable inner essence residing in 'the Heart of a Man' (I, i, 14–15), but the language keeps pressing the residence of manly reality outward, to the minds of other manly men with whom one interacts in public deeds—who know one's 'character', recognize one's 'honour', the worth of one's 'Word', remember one's 'glory', preserve one's 'Fame' (I, i). Embroidery, the reading of romances, preoccupation with dress, the spleen (I, ii), are the gendered occupations of 'the Life of a Woman' (I, i, 52), which is not to live as something distinct—womanly—but as something *not-manly*, not truly or fully existent and therefore debased: manly 'Character' is opposed to womanish 'Infamy', 'Honour' to 'Cowardise', 'Death with Fame' to 'Life with Shame', one's 'Word' to the pleasure of breaking promises, integrity of being to natural variousness, sword to tongue, duty to country to obedience to mama, resolution to pity, freedom to captivity (I, i, Air XXXVI; III, iii, 18–19, Airs L, XXXIII). In short, whatever one's qualities of generosity, courage, resolution, confidence, one cannot be a 'Man' unless one is recognized to be so by other 'Men', and to be visible requires definition against the contrasting background. 'Honour' is in the recognition; it is for this reason that Achilles becomes dishonoured by his disguise: 'my Honour is already sacrific'd to my Duty. That I gave you when I submitted to put on this Womans Habit' (I, i, 30–2).

Dependency upon the recognition of others for the empowerment of one's identity is only a step away from our final category, in which the reality *arises out of* how we are apprehended by others. Deidamia fears that Achilles will seem to her sisters to be a man because 'whenever I look upon you, I have always the Image of a Man before my Eyes' (II, x, 97–8). The greater part of *Achilles* is given to investigating the reality of this kind of identity wherein what Achilles *is* is only what he is believed to be by Lycomedes—a young girl. When Deidamia sees in Pyrrha the image of a man, she discerns what she *knows* but also projects what she *desires*; for Lycomedes, however, Pyrrha is his desire alone.

The Lycomedes plot is the most interesting part of *Achilles*, for it is entirely Gay's own contribution to the legend; he emphasizes its importance by giving it the greater part of his

dramatic time. Its basis is the stock situation in theatre—soon
to become the stock situation in the novel as well—in which the
young heroine is exposed to unwelcome sexual advances from a
man, usually older or of a higher social position, whom she
ought to be able to look to for protection. This plot comes into
Achilles, we have noticed, from *Polly*, where Gay used it in its
'Potiphar's wife' variant. His adding the twist of the travesty to
the scene moves its concern from the question of sex to the
question of gender and stresses how largely the harassment is a
function of power rather than of true sexual desire. In Gay's
version of the Achilles plot (unlike Rolli's), Thetis, pretending
to be 'a distress'd *Grecian* Princess' (I, i, 68), asks Lycomedes to
allow her 'daughter Pyrrha' to share the education and pastimes
of his girls. Lycomedes does not believe the reasons Thetis gives
for making her request, but, when his aide Diphilus flatters his
vanity by suggesting that the 'most delicious Piece' he admires
might be 'had' (I, v, 3, 12), he cannot find any other explanation
for the girl's being left behind than that the women hope that he
will make the girl his mistress. In other words, the girl exists for
him only as a blank onto which he projects his own fantasies; he
cannot summon up the thought that she might have a mode of
being beyond his awareness or imagination. Though he can see
clearly that Pyrrha's behaviour—for example, her vehemently
denouncing Diphilus as 'a Pimp, a Pandar, a Bawd' (II, i,
34)—is not overtly encouraging, he eagerly accepts Diphilus's
construction that the girl's language is a matter of 'ill-breeding'
and her attitude an 'affectation' covering 'Modesty' (II, iv, 31),
which therefore expresses the receptiveness he desires: 'She had
all the Resentment and Fury of the most complying Prude' (II,
iii, 19–20).

Lycomedes begins his effort to possess the girl by sending an
agent to attempt to buy her with gifts. Next he offers the
presents personally. Next he tries to beguile her with flattery.
He declares his passion. Indifference and resistance become
imperatives for aggressive love-making:

> To save the Appearances of Virtue, the most easy Woman
> expects a little gentle Compulsion, and to be allow'd the Decency
> of a little feeble Resistance. For the Quiet of her own Conscience
> a Woman may insist upon acting the Part of Modesty, and you
> must comply with her Scruples. (II, iii, 36–41)

When the last tactics seem not to work, he quickly turns to trying rape:

> When the Fort on no Condition
>   Will admit the gen'rous Foe,
> Parley but delays Submission;
>   We by Storm shou'd lay it low.[30]

$$\text{(II, iv, 65–8)}$$

The burlesque battle this conceit introduces functions in comic terms to release the tension in the scene. We must not leap to the supposition, however, that the playwright thereby trivializes the kind of oppression he has been dramatizing. As Pyrrha, Gay's underdog is endowed with precisely the invincible power that Lycomedes's whole attitude presupposes—and that the very idea of Hero embodied in Achilles presupposes—to be utterly absent in women (i.e., non-men): 'Am I so ignominiously to be got the better of! . . . By a Woman!' (II, iv, 99, 101). Humiliated, Lycomedes takes the still-all-too-familiar recourse of blaming the victim:

> *Achilles*: Who was the Aggressor, Sir?
> *Lycomedes*: Beauty, Inclination, Love. (II, v, 24–5)

When Lycomedes becomes finally convinced that the girl cannot become his own possession, he does not enlarge his perception of her from object to person, but merely comes to look upon her as something disturbing to be got rid of. Candidly stating what most people act upon but do not admit to themselves about someone whom they have injured, he declares: 'Her Presence just now wou'd be shocking.—I cou'd not stand the Shame and Confusion' (II, viii, 30–1). He therefore joins in with his wife's plans to marry her off to the (as it happens, uninterested) man of their choice.

'When shall I appear as I am', says Achilles to himself, to be able to 'extricate my self out of this Chain of Perplexities!—I have no sooner escap'd being ravish'd but I am immediately to be made a Wife' (II, x, 65–8). He is clear that these torments occur because he is gendered as female, even though he may not realize the link between the intended marriage and the failure of the attempted rape. Gay's plot makes explicit how, in a society with a double standard, women are forced to destroy each other: Queen Theaspe, whose status derives from her husband, looks through his eyes to see the object of his desire ('I can see her [Pyrrha's] Faults, Sir. I see her as a Woman sees a Woman. The Men, it seems, think the aukward Creature handsome' (I, vi, 16–18)). She confirms the men's deduction as to why Pyrrha has been left behind: 'The Woman, no doubt, depends upon it, that her Daughter's Charms are not to be resisted' (I, vi, 97–8). She is attuned to proclivities in her husband before he is even aware of them; she feels jealousy, well-placed, but before the event. Diphilus is able to use her jealousy as an argument to persuade Lycomedes to pursue the affair; the evidence that women are (merely) objects of men's desire comes, then, not just from the men but also from other women's jealousy and anxiety.

The young girl is therefore perceived in sexual terms by the persons she must look to for protection. By the travesty Gay makes this quite clear: Achilles's attractiveness to young men, presumably by virtue of his felt qualities of heroism and leadership, is, because of his gender, interpreted as the sexual charm of a belle (by Diphilus, II, v, 96–7, by Theaspe II, vi, 13–14). His enthusiastic admiration, when Theaspe asks him how he likes Periphas, for the man's wonderful 'Impatience . . . to serve . . . at the Siege of *Troy*' (II, ix, 9–10), she misreads in the same way. The predicament for women in an oppressive society is that young girls require protection, but because of hypocrisy and the double standard it is *assumed* that they are being put forward not for protection but for advantage through covert sex. It is the inexperienced and little-aware girl who has the greatest chance for advantage, while, for men, experience, wealth, and self-confidence offset the natural attractions of youth. What is 'experience' for 'experienced women' is the coming to awareness of the arrangements and how they work, but, as Gay shows, that very awareness acts to propel the oppression forward upon other women.

What a woman must do—and is entitled to do—in the face of unwelcome attentions Gay expresses through Parthenia in *Dione*. Gay supports her point of view by arranging his plot so that her wishes can be fully met, and in order to do so he was obliged to cast his play as a tragedy, for him not at all a comfortable mode.[31] Because of her exceptional beauty Parthenia persistently finds herself attracting men's desire; a man puts the

argument to her: 'What heart is proof against that face divine?/
Love is not in our power' (I, iii, 11–12). But she refuses to
accept that someone else's desire should obligate her when she
had done nothing to encourage it:

> If e'er I trifled with a shepherd's pain,
> Or with false hope his passion strove to gain;
> Then might you justly curse my savage mind,
> Then might you rank me with the serpent kind:
> But I ne'er trifled with a shepherd's pain,
> Nor with false hope his passion strove to gain:
> 'Tis to his rash pursuit he owes his fate,
> I was not cruel; he was obstinate.
>
> (I, iii, 13–20)

And she goes on with what one might call a Whig feminist credo:

> Why will intruding man my peace destroy?
> Let me content, and solitude enjoy;
> Free was I born, my freedom to maintain,
> Early I sought the unambitious plain.
>
> (I, iii, 25–8)

She sternly advises that her suitor be 'Bid . . . his heart-consuming
groans give o'er, . . . be wise,/ Prevent thy fate' (I, iii, 37, 39–
40). Lycidas's disregard of her insistence that he take responsibility for his own life (or, his disregard of the autonomy of
nature) brings death to himself and Dione but leaves Parthenia
unmated and unharassed, as she had wished.

By the time of *Achilles* the question of women's right—or
desire—to live unmolested had become a topical issue through
the sensational Charteris case, which had dramatized the social
factors as blatantly as can be imagined. Colonel Francis Charteris
had amassed a huge fortune by graft, gambling, close-dealing
and chicanery. He had been censured before the House of
Commons for taking pay-offs as an officer. He was known by his
male visitors to run his household of maid-servants as a brothel.[32]
He had been found guilty in Scotland of raping a woman at
pistol-point on a public road, but had been pardoned by George
I. In February 1730 he was found guilty of raping a recently
hired serving-maid in his London house and was sentenced to
hang. Vast quantities of his property, which had become forfeit,
were then seized by various public officials, and in due course

bought back by his son-in-law, the Earl of Wemyss, for very large sums. On 10 April he was pardoned by George II. Charteris was a well-known public figure, whose life had touched many of both sexes and all social classes in various parts of Great Britain, and his case attracted great interest. Day-to-day details, particularly between the trial and pardon, were widely reported and reprinted in the numerous London newspapers, and there flourished a complement of ballads, 'lives', portraits, and journalistic commentary.

Charteris's defence declared that the woman had been sleeping with him for many nights and that she had many times joked with other servants about his being impotent.[33] Some people (Addison, for example) preferred to fancy that this was true, in order to secure the piquant irony that Charteris 'having daily deserved the GIBBET for what/he *did*,/Was at last condemn'd to it for what he *could*/not *do*'.[34] Implicit in Charteris's defence—and accepted, though perhaps not faced, by those who liked the irony—was the idea that the rape charge was false. This is not far from the idea that *all* rape charges are false, that there is in fact no such thing as rape—'The late King [George I], as likewise Queen Elizabeth', Viscount Percival observes, predicting Charteris's pardon as early as 28 February, 'would never suffer a man condemned for a rape to be executed, as not believing it possible for to commit the crime unless the woman in some sort consented'.[35] The physical vulnerability of the woman's body to the man's invasion is opposed to the legal vulnerability of the man to the woman's accusation. In Charteris's instance the sex difference was underscored as a class difference, not only between master and serving-maid, but also between jurymen and Privy Council. Satirical editorials began to comment that, inasmuch as members of the upper class did not count rape a crime but instead something called 'gallantry', those with money and influence ought to be licensed to do it freely; this would spare useless trials, clarify social distinctions, and teach the lower classes—particularly lower-class women—their place.[36]

Gay followed this case—in fact he wrote to Swift just at the moment that Charteris was about to be pardoned:

> today I dine with Alderman Barbar the present Sheriff who holds his feast in the city. Does not Chartres' misfortunes grieve you, for

203

that great man is like to save his life and lose some of his money, a very hard case![37]

Gay's thoughts run as they do because Barber had been one of the three officials involved in the seizure of Charteris's forfeited goods, payment for which was still being negotiated,[38] and he was doubtless looking forward to talk of the case at the dinner. Gay probably heard other stories about Charteris from the Duke of Queensberry, whose mother is said to have been cheated of several thousand pounds by him at cards in a single evening.[39] After the pardon, interest in Charteris did not fade; rather, he became a symbolic figure of public corruption for artists of greater imaginative scope: Swift compares him to the recently-appointed English Dean of Fern in Ireland, who was indicted for rape on 6 June; *The Craftsman* and other political writers establish him as a satirical surrogate for Robert Walpole; Hogarth depicts him leering at Moll Hackabout, just disembarked from the York coach; Pope cites him in the *Epistle to Bathurst* as evidence that wealth is no index of moral worth.[40] All these works appeared in the period between Charteris's pardon and the opening of *Achilles* in February 1733.

The context in 1730 also generated Fielding's *Rape upon Rape*,[41] which, targeting its satire against the venal Justice Squeezum and his associates, builds a plot out of false charges of rape, accusations of false charges of rape, and charges of conspiracy to bring false charges of rape. For Fielding rape is rather more a term of utterance than a frightening and opprobrious reality:

> But, Ladies, did not you too sympathize?
> Hey! pray, confess, do all your Frowns arise
> Because so much of *Rape* and *Rape* we bawl?
> Or is it, that we have no *Rape* at all?
>
> Indeed, our Poet, to oblige the Age,
> Had brought a dreadful Scene upon the Stage:
> But I, perceiving what his Muse would drive at,
> Told him the Ladies never would connive at
> A downright actual *Rape*—unless in private.[42]

'Jokes about rape', writes Ian Donaldson, 'characteristically imply that the crime may not in fact exist; that it is a legal and social fiction, which will dissolve before the gaze of humour and the universal sexual appetite.' Fielding validates his knowing implication by having a woman speak the lines quoted, thus exposing the 'disparity between a woman's words and her actual desires' that such jokes presume.[43] Fielding discounts 'rape' by locating it as an encounter between men and women of the same high and sophisticated social class. Fielding's outlook is that of a man of this class, classically educated, confident, forward, whose social and financial ascendancy encourage him and his fellows to understand that the desires of others correspond to their own.

Gay began to formulate *Achilles* sometime in the wake of the Charteris case. Certainly, even if we resist accepting the partisan impulse to which *The Daily Journal* and *Achilles Dissected* attribute its genesis, we must acknowledge that it arises out of the temporal context in which people, certainly the people in Gay's circle, knew the configuration of sexual desire among persons at Court—the King, the Queen, Mrs. Howard, Lord Hervey (the Vice Chamberlain)—and knew that symbols inviting identification with Walpole's administration would be read in a partisan way. The duel between Ajax and Periphas, for example, could recall that between Pulteney and Hervey in January 1731 over the former's putting into print innuendos about the nature of Hervey's passion for Stephen Fox.[44] Since *The Beggar's Opera*, as Gay was well aware, the theatre had become more and more explicitly partisan and satirical of Walpole and the Court.

However much *Achilles* may have arisen out of this context, and whatever invitation it could be perceived to offer party journalists to politicize its genesis, intention and meaning, the fact is that, for Gay, public corruption was always less interesting and acutely felt than the tyranny of one individual over another. In the figure of the travesty Achilles, Gay saw a means—in a light context that would not be resisted—to signal to men of Fielding's background and mentality an indirect but telling point about themselves in their personal conduct. To the legend, Gay added Lycomedes's pursuit of Pyrrha. Lycomedes's attempted rape of Pyrrha, the culmination of this extensive part of *Achilles*, invokes by inversion, for the classically-aware segment of his audience, the rape of Deidamia *by* Pyrrha in Ovid's version, where the idea of rape was added to the old tale. One might wish to argue, in fact, that the epigraph from Ovid's

Metamorphoses on the title page of *Achilles* be construed as a
significant misdirection to the right author but the wrong text.

What I have not mentioned so far is the context in which
Ovid invokes the tale. Many of my readers will be surprised to
learn that what is today called 'date-rape' has for generations of
'gentlemen' been sanctioned by classical authority. In *Ars
Amatoria* Ovid, the sophisticated instructor of the inexperienced
young man, assures him that he need have no hesitation in
raping his girl if she does not readily yield:

> oscula qui sumpsit, si non et cetera sumit,
>   haec quoque, quae data sunt, perdere dignus erit.
> quantum defuerat pleno post oscula voto?
>   ei mihi, rusticitas, non pudor ille fuit.
> vim licet appelles: grata est vis ista puellis:
>   quod iuvat, invitae saepe dedisse volunt.
> quaecumque est veneris subita violata rapina,
>   gaudet, et inprobitas muneris instar habet.
> at quae, cum posset cogi, non tacta recessit,
>   ut simulet vultu gaudia, tristis erit.

(I, 669–78)[45]

Henry Fielding himself (though years later) was to put out a
'modernization' of the Ovid with quite a close translation of
these particular lines:

> Now when you have proceeded to Kisses, if you proceed no
> farther, you may well be called unworthy of what you have
> hitherto obtained. When you was at her Lips, how near was you
> to your Journey's End! If therefore you stop there, you rather
> deserve the Name of a bashful 'Squire than of a modest Man.
>
> The Girls may call this perhaps Violence; but it is a Violence
> agreeable to them: for they are often desirous of being pleased
> against their Will: For a Woman taken without her Consent,
> notwithstanding her Frowns, is often well satisfied in her Heart,
> and your Impudence is taken as a Favour; whilst she who, when
> inclined to be ravished, hath retreated untouched, however she
> may affect to smile, is in reality out of Humour.[46]

To support this advice Ovid adduces various instances of women
who came to dote on their rapists, most importantly 'the well-
known story, worth repeating nevertheless' (*fabula nota quidem,
sed non indigna referri* (I, 681)) of Achilles and Deidamia. As
rhetorically Ovid claims ascendency over his pupil by the skilful

anticipatory blocking action of the terms *rusticitas* and *pudor* (I, 672), which pressure the young man to act as he directs, so does he sustain his posture by daring to mock even Achilles, in his disguise, who conceals his manhood behind a skirt (*veste virum longa dissimulatus* (I, 690)) and who messes about with spindles and wool. But, he observes, Deidamia certainly found out that he was a man (*vir, viri*)—and it was by force (*vis, vim, vires*):

> *haec illum stupro comperit esse virum*
> *viribus illa quidem victa est, ita credere oportet:*
> *sed voluit vinci viribus illa tamen.*

(I, 698–700)

She wanted to be conquered by force, and afterwards when he was going off to Troy she kept begging him to stay. As Fielding puts it:

> He ravished her, that is the Truth on't; that a Gentleman ought to believe, in favour of the Lady: but he may believe the Lady was willing enough to be ravished at the same time.[47]

Gay calls up this passage—the example, the very advice (in lines already quoted)—and by moving Achilles from agent to recipient enforces a reassessment of the advice from within the consciousness of the woman whom Ovid keeps silent until she has been subdued. The burning male consciousness of Achilles invites his fellow Fieldings, or Ovids, to recognize what it might be to suffer and be silent, while, for those of Gay's audience gendered female, the concealed power replots Ovid's tale so that the would-be rapist becomes the booby object of ridicule. Alas that it takes a John Gay to be able both to see what Ovid's attitude implies for women and to express to men what he sees. The characteristic duality of his symbols, his forms and his modes reflects the dependency of his life and both enables him to speak and withholds what he would say. While, through Gay's comedy, women who are sexually harassed become empowered by the representation of Pyrrha, at the same time the figure of Pyrrha must suggest that to become empowered they must become what they cannot become, a hero and a man.[48]

My argument is not that Gay is a feminist *per se*, but that the predicament of women represents one mode of the wider condition of dependency, the dynamics and abuses of which

Gay knew all too well in his own life, and which he probes in terms of many kinds of social relationships in his writing. Many other modes of dependency, not touched upon in this paper but well worth attention, can be found in the very piece we have been considering. Gay's duples, such as Pyrrha/Achilles, enable him to render the dependent's unresolved adherence to, and rage against, the social system in which he or she is both sustained and suppressed. Gay's art can make us hear simultaneously the voice (or the eloquent silence) of acquiescence *and* the voice of rage, as the inner ears of dependents hear. And by the very means of something apparently inconsequential—a burlesque, a ballad opera—perhaps Gay beguiles some of the powerful to hear the double voices, too.

NOTES

1. For example, Sue-Ellen Case, 'Classic Drag: The Greek Creation of Female Parts', *Theatre Journal*, 37 (1985), 317–27, or David Mayer, 'The Sexuality of Pantomime', *Theatre Quarterly*, 4, 13 (1974), 60, 63.
2. John Harold Wilson noticed in 1958 the sexual dimension added to 'page' or 'breeches' parts (such as Shakespeare's Rosalind and Viola) when after the Restoration they came to be played by women. He points out (quoting Mandeville's *The Fable of the Bees*, Remark P) that they provided a unique, sanctioned public opportunity for men to look at women's legs and thighs in an era when skirts came to the floor (*All the King's Ladies: Actresses of the Restoration* (Chicago, 1958), p. 75). Quite apart from consideration of the practice of cross-casting, he finds that, out of about 375 new or altered plays first produced in London beween 1660 and 1700, eighty-nine contained rôles for women dressed as men (p. 73). New parts of this sort continued to be written after the turn of the century, as we see, for example, in *The Recruiting Officer* (the most performed play of the period before *The Beggar's Opera*) or in Gay's *Dione* and *Polly*.
   The advent of actresses at the Restoration had quite different consequences for travesty of the opposite kind. Actors who before the Commonwealth had been trained to play women found difficulty now in getting parts, and few new rôles calling for men to appear as women were written; R. C. Sharma finds only one, in Farquhar's *The Constant Couple*, within the plays he surveys (*Themes and Conventions in the Comedy of Manners* (New York, 1965), p. 184). In theatre the scope of female travesty tended to dwindle to the occasional rôles that could be played as a comic 'dame', a representation, Mayer points out, that projects considerable hostility to,

and ambivalence about, women (see note 1). (Opera, incidentally, has quite a separate history during this period with respect to travesty.)

In this theatrical context Gay's travesty rôle of Achilles seems modally unique, projected along a psychological plane that burlesques women no more than men. Whatever comic latitude the actor may feel he is invited to take throughout most of the play, he must embody an attractive person fit to be a hero, and one of the young marrying couple, at the end. The ideas of youth and manliness combined with the idea of the dependent young girl suggest quite different psychological features from those of the dame. We do not know whether Gay gave indications about casting and in any event he was dead before the play was worked out in rehearsal, but the actor so cast, Thomas Salway, seems to support the resonance I suggest. Apparently in his mid-twenties, he counted as a singer in Rich's company (he was a tenor); from his rôles he appears to have been capable of slapstick, comedy and second-line romantic parts (Edward A. Langhans, draft of 'Salway', to be published in the *Biographical Dictionary of Actors* [&c.] *1660–1800*, ed. Philip H. Highfill, Jr., *et al.*).

3. See, for example, Phyllis Rackin's insightful study of the figure in an earlier period, 'Androgyny, Mimesis, and the Marriage of the Boy Heroine on the English Renaissance Stage', *PMLA*, 102 (1987), 29–39, which unfortunately appeared too late for me to use in preparing this essay.

4. Little critical attention has been given to *Achilles*. Contemporary party journalists—a reviewer in the *Daily Courant* (16 February 1732/33) and an 'Atex Burnet' (see note 16)—pretended to discover in it a satire of George II's household and of Walpole. Howard Erskine-Hill, touching upon the work briefly but approvingly in 'The Significance of Gay's Drama', sees the disguised Achilles as the 'truth-bearer' giving moral weight to the form of farce (Marie Axton and Raymond Williams (eds.), *English Drama: Forms and Development: Essays in Honour of Muriel Clara Bradbrook* (Cambridge, 1977), pp. 160–61). Sven M. Armens finds Gay non-judgemental—ribald, comical, light—about the men's sexual politics that form the plot of *Achilles*, but sees the work as 'studded' with 'sharp and even misogynistic comments' about women (*John Gay: Social Critic* (New York, 1954), pp. 142–46). In his valuable study, 'John Gay's *Achilles*: The Burlesque Element', Peter Lewis sets forth the burlesque relationships of the work to heroic drama, Italian opera, and sentimental comedy (*Ariel*, 3 (1972), 17–28). But none of these critics address the aspects of *Achilles* I wish to consider.

5. This is the only source that gives Ajax as Ulysses's companion; Statius and Philostratus have Diomede (and Argytes, noticed but unnamed by Philostratus, to blow the trumpet); Hyginus indicates, but does not name, one or more companions; Apollodorus indicates no companions (for references, see note 10).

6. T. Folkma, sculp. (1722), 'Achilles disguised like a Woman, is discovered by Ulysses', S. le Clerc, invent., *Ovid's Metamorphoses* (Amsterdam, 1732), p. 419.

7. Published for the same bookseller (William Keble) and advertised in the

same notice that announces publication of Gay's *Wine* (*Daily Courant*, 22 May 1708). Ajax's speech is by Nahum Tate.

8. *Ovid in Masquerade, being, A Burlesque upon the xiii^{th} Book of His Metamorphoses, containing the Celebrated Speeches of Ajax and Ulysses. . . . By Mr.* Joseph Gay. London: for E. Curll, 1719 [1718]. Foxon enters the item under John Durant de Breval, but advises caution, 'since the pseudonym Joseph Gay was also used by Francis Chute'.

9. Also circulating would have been the seventeenth-century translations of the passage in George Sandys's *Ovid's Metamorphosis English'd* (1626, 1628, 1632, 1638, 1640, 1656, 1664, 1669, 1678, 1690); and in two versions of Book XIII: *Wisdoms Conqvest* (1651), sometimes assigned to Thomas Hall; and P[atrick] K[er]'s *Logomachia* (1690).

10. The Achilles-in-Scyros story is told or alluded to in the following classical texts: *Greek*: Apollodorus, *The Library*, III, xiii, 8; Bion (or Pseudo-Bion), II; Euripides, *Skyrioi*; Paulus Sileniarius (*Greek Anthology*), V, 255; Pausanias, I, xxii, 6; Philostratus the Younger, *Imagines*, I; *Latin*: Horace, *Odes*, I, 8; Hyginus, *Myths*, XCVI; Ovid, *Ars Amatoria* (hereafter *AA*), I, 681–704, *Metamorphoses* (hereafter *M*), XIII, 162–70; Pliny, *Natural History*, XXXV, 134; Seneca, *Troades*, 212–15, 343–44, 570–71; Sidonius, *Carmina*, IX, 140–43; Statius, *Achilleid*, I, 5–6, 142, 270–72, 283–381, 533–35, 560–674, 709–960.

11. *sed opertae conscia culpae/cuncta pavet tacitasque putat sentire sorores* (*Achilleid*, I, 562–63; Loeb edition of *Statius*, ed. J. H. Mozley (London and New York, 1928)).

12. *Deidamia and the Love Affair*: not in *M* (but as intrigue mentioned by Sandys (1632 only), Ker); *as intrigue*: Apollodorus, Philostratus, Seneca; *as rape*: *AA*, Statius; Bion's 'stolen joys/espousals' could be read as either, according to whether they are considered 'unknown to others' or 'stolen from Deidamia'; Sidonius's language is coy, but seems to allude to Statius's *mise en scène*. *Achilles Spinning*: not in *M*; in *AA*, Statius, Bion. *The Group of Lycomedes's Daughters*; not in Ovid (but mentioned by Sandys); in Statius, Bion, Philostratus, Hyginus, Pausanias (also reporting Polygnotus), Sidonius. *The Trumpet*: not in Ovid; in Statius, Apollodorus, Hyginus.

13. Eric Arthur Barker rejects its attribution to Bion (*Oxford Classical Dictionary* (1949), p. 138). This piece is not in the following volumes that might have contained it: Thomas Stanley, *Poems* (1651); Theocritus, *Idylliums*, trans. Creech (2nd edn., 1713); Moschus and Bion, *Idylliums*, trans. Cooke (1724); Thomas Cooke, *Tales* (1729).

14. Act, scene, and line references are to the texts of Gay's plays in *DW*, from which all quotations are taken (roman and italic reversed in predominantly italic passages such as Airs).

15. The fragment breaks off at this point; 'A veritable cliffhanger', remarks Professor Peter Westervelt of Colby College, to whom I am grateful for providing a literal translation where the Loeb edition (*The Greek Bucolic Poets*, trans. J. M. Edmonds (London and New York, 1919), pp. 398–401) was seduced into a false Spenserian style.

16. *Achilles Dissected: Being a Compleat Key of the Political Characters In that New Ballad Opera, Written by the late Mr. Gay. An Account of the Plan upon which it is*

founded. *With Remarks upon the Whole . . . To which is added, The First Satire of the Second Book of Horace, Imitated in a Dialogue between Mr. Pope and the Ordinary of Newgate* (London, 1733), p. 1; Burnet's identity is unknown, despite his being confused sometimes with the author of the accompanying poem, Guthry, or with Tom Burnet.

17. Loeb translation: *vi potitur votis et toto pectore veros/ admovet amplexus* (I, 642–3); translations from Latin, when not otherwise credited, are my own.

18. *Pelea virgo*, 'the daughter of Peleus', is whom Thetis asked to leave behind; Achilles is Peleus's son. But in ending the passage with these words, Statius's principal opposition is not of female child to male child, but of what is lesser than man (woman), hence shameful, to what is greater than man (hero), hence awesome.

19. Observe, for example, the actively misleading language of even quite recent scholars in describing Achilles's rape of Deidamia in Statius and Ovid: 'The event [Ulysses's disclosure of Achilles] was told . . . at some length by Statius in his *Achilleid*. The courtship of Deidamia was recorded by Bion and by Ovid in his *Art of Love*' (Wilmon Brewer, *Ovid's Metamorphoses in European Culture*, rev. edn. (Francestown, New Hampshire, 1978), II, 1419); 'Gay's principal source [for *Achilles*] seems to have been Statius, but the story also appears in Bion and Ovid' (John Fuller, 'Introduction', [*DW*, I, 59]). Fuller gives no citations for Bion and Ovid and no indication that the Scyros episode is treated *twice* in Ovid, and he discusses the treatment of the love affair in these authors no further.

20. King 'endeavour[s] . . . to give Readers of both Sexes some Ideas of the Art of Love; such a Love as is innocent and virtuous'; to this end, he manipulates Ovid's text, which he prints in blocks as footnotes, re-arranging the material and taking occasion to omit a number of lines; furthermore, he neglects to translate some of the Latin he actually prints. Ovid's advice that prompts the Achilles story is entirely omitted, as is the rape (although King does recount the rape of the Sabines); here it is Deidamia who initiates the affair, which King represents as the consequence of avoiding military service: 'Thus whilst we Glory's Dictates shun,/ Into the Snares of Vice we run' (*The Art of Love: In Imitation of Ovid De Arte Amandi* (London, 1708—dated by Foxon, who also records the reissue, which I have not seen), pp. vii, 59–64). Gay would have been aware of this edition, for the announcement of its publication follows immediately on the page of the *Daily Courant* the announcement of his own *Wine* (22 May 1708). By 1711, at least, Gay knew King, whose destitute plight he mentions with compassion in *The Present State of Wit* (*PP*, II, 449). If he also knew King's text, Gay must have enjoyed its burlesque, which has affinities with themes he would develop in *The What D'Ye Call It*—when Deidamia's pregnancy is about to be discovered, Achilles runs off into the army in order to avoid punishment. For *Achilles* Gay may have taken hints from King's modernization for Thetis's instructions to her son concerning women's dress, posture, movement and mannerisms (which have their source in Statius, not Ovid) and for the substitution of embroidery work for spinning.

21. Ovid may have received the rape from a lost Greek tradition (as represented by papyrus Hypothesis, cited by T. B. L. Webster, *The Tragedies of Euripides* (London, 1967), pp. 95–6).

22. The child was called Neoptolemus or Pyrrhus; he appears in *The Iliad* as Achilles's son, even if the Scyros episode does not. Shortly before arriving at the Scyros tale in his speech in the *Metamorphoses*, Ulysses mentions Pyrrhus of Scyros as Achilles's son (and therefore logical recipient of the contested armour if it is to be awarded on the grounds of kinship), but Ovid does not clearly connect his origin to the time Achilles dwelt in disguise. Statius of course treats these connections in the episode fully.

23. *PP*, I, 206 (Commentary, II, 581). The classical sources Gay associates with his garb and reverie are worth noticing, all together forming an imaginative cluster that could have influenced the choice and shaping of *Achilles*; Dearing (*PP*, II, 583) observes that it is not Venus (*Aeneid*, I. 229ff.) but Thetis, appealing on behalf of Achilles (*Iliad*, I, 501), who holds Zeus 'under the chin'.

24. I have not been able to see the 1741 libretto; my knowledge of the plot of *Deidamia* is taken from the summary by Edward J. Dent ('The Operas', in Gerald Abraham (ed.), *Handel: A Symposium* (London, 1954), pp. 59–62), and from Winton Dean's broadcast commentary accompanying a B.B.C. radio performance (ca. 1974) of which I heard an imperfect transcription.

25. Samuel Garth (ed.), *Ovid's Metamorphoses* (London, 1717), p. 443; Ovid has *decepterat omnes . . . sumptae fallacia vestis: arma . . . anima motura virilem* (XIII, 163–66), the last phrase being translated literally as 'to tempt a manly mind' by Sandys, *Wisdoms Conqvest* and Theobald.

26. Burnet, who of course took the view that a number of writers were involved in finishing *Achilles*, is the first to state that the '*Prologue . . . was written by Mr. Pope*' (p. 2); Norman Ault provides an extensive argument to support this attribution ('The Prologue to *Achilles*', *New Light on Pope* (London, 1949), pp. 215–21). Fuller accepts Ault's argument and deploys Ault's evidence in a series of footnotes (*DW*, II, 390). Maynard Mack, however, in his review of Ault's book finds the argument unconvincing (*PQ*, 29 (1950), 291), and, *pace* Ault, John Butt places it among the less plausibly attributable to Pope of the 'Poems of Doubtful Authorship' considered for volume VI of the Twickenham Pope (Norman Ault and John Butt, (eds.), *Minor Poems*, (London and New Haven, 1964), p. 457).

27. This alludes to Dennis's description of Pope's *Homer* as a translation in which 'there are Twenty Prosaick Lines, for One that is Poetical.' 'Where the Original is pure, the Translation is often barbarous,' he writes: 'In short, the HOMER which LINTOTT prints, does not talk like HOMER, but like POPE' (*Remarks Upon Mr. Pope's Translation of Homer* (London, for E. Curll), 1717, pp. 10–12).

28. The considerable differences in the *dramatic structure* of the performed *Achilles* described by Burnet in *Achilles Dissected* and the version appearing in the printed edition do imply that rearrangements and perhaps re-writing of this aspect of the work may have taken place in rehearsal and during the run. *Achilles* opened on 10 February; Burnet's pamphlet is dated 12 February (leaf B1ʳ), but one should note that it extracts (at

length) the review appearing in the *Daily Courant* of 16 February; *Achilles* was published on 1 March (*Grub-street Journal*). One song, probably (as Fuller points out (*DW*, II, 391)) from the end of III, ii, with the lines

> Hercules's Shirt[-*a*]
> Which burnt him all to---Dirt[-*a*],
> And set him all on a Fire-a,
> [*Contriv'd by his Deianira*]

(*Daily Courant*, with bracketed variants from Burnet), may have been cut in response to their ridicule. Scholars of Gay have noticed this song (if not its variants), but no commentator, so far as I am aware, has discussed the changes in structure. The structure Burnet describes is as follows: Act I: 'our young Hero burns for his Deidamia, and she sighs for her Achilles'; Lycomedes desires Pyrrha; Act II: Lycomedes's pursuit of Pyrrha and Theaspe's jealousy; Act III: Lycomedes's attempted rape of Pyrrha; duel between Ajax and Periphas; revelation of Deidamia's sexual knowledge of Pyrrha's masculinity; Ulysses's disclosure of Achilles's identity (pp. 2–5). In the revised version the Lycomedes plot is disposed of before the Deidamia plot is begun, and several of the climaxes are moved back from Act III to increase the dynamics of Act II. These alterations do not affect the main argument of this paper, which attributes the exploration of sex and gender identity in the work to Gay and which finds greatest interest in the part of the story that Gay added, the Lycomedes plot, which in Burnet's version occupies even more of the play than in the version we read.

29. 'Thus Ladylike he with a Lady Lay,/ Till what he was her belly did bewray' (Heywood, tr., *AA* (1650 edn.), p. 30); see also King translation, *AA* (1708), p. 63.

30. Some earlier translators anticipate Gay in making the implicit analogy explicit in their diction: 'Yet will she fight like one would loose the field' (Heywood, p. 29); 'Who e'er retreats, when he thus far has gone;/ How almost was He Master of the Town!' and 'The Siege [of a Royal Virgin] much safer, . . . by Force, he won the Field' (Hoy translation, *AA* (1682), pp. 40, 41). For the use of this metaphor in Ovid and elsewhere in antiquity, see Molly Myerowitz, *Ovid's Games of Love* (Detroit, 1985), pp. 205–6, n. 78.

31. The play was never performed and has attracted few readers. Shortly after *Achilles* opened, however, an operatic adaptation set by Johann Friedrich Lampe using Gay's plot of *Dione* and some of his dialogue for the recitative ran briefly from 23 February 1733 (Fuller, *DW*, I, 36; *The London Stage 1660–1800*, Part 3 (1729–1747), ed. Arthur H. Scouten (Carbondale, Ill. 1961), p. 273.

32. *Diary of Viscount Percival, Afterwards First Earl of Egmont*—Historical Manuscripts Commission, *Manuscripts of the Earl of Egmont*, I (London, 1920), 75 (28 February 1730).

33. *The Proceedings at the Sessions of the Peace, and Oyer and Terminer, for the City of London, and County of Middlesex held At Justice-Hall in the Old Bailey, on Friday the 27th of February . . . upon a Bill of Indictment found against Francis Charteris,*

Esq; for committing a Rape on the Body of Anne Bond, of which he was found Guilty ((London), 1730). A fuller version of the trial appears in *Select Trials, for Murders, ... at the Sessions-House in the Old-Bailey. . . . Vol. II: From the Year 1724, to 1732, Inclusive* (London, 1735), pp. 339–51; this text also covers subsequent events beyond his death in 1732 by collating and reprinting the newspaper coverage. A brief notice of Charteris's life by Pope can be found as annotation to the *Epistle to Bathurst*, l. 20 (F. W. Bateson (ed.), *Epistles to Several Persons (Moral Essays)*, 2nd edn. (London and New Haven, 1961), pp. 85–6—vol. III, ii of the Twickenham Pope). A fuller summary occurs in the *Dictionary of National Biography*. A good modern account, directed towards his meaning for Hogarth, can be found in Ronald Paulson, *Hogarth: His Life, Art, and Times* (New Haven and London, 1971), I, 244–51.

34. 'An Epitaph' (beginning, 'Here lieth the body of Colonel/Don Francisco'). It was printed in the *London Magazine*, 1 (April 1732), 39, in the *Gentleman's Magazine*, 2 (April 1732), 718, and also in the Pope-Swift *Miscellanies, The Third Volume* (1732), with the *Select Trials* (1735) (n. 33), and as part of Pope's footnote (*Epistle to Bathurst*, l. 20n (n. 33)), where its attribution to Arbuthnot is made.

35. *Diary*, I, 75.

36. *Grub-street Journal* (12 March and 9 April 1730).

37. *Letters*, pp. 90–1 (31 March 1730).

38. For the seizure: *Daily Courant* (28 February), *London Evening Post* (26–28 February), *Daily Post* (28 February), *Monthly Chronicle* (27 February). For the payment: *Daily Journal* (31 August). Sheriff Barber's share was £1,650.

39. E. Beresford Chancellor, *Col. Charteris and the Duke of Wharton—The Lives of the Rakes*, III (London, 1925), 62–3.

40. 'An Excellent New Ballad: or, The true Eng-sh D--n to be hang'd for a R-pe', *The Poems of Jonathan Swift*, ed. Harold Williams, 2nd edn., II (Oxford, 1958), 516–20; it appeared in the *Grub-street Journal* of 11 June 1730. *The Country Journal; or, the Craftsman*, 8 August 1730, and *An Answer To One Part of a late Infamous Libel, intitled, Remarks on the Craftsman's Vindication of his two honourable Patrons; In which The Character and Conduct of Mr. P. is fully Vindicated In a Letter to the most Noble Author* (London, 1731), pp. 43–4, sometimes attributed to William Pulteney. 'A Harlot's Progress', Plate 1; the painting of the series may have been finished in September 1731; the prints were published on 10 April 1732 (Ronald Paulson, comp., *Hogarth's Graphic Works* (New Haven and London, 1965), I, 141, 144). The *Epistle to Bathurst* was published on 15 January 1733.

41. Bertrand A. Goldgar, *Walpole and the Wits: The Relation of Politics to Literature, 1722–1742* (Lincoln, Neb., and London, 1976), pp. 105–10.

42. 'Epilogue. Spoken by Mrs. Mullart', *The Coffee House Politician; or, the Justice Caught in his own Trap* (London, 1730) leaf A3^r; italic and roman reversed. *Rape upon Rape; or, the Justice Caught in his own Trap* opened on 23 June 1730 and was immediately published (*London Evening Post*, 23/25 June). When the play reopened in November its title was softened to *The Coffee House Politician; or, the Justice Caught in his own Trap*; the text was reissued under this title with altered front matter, including revision of the

epilogue. The quotation is from this revised epilogue.

43. Donaldson, *The Rapes of Lucretia: A Myth and its Transformation* (Oxford, 1982), pp. 87–9, which also treat other flippant references to rape in English plays of the period. Donaldson's thoughtful and intelligent study provides a valuable consideration of the theme of rape in literature and art.

44. See Romney Sedgwick, 'Introduction' to John, Lord Hervey's *Some Materials towards Memoirs of the Reign of King George II* (London, 1931), I, xxii–xxx, and Robert Halsband, *Lord Hervey: Eighteenth-Century Courtier* (Oxford, 1973), pp. 108–18, 144. It is plausible that Gay might have been led to think of a 'Master-Miss' at Court as a comic subject, in the context of gossip about Hervey in 1731, perhaps in banter with political friends. In *Achilles Dissected*, Burnet, already having indicated that Gay's Lycomedes might not have been '*ignorant of the sex of* ACHILLES', insinuates that 'the *Duel* fought between that Hero AJAX and a *Great* LORD, [is] a plain Representation of what lately happened between a *Little* LORD and a *Great* COMMONER' (pp. 12, 13); Gay's version of the duel (if it is that) belatedly lags after the immediate spate of satires inevitably following the event—*An Epistle from Little Captain Brazen, to the Worthy Captain Plume, The Countess's Speech To her Son Roderigo, The Duel; A Poem, Pulteney: or, the Patriot,* and others—which had laid the ground for comic interpretation. One might note that Hervey, writing of *Achilles* to the Duke of Richmond on 17 February, singles out Ajax as 'the only part that has the least pretence to humour', though rather more owing to the actor Hall than Gay, in an otherwise dull piece (The Earl of Ilchester (ed.), *Lord Hervey and His Friends: 1726–38* (London, 1950), pp. 162–63).

45. Latin texts of *AA* are conflated from A. S. Hollis's edition of Book I (Oxford, 1977), pp. 26–7, and J. H. Mozley's Loeb edition, rev. G. P. Goold (1979), pp. 58, 60.

46. Fielding, *Ovid's Art of Love Paraphrased, and Adapted to the Present Time. With Notes. and A most Correct Edition of the Original. Book I* (London, 1747), p. 75. The 1760 edition of this work, which bears the title *The Lovers Assistant, or, New Art of Love*, is edited by Claude E. Jones as Augustan Reprint 89 (Los Angeles, 1961). See Ovid, *The Erotic Poems*, trans. Peter Green ((Harmondsworth), 1982), for an excellent modern translation.

47. Fielding, p. 79.

48. Gay's indirection, or a blunter social sanction, seems to have got his message across to Fielding to some degree by 1747, for he prefaces his treatment of the Achilles passage with a disclaimer (however ironic) for modern times: 'Ravishing is indeed out of fashion in this Age; and therefore I am at a loss for modern Examples; but ancient Story abounds with them. . . . Though the Story of *Deidamia* was formerly in all the *Trojan* News-Papers, yet my Readers may be pleased to see it better told' (p. 77).

10

John Gay's Monument

by YVONNE NOBLE

To his contemporaries Gay's contribution to English culture seemed so central and unquestionable that not merely was a monument put up for him in Poets' Corner of Westminster Abbey, but his funeral was held there and he was actually buried at that site. Pope and the Queensberrys took pains to mark his grave with an imposing monument charged with significance. As a work of art the monument is notable in many ways: it is an important sculpture by Rysbrack (worth a plate in the *Sculpture in Britain: 1530 to 1830* volume of the standard reference series, the Pelican History of Art)[1]; it bears an epitaph by Alexander Pope; it bears an epitaph by Gay himself (the famous 'Life is a Jest' epigrammatic couplet); it bears—what John Kerslake, compiler of the catalogue of *Early Georgian Portraits* for the National Portrait Gallery, tells me is extremely rare—an authentic portrait of Gay.

Distressingly, this great object cannot be seen. The Abbey found it necessary to move Gay's monument and the matching one for Nicholas Rowe from their places on the south wall of Poets' Corner when medieval wall paintings were discovered behind them in 1939, since when they have been kept in safekeeping but inaccessible in the triforium. A so-far insuperable obstacle to the return of Gay's monument has been that the Abbey has no space in which to display it safe for public access where the stones could remain free from weathering. Supposing that a site could be found or prepared, a further task would be to raise the funds to pay for the moving and installation. The present arrangements, however, are obviously highly unsatisfactory because there can be no public encounter with this important work, because the aims of the donors are frustrated, and not least because Gay is not only stripped of his memorial but furthermore left dishonoured by an unmarked grave. Circumstances that are highly unsatisfactory at the 300th anniversary of Gay's birth will become scandalous if left to obtain at the similar anniversary of his death.

Readers having suggestions how the dilemma might be resolved and those who might at some later time be willing to contribute money are invited to write to me now or in future, at 53 New Dover Road, Canterbury, Kent CT1 3DP, England, or at Box 156, Finleyville, Pennsylvania 15332, U.S.A. The recently retired Dean of Westminster, Dr. Edward Carpenter, proposed putting down a slab or plaque for Gay in the South Choir Aisle near those for Noel Coward and Sybil Thorndike. Members of the Gay conference in Durham, July 1985, preferred to delay providing a second memorial in order to continue seeking a means of bringing the original monument back into view, while perhaps placing a small marker upon the actual site of Gay's grave in Poets' Corner.

The climate of recent study on Gay has made us aware how much Swift's and Pope's stress on Gay's lack of patronage was a strategy to discredit a Prime Minister and a régime that they saw as anti-intellectual and hostile to native art. The monument was designed and placed as an enduring censure to 'the Great' powers of the ilk. Thus Pope could write afterwards in the *Epistle to Arbuthnot*:

> Blest be the *Great!* for those they take away,
> And those they left me—For they left me GAY,
> Left me to see neglected Genius bloom,
> Neglected die! and tell it on his Tomb;
> Of all thy blameless Life the sole Return
> My Verse, and QUEENSB'RY weeping o'er thy Urn!
>
> (255–60)[2]

Now of course the lines are doubly ironic, bitterly absurd. It is possible to imagine, however, that Pope's message might regain some force for this and the coming centuries if the stones were allowed to speak again. It is possible to imagine that even the

occasion of the monument's restoration to view could be found
eloquent with this tongue.

NOTES

1. Margaret Whinney ([Harmondsworth], 1964), pl. 67B. It is also illustrated
   in M. I. Webb's *Michael Rysbrack, Sculptor* (London, 1954), pl. 31.
2. John Butt (ed.), *Imitations of Horace* (London and New Haven, 1961),
   p. 114. Vol. IV of the Twickenham Edition of *The Poems of Alexander Pope*.

Notes on Contributors

STEPHEN COPLEY is Lecturer in English at University College, Cardiff. He has edited *Literature and the Social Order In Eighteenth-century England* (1984), an annotated collection of documents providing a context for several Scriblerian themes, and also Fielding's *Joseph Andrews* (1987). He is at present editing a volume of essays on Romanticism.

ALAN DOWNIE is Senior Lecturer in English at Goldsmith's College in the University of London. He has written widely on the historical background to eighteenth-century literature. His most recent work includes *Robert Harley and the Press: Propaganda and Public Opinion in the Age of Swift and Defoe* (1979) and *Jonathan Swift, Political Writer* (1984). He is also an editor of the *Scriblerian*.

BREAN S. HAMMOND is Senior Lecturer in English at the University of Liverpool. He has written a study of Pope's later years, *Pope and Bolingbroke: A Study of Friendship and Influence* (1984) and also a more general treatment of Pope's work in the Harvester New Readings series, *Pope* (1986). His most recent work has been on Swift with his contribution on *Gulliver's Travels* (1988) to the Open University Press's 'Guides to Literature' series. He is also Editor of the *British Journal of Eighteenth-century Studies*.

IAN HAYWOOD is a Tutor for the Open University. He is the author of *Faking It: Art and the Politics of Forgery* (1987).

PETER LEWIS is Senior Lecturer in English at the University of Durham. He is a specialist in eighteenth-century drama. He has edited *The Beggar's Opera* (1973) and contributed a volume on the play (1976) to the 'Studies in English Literature' series. His most recent work has been a study of *Fielding's Burlesque Drama* (1987).

YVONNE NOBLE is a freelance writer and editor who lives in Canterbury, Kent. She has edited the 'Twentieth-century interpretations' volume on *The Beggar's Opera* (1975) and is currently editing the play, complete with notes on the original score.

219

John Gay and the Scriblerians

PAT ROGERS is De Bartolo Professor in the Humanities at the University of South Florida at Tampa. He is one of the leading critics and literary historians of the period. He is the author of several full-length studies of Scriblerian literature, including *Grub Street* (1972), *The Augustan Vision* (1974), *An Introduction to Pope* (1976), *Henry Fielding* (1979), *Robinson Crusoe* (1979), *Literature and Popular Culture in Eighteenth-century England* (1985) and *Eighteenth-century Encounters* (1985). He has also edited the Critical Heritage volume on Defoe (1972), the *Complete Poems* of Swift (1983), and, most recently, the *Oxford Illustrated History of English Literature* (1987).

CAROLYN WILLIAMS is Lecturer in English at the University of Reading. She has written generally on the portrayal of women in the period's literature, drama especially, and is currently writing a study of Sexuality in Pope's Homer.

NIGEL WOOD is Lecturer in English at the University of Birmingham. He has written on *Swift* (1986) for the Harvester New Readings series and his consideration of Samuel Johnson as a literary critic will appear in 1990. At present he is engaged on an annotated edition of Johnson's *Dictionary*.

TOM WOODMAN is Lecturer in English at the University of Reading. He has contributed a study of Thomas Parnell (1985) for the Twayne's English Authors Series and his *Poetry and Politeness in Pope* will appear in 1989.

Index

221

Index

Index

223

Index